SEMEIA 56

Social Networks in the Early Christian Environment: Issues and Methods for Social History

Guest Editor:
L. Michael White

SEMEIA 56

Copyright © 1992 by the Society of Biblical Literature

All rights reserved. No part of this work may be reproduced or transmitted in any form or by any means, electronic or mechanical, including photocopying and recording, or by means of any information storage or retrieval system, except as may be expressly permitted by the 1976 Copyright Act or in writing from the publisher. Requests for permission should be addressed in writing to the Rights and Permissions Office, Society of Biblical Literature, 825 Houston Mill Road, Atlanta, GA 30329, USA.

ISSN 0095-571X
ISBN 1-58983-132-2

Printed in the United States of America
on acid-free paper

CONTENTS

Contributors to This Issue v

Editor's Preface vii

I. PROLEGOMENA: SOCIAL NETWORKS AND SOCIAL HISTORY

1. Finding the Ties that Bind: Issues from Social Description
   L. Michael White 3

2. Social Networks: Theoretical Orientation and Historical Applications
   L. Michael White 23

II. MAPPING SOCIAL NETWORKS IN THE ENVIRONMENT

3. Benefactor/Patronage Networks in the Urban Environment: Evidence from Thessalonica
   Holland Hendrix 39

4. Oracles and Their Society: Social Realities as Reflected in the Oracles of Claros and Didyma
   Thomas L. Robinson 59

5. Elite Networks and Heresy Accusations: Towards a Social Description of the Origenist Controversy
   Elizabeth A. Clark 79

III. NETWORK MODELS AND DYNAMICS IN HISTORICAL CONTEXTS

6. "By the gods, it's my one desire to see an actual Stoic": Epictetus' Relations with Students and Visitors in His Personal Network
   Ronald F. Hock 121

7. Christ as Patron in the *Acts of Peter*
   Robert F. Stoops, Jr. 143

8. Epidemics, Networks, and the Rise of Christianity
   Rodney Stark 159

WORKS CONSULTED 179

CONTRIBUTORS TO THIS ISSUE

Elizabeth A. Clark
  Department of Religion
  Duke University
  Durham, NC 27706

Holland Hendrix
  Union Theological Seminary
  Broadway and 120th Street
  New York, NY 10027

Ronald F. Hock
  School of Religion
  University of Southern California
  University Park
  Los Angeles, CA 90089

Thomas L. Robinson
  Union Theological Seminary
  and TLR Services
  205 Crescent Ave.
  Leonia, NJ 07605

Rodney Stark
  Departments of Sociology and Comparative Religion
  University of Washington (DK–40)
  Seattle, WA 98195

Robert F. Stoops, Jr.
  Department of Liberal Studies
  Western Washington University
  Bellingham, WA 98225

L. Michael White
  Department of Religion
  Oberlin College
  Oberlin, OH 44074

Editor's Preface

The articles in this volume arose from the research program of the Social History of Early Christianity Group (now called the Social History of Formative Christianity and Judaism Section) of the Society of Biblical Literature. The interest in networks began with some preliminary suggestions of future avenues of research in the social history of the early Christian movement. This idea led to a session on the topic, but other papers in subsequent years have continued to pursue the issue.

These studies are brought together in this volume of *Semeia* for two primary reasons: first, in order to introduce network theory and analysis; second, to show direct application of this approach to social history research on early Christianity and its Hellenistic-Roman environment. Because network theory is a highly technical issue unto itself, it will be necessary to offer some general introductory comments in the Prolegomena section. Moreover, it has been decided to compile the bibliographies of all the papers into a single list of works consulted, which is given at the end of the volume. It is hoped that this will make available in a ready fashion both works on network theory and works on the historical topics treated in the individual articles. One further note is required on the nature of sources cited in the studies. In keeping with *Semeia* format, modern authors are generally cited in the text (unless the references are too lengthy) using APA style. However, for citations of ancient sources, especially inscriptions or text references in original languages, traditional footnotes have been retained. This has been done in part because of the quantity of such references in certain specialized studies (as, for example, when the only available full text is in either Greek or Latin original). This retention of historical format will ensure that those who wish to pursue lines suggested in the historical analysis will have at their disposal the relevant source materials.

All the studies presented here are careful historical studies informed by sociological and anthropological methods. The volume has been organized as follows. The Prolegomena presents two studies by L. M. White to introduce the topic of networks. The first of these attempts to show the relevance of network analysis by examining evidence for the social "connectedness" of groups and individuals in Roman society. The second, then, offers a theoretical orientation to network analysis followed by a discussion of areas of applicability to social history.

The three studies in Part II take the methods of network analysis into the historical arena in order to "map out" specific cases in detail. The sources range from literary historical to archaeological and epigraphic remains, and so present diverse problems of application. Holland Hendrix studies epigraphic remains of benefaction and patronage in the urban environment of Thessalonica to assemble a pattern of network relations. Thomas Robinson undertakes primary archaeological analysis of the two Apolline oracles of Claros and Didyma in order to see how each related to local society and clientele by creating networks of relations. Elizabeth Clark provides a detailed analysis of relations between Jerome and Rufinus and their respective supporters by careful examination of references to these individuals in the letters and other primary sources.

The three studies in Part III then attempt to show how an awareness of network theory and analysis provides new insights into the intellectual and religious environment. Ronald Hock looks at the way the renowned Stoic Epictetus interacted with students and others in his school at Nicopolis in order to throw new light on the social context for Epictetus' philosophy and self-presentation. Robert Stoops looks at the role of patronage, both as relationship and as symbol, in the apocryphal *Acts of Peter*. Finally, by way of conclusion, Rodney Stark shows how recognizing the effects of network ties among individuals in the Roman world, especially during times of crisis, can help to explain the numerical growth of Christianity in the second and third centuries.

L. M. White
Oberlin, Ohio

PART I

PROLEGOMENA
SOCIAL NETWORKS AND SOCIAL HISTORY

FINDING THE TIES THAT BIND:
ISSUES FROM SOCIAL DESCRIPTION

L. Michael White
Oberlin College

ABSTRACT

This study shows the value of analyzing social networks as a feature of social history within the early Christian environment. One of the long-standing questions of early Christian studies has been the social progress of the movement. Given the usual assumptions of the lower-class origins of the movement, Christianity's eventual success in cracking into the ranks of the old pagan aristocracy comes as something of a surprise. Recent work in network theory as applied to processes of religious conversion holds that such conversions do not depend upon ideological appeal alone, but rather on the social ties between individuals. Recent work in the social, political, and economic structures of the Roman world suggests, moreover, that new attention needs to be given to the interconnectedness of life up and down the social ladder. This study argues that the two sets of observations need to be correlated more carefully by applying network analysis to the social history. In particular, the evidence suggests that religious cell groups or conventicles offered an important set of social links within the urban environment of the Roman world. The point is demonstrated through analysis of several historical case-studies.

Cliques and Social History in the Roman World

My, but the old Roman aristocracy was a cliquish lot. Even the likes of a Cicero felt the sting of being belittled as an outsider—*nouveau riche*, a "new man" (*novus homo*). In the eyes of his political opponents he was a Johnny-come-lately pretender to the "nobility" (*nobilitas*) of the old order.[1] Yet M. Tullius Cicero and his family had risen to the ranks of the senate, and he held the office of consul during an important period of Rome's accession to world power. What is interesting in this rather well-known case is Cicero's ability to weave coalitions and barter power among the political factions of his day. Nor was it an intellectual exercise alone. Cicero's philosophical and political writings must be understood in their social context.

Cicero played the politics of contacts and alliances well, even though he ultimately got caught in the political crossfire between the factions of Julius Caesar and the republicans. Still, it is interesting to notice some of the less abstruse elements of Cicero's actions in this vein; he provided dowries to the marriageable daughters and secured posts for the sons of his "friends" within the aristocracy.[2] Similarly, his contemporaries Crassus and Julius Caesar made no-interest "loans" to other senators (Gelzer:114, 117), while normal interest rates ranged from 6–12 per cent. The intent of both actions was to insure their "friendship" (*amicitia*), meaning both social ties and political support (Gelzer:101–110). After all, *amicitia* served as a polite synonym for "party" politics (Taylor:7, 68–69). A century (and more) later one finds Pliny the younger, now under imperial influences, still pursuing the same order of social life among the senatorial aristocracy.[3] Not much had changed in the course of the Augustan revolution. Indeed, if anything the bonds of patronage networks were becoming even more important (Syme, 1960:369–380). The social changes since the late republic tended to increase social tension and competition, not so much between the orders, but between cliques and factions within the aristocracy. The coin of the realm was power and influence (Wood:40).

In the Roman world it was not enough to be rich, though wealth surely made it easier to get along. No, it was far better to be well-born, or at least well-connected, as well as rich, if one wanted the highest prestige and status (*dignitas*) in Rome's social order. Status had its marks of connectedness: "the farther back . . . , the more . . . , the closer to Rome" (MacMullen 1974:122). Sometimes the old nobility, even Cicero himself, could get on with less, assuming those other connections were managed properly (cf. MacMullen, 1974:117; Wistrand:28). It was a social order they guarded jealously, even after it had begun to erode. Seemingly a noble quest, its excessive strivings were scorned by Lucretius:

> vying by wits inborn, contending for nobility,
> striving night and day by glorious industry
> to rise to preeminence in wealth and power to seize.
> O wretched minds of humankind, O hearts blind![4]

The Epicurean critique was leveled at the "vainglories" (*kenodoxiai*) of the uninitiated that keep them mired in worldly pursuits. The antidote was retreat into the garden of philosophy and true friendship, whether at Athens or Herculaneum (cf. Frischer:73). No wonder during Roman times that Epicurean cells should have been labeled misanthropic, disruptive, and dangerous (cf. MacMullen, 1966:53). Yet, their criticisms, and even their own social organization (especially in the early Empire), reflect the social structures in which they worked. Order, class, status, wealth, and power—these were the foundation stones on which the superstructure of the Roman social pyramid was erected (Gelzer:14–25; MacMullen, 1974:88–94; Wistrand:5–7). But of course, these were dominated by the *old boys* of old Rome itself in a descending scale from the senators, to equestrians, plebs, freedmen, and slaves. Race (or ethnicity) and gender formed their own sub-index to this scale, inherently on a half-step down at every level.

This social structure viewed at some distance must appear to be a daunting escarpment. So, how can one explain the fateful encounter that eventuated between the old Roman aristocracy and the emergent Christian church? The age-old question asks how a persecuted minority begun by Judaean peasants could have penetrated to the heart of old Rome and captured the aristocracy and the empire itself. The traditional picture of how the Christians' movement fared was derived from Eusebius but filtered through the neo-orthodox theological perspectives of Adolf Harnack and others. The result was a triumphalist model of the victory of the Christian message over the social orders it encountered (White, 1985:97–104).

It is significant, however, that those who opposed the spread of Christianity rarely worried about ideological or doctrinal matters in the early stages. The diffusion of Christianity came to be viewed as a contagion, a malignancy in the body politic, using a metaphor that had already been leveled against Jews and others.[5] Typically, the sense of alarm is directed at the segments of society where the infection had festered. While some caviled at deception of the poor and ignorant, of "women, children, and slaves," others found the threat especially in the ranks of the elite.[6] Still, what most alarmed earlier Roman detractors was that attachment to these foreign "superstitions" disrupted the social structures. As Tacitus notes,

> The Jews are very loyal toward one another, and always ready to show compassion, but toward every other people they display only contempt and enmity.... Those who are converted to their ways follow the same practice, and they are tainted by no teaching sooner than to despise the gods, to disown their country, and to regard parents, children, and siblings as of little account.[7]

There is a certain irony that a Roman aristocrat, of all people, should decry misanthropic cliquishness on the part of Jews or Christians. Yet, these three threatened areas—gods, country, and family—mark a symbolic equation that gave definition to the moral structure of the social order and hence what was sacred to the Roman sense of orderliness in terms of relationships and values.[8]

It was this historical observation that first began to raise the question of social networks for me a few years ago (White, 1985). Arising out of several currents of social world studies, treatments of Christian origins had begun to reassess their social standing, especially in Pauline communities (Malherbe:29–47; Meeks:51–73). With this reassessment arose new questions of both the courses and the process of diffusion of Christianity within the Roman social order. New studies of the religious environment and of the social structures themselves contribute to a revised panorama. Some discussions have focused on social mobility in the Roman empire, with an eye toward the upward movement of Christians into the aristocracy (M. K. Hopkins; A. H. M. Jones, 1963:30; Finn). Others have reexamined the notion of adherence and conversion (MacMullen, 1985:67–81) and questioned whether the social structure really changed with the "Christianization" of the empire (MacMullen, 1981:94–130; 1984:1–9).

It must be noticed that cliquishness was not limited to aristocratic circles alone. In a highly stratified social environment, where few individual voices below the highest echelon could even be heard (much less heeded), the population groups of Rome found it practical to assemble their own choruses. When singing-for-supper before Emperor and Senate, it helped to be identified by "vicinity" (from *vici*, the street associations), whether it was Tannery Row in Rome itself, a league of Asian cities, or the Guild (cf. MacMullen, 1974:68–69). Group connectedness, coalition dynamics, was tantamount at times to voluntary "ghettoizing" in large urban centers. People formed identity groups by neighborhoods, ethnic groups, hometowns, guilds and occupation, or other factors. In most cases religious identities were prominently displayed. It also helped to have well-connected sponsors or patrons. Being part of a group gave voice and some sense, however small, of power (MacMullen, 1974:67–87). Thus, in more recent discussions of the fourth century, when the empire was becoming at least nominally Christian, some studies have looked at group loyalties not in terms of adherence to the ideological content alone but rather in terms of social structures and ties (cf. Brown, 1972:166–172). The question then begins to refocus on the degree to which the social structures of the Roman world were undergoing change either contemporaneous with or as a result of the emergence of Christianity (Alföldy:183; White, 1985:126). As a result, one begins to look at the way Christians came to be associated with networks of power and influence in the Roman world.

Ties that Bind: The Case of the Pagan Revival

From the later end of the historical spectrum, the genteel battle over the altar of Victory in 382–384 CE is an instructive case. It began when the new Caesar in the West, Gratian (375–383), was persuaded to divest his reign of the visible trappings of "paganism." He renounced the imperial title of *pontifex maximus* (379) and confiscated the sacred coffers and endowments of the priestly colleges and temples (381). But the final blow came in 382 when he removed from the Senate the altar of Victory that had been restored under Julian. These decisions clearly reflected Gratian's favoritism toward Christian ideals, but were strongly influenced by his social ties to the new bishop of Milan, Ambrose. It is not insignificant that Aurelius Ambrose, the son of a praetorian prefect, had been selected (in 374) from his office as consul of the Italian praefecture of Aemilia and Liguria to succeed the Arian bishop Auxentius. His influence over Gratian came largely through these same aristocratic circles. Among its leading figures stood the professor and poet Decimius Magnus Ausonius, who had been Gratian's tutor. Ausonius was appointed consul in 379. Indeed, Ausonius also secured political offices for several members of the pagan Symmachus' family, including appointment of a brother, Celsinus Titianus, as vicar of Africa (cf. MacMullen 1988:77). Symmachus himself had served as consul of Africa in 373–74. This connection may help to explain how Aurelius Symmachus, who would author the plea for restoration of the Altar of Victory (Barrow), had come to recommend the young Augustine to Ambrose for the post of teacher of rhetoric at Milan. For his brother Celsinus Titianus, though likewise a staunch "pagan" (*pontifex Solis et Vestae*), was apparently married to a daughter (or sister?) of the Christian aristocrat, Anicius Auchenius Bassus, urban prefect in 382, another intimate of Ausonius.[9]

What one begins to see is the interconnected web of social as well as political loyalties and influences that lurk just below the surface of the ideological debates. This is nowhere clearer than in the person of Q. Aurelius Symmachus Eusebius, *vir clarissimus* (*v.c.*), who as urban prefect of Rome in 384 was the spiritual as well as social anchor of the old pagan aristocratic circle. Aurelius Symmachus was "connected." He engaged in professional as well as friendly correspondence with both Ausonius and Ambrose, whom he had known for some years. He had also been the young political protégé of one of the best known "pagans" of his day, Vettius Agorius Praetextatus, *v.c.*.

As praetorian prefect of Achaia and urban prefect of Rome under Julian, Praetextatus had been instrumental in the first flap over the altar twenty years earlier. Subsequently he retired from public office, but obviously remained quite active behind the scenes in the pagan aristocracy. Praetextatus' wife, Fabia Aconia Paulina, was also prominent in the so-called "pagan revival," as their joint epitaph makes clear.[10] While stationed as praefect of Achaia (under Julian) they both became initiates in a number of the mysteries and renowned as protectors of the ancient rites. A sister (or niece?), Praetextata, was married to the urban vicar (and former consular of Campania) Julius Festus Hymetius.

This is the pagan Festus Hymetius who incurred the wrath of Jerome while the latter was in Rome at this same time (c. 382–385) as secretary to Pope Damasus.[11] The occasion for this bitter confrontation was Hymetius' resistance to the ascetical Christian leanings of his young niece, Julia Eustochium, the daughter of Jerome's most ardent patron, Paula (Kelly:92, 96–98; cf. Clark, 1979:63). The daughter, however, still a child, legally had come under the care or "keeping" (*tutela*) of Hymetius (by right of *patria potestas*) since her own father and Paula's husband, Julius Toxotius, had recently died (c. 379, cf. Kelly:92). Under Hymetius' guardianship an appropriate marriage was arranged for her. Thus, Julia Eustochium could look to a mixed religious environment even within her own aristocratic family. Her mother was a fervent Christian ascetic and principal in both monastic development and in theological controversies. (See the article below by Elizabeth Clark.) Her paternal aunt and de facto guardian for a time was the niece of Praetextatus, the most renowned defender of the old Roman religion.

It is not surprising, then, that tensions would run high over Festus Hymetius' decision. Hymetius himself came under political scrutiny. Religious rivalries at the court of Valentinian might have had a role in earlier charges of embezzlement and conspiracy brought against Hymetius (371–72). Still, family connections with the likes of Praetextatus made it possible to have the trial heard before the Senate with a far more favorable outcome (cf. Arnheim:179–180). So, it seems that Hymetius had returned from temporary banishment after the death of Valentinian (375) to resume his active role in pagan life at Rome at just this important moment. As Praetextatus' colleagues began to rally around the cause of the Altar of Victory, the battle was being waged on yet another front within the old aristocratic families.

It is indicative of Praetextatus' prestige within the old pagan circles at Rome that in 385 he was posthumously given the unheard-of honor of a statue dedicated to a man by the Vestal Virgins. In return, Fabia Paulina gave an honorific statue of the chief Vestal Virgin, Coelia Concordia. In addition to her support of traditional religion, Paulina represented bonds to several of the old senatorial families, the Maecii Gracchi and the Fabii, through her father Aco(nius) Catulinus Philomathius (formerly vicar of Africa and praetorian prefect for 341). She was also related by marriage, therefore, to Fabius Titianus, who (alongside her husband) held a priesthood in the pontifical college known as *quindecemviri sacris faciundis*.[12]

One of Fabia Paulina's cousins, a daughter of this same Fabius Titianus, had married L. Aurelius Avianus Symmachus Phosphorus, another member of the *quindecimviri sacris faciundis*. Their children included Aurelius Symmachus Eusebius and Celsinus Titianus (Arnheim:78–79). No wonder the younger Symmachus should become the political protégé of Praetextatus. Fabia Paulina and Praetextatus were further interrelated to M. Maecius Memmius Furius Burburius Caecilianus Placidus, a praetorian prefect under Constans, who held the priesthoods of *pontifex major* and *quindecemvir sacris faciundis*.[13] Paula (the sister-in-law of Hymetius and Jerome's patroness) was the daughter of Blesilla, who in turn was the daughter (or sister?) of this same Maecius Memmius Furius Burburius Caecilianus. Meanwhile, Aurelius Symmachus himself married Rusticiana (a name recalling the virtues of old Rome), the daughter of Memmius Vitrasius Orfitus Honorius, another close kinsman of both Praetextatus and Maecius Memmius Furius Burburius Caecilianus. Vitrasius Orfitus held all three republican magistracies under Julian. He also held priesthoods in three of the oldest priestly colleges—the Priests of Vesta, the Priests of Sol, and the *quindecemviri sacris faciundis*.[14] Praetextatus held these same three priesthoods at about the same time.

The last priestly office, the *quindecemviri* (*XVviri*), becomes a significant link, since it comprised a very elite group of fifteen ex-consuls who served as guardians of the Sibylline books. The *pontifices maiores*, equally elite, oversaw the festival calendar and the allocations of sacred space within the city. Aurelius Symmachus' daughter was married to Virius Nicomachus Flavianus the younger, son of the praetorian prefect of the same name while Symmachus was urban prefect. A famous ivory diptych celebrates the union of these two families with symbols of traditional pagan values represented as priestesses of Ceres/Demeter-Magna Mater and Jupiter/Liber at sacrifice (cf. Bloch:212). The elder Nicomachus was related to the houses of the Caeionii and the Anicii that had intermarried at an earlier stage. He also served as *pontifex maior* alongside Aurelius Symmachus in the pontifical college.[15] While Aurelius Symmachus held only this one priesthood, his father, Avianus Symmachus, had been both *pontifex major* and *XVvir*, the latter during the same time as both Vitrasius Orfitus and Praetextatus.[16] Aurelius Symmachus' political patron, Praetextatus, preparing to return to public life as consul designate for the following year, might have stood at his elbow as the third *relatio* concerning the altar was being addressed to the new emperor Valentinian II in 384 (Bloch:199; Seeck; Barrow:10–12). Unfortunately, Praetextatus died in the Autumn of 384, a turn of events Jerome noted with far too much self-satisfaction.[17]

The "pagan revival" was a family affair among the *clarissimi* centered in two sets of primary relationships: the first, kinships and intermarriages among the old senatorial families of Rome; the second, membership in the elite (virtually hereditary) priestly colleges of the old civic cult. It was a tight clique, a network. [See Fig. 1.] Nor is it mere accident that the circle of *clarissimi* around Symmachus (including Praetextatus, Vitrasius Orfitus, Decius Albinus, Priscus Attalus, Virius Nicomachus Flavianus, and his son Nicomachus Flavianus) all had villas on the Bay of Naples (D'Arms,

1970:203–232 [Catalogue II]). Aurelius Symmachus himself had six estates there, and a number of his important contacts and appointments were mediated through this elite enclave of Romans-on-holiday in Campania (cf. D'Arms, 1970: 227–229). Yet the local networks of Campanian influence and patronage become important, too.

Further interconnections were manipulated and enhanced by the noble women, most of whom carried the equivalent title *clarissima femina* (*c.f.*). Praetextatus and Vitrasius Orfitus were both members of the college of *Pontifices Solis*, as was Caeionius Rufius Volusianus, the son of C. Caeionius Rufius Volusianus Lampadius and Caecinia Lolliana. The younger Volusianus, like Praetextatus, was a hierophant of Isis. The wives and/or mothers had their own contacts through prominent religious offices, as with Fabia Aconia Paulina and Caecinia Lolliana through the cult of Isis.[18] As will become more evident below, from here the contacts can also go down the social register, as in the case of Q. Fabius Ingenuus, a freedman of Fabius Titianus (named above), and hence also loosely linked to the family of Aurelius Symmachus through his mother. This aspiring freedman was *sevir Augustalis* in the local imperial cult of Regium, while together with his wife, Fabia Candida, the couple made a joint dedication to the cult of Isis and Sarapis.[19] The number of social interconnections, then, are multiplied and thereby strengthened in effect.

There are, then, five different types of bonds between the individual members of the pagan "inner circle" of Symmachus that help to reinforce its internal cohesion; they include direct kinship, marriage, high imperial offices (especially in Africa, Campania, and Rome), the elite priestly colleges (especially the *pontifices maiores* and the *XVviri sacris faciundis*), and other "neighborhood" connections [Fig. 1]. Clearly, the familial relations alone, or even the regional ties in Campania, do not suffice to explain why some individuals in Symmachus' larger network of contacts show up as pagan defenders. Among these same families there were several prominent Christians of equally high rank who are within Symmachus' reach; many were interrelated by marriage as well. What emerges as the most significant set of indicators for this particular situation is the intersection of the kinship/marriage links with membership in the elite priestly colleges. The bone of contention, of course, was the legacy of control for nominations to proconsular (i.e. consular and praefect) offices in Rome, Campania, and Africa, and hence for adlection to the Senate and the clarissimate (cf. Arnheim:104–105). The major change that had occurred by Symmachus' time was that the *cursus honorum* for senators and consular offices no longer passed invariably through the pontifical colleges. There were new modes of access through Christian networks, as the cases of Ausonius and Ambrose illustrate.

Fig. 1: **THE CIRCLE OF AURELIUS SYMMACHUS**

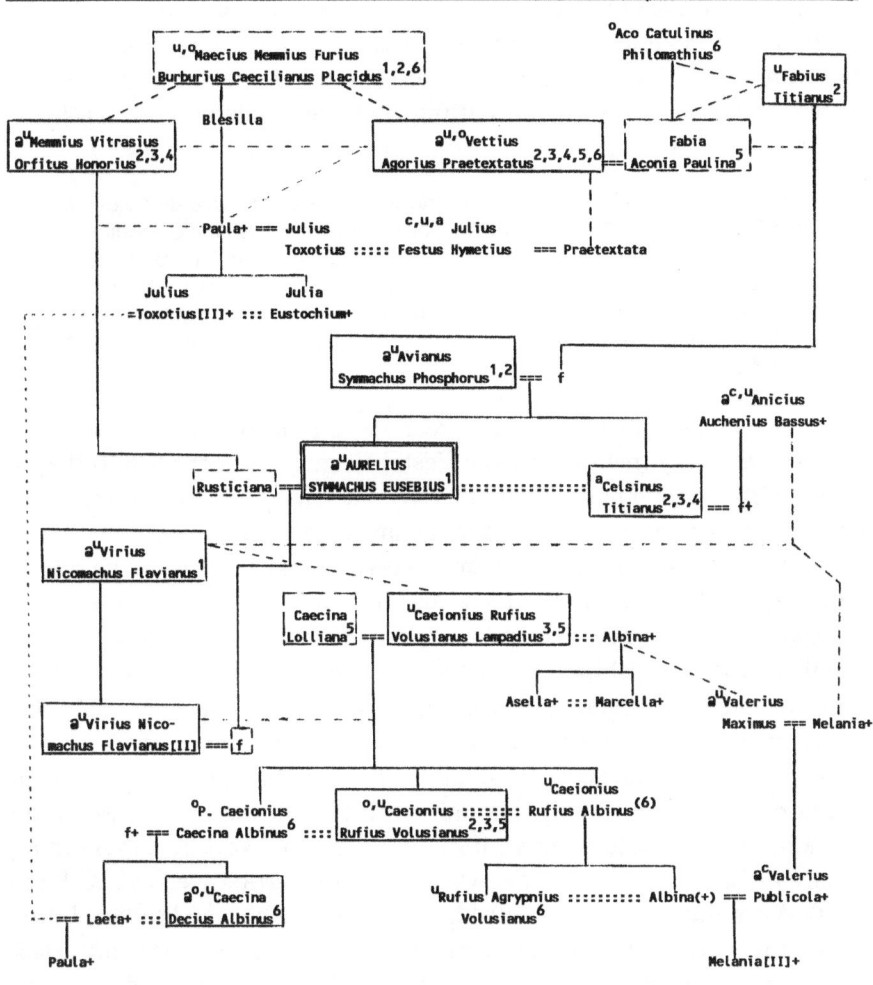

KEY Kinships: ——— *direct filiation*;   :::: *sibling*;   ---- *other kin*;
     Marriage ===;   Neighbors/Campanian Villas a
     Offices: u -Rome *(urban or praetorian praefect)*; c - Campania *(proconsular or vicar)*; a -Africa *(procon. or vic.)*; o -other Prov. *(procon. or vic.)*.
     Priesthoods: 1 -*Pontifex maior*; 2 -*XVvir sacris faciundis*; 3 -*Pont. Solis*; 4 -*Pont. Vestae*; 5 -*Sacerd. Isidi*; 6 -*augur* or *pont.* ?
     Other: + = Christian;   f = wife/daughter not named;   () = probable

The so-called debate over the altar of Victory, therefore, had deeper social roots. More was at stake than the decoration of the curia. When Gratian renounced the pontifical robes as part of his imperial demeanor, he was effectively denying the traditional social ties (since Augustus) of the emperor (as *pontifex maximus*) to the colleges of priests (especially the *pontifices maiores* and the *XVviri sacris faciundis*) and the related circles of the traditional civic cult. By confiscating their treasuries and their endowments Gratian was undercutting their very existence. Thus, Symmachus' plea is telling:

> Shall noble virgins [the Vestals] and those who serve the sacred offices [the Pontifices] concerned with our destiny be the exceptions [to the guarantees of private bequests in the name of piety]? What is the good of dedicating a holy body to the well-being of the state, of buttressing the eternity of the empire with divine support, of directing friendly virtues toward your arms and regiments, of offering prayers for the benefit of all, if at the same time you do not offer justice to all?[20]

Symmachus' plea for the altar was really a call for tolerance and maintenance of the very institutions, the Vestal Virgins and pontifical colleges, whose virtues it symbolized, and thereby a defense of the social structures of the city's pagan aristocracy—once again, gods, country, family.

Ultimately, Symmachus was unsuccessful in trying to stem the tide of Christian influence, even though he and his allies (including Praetextatus, his son-in-law Nicomachus, and Caeionius Rufius Albinus) continued to dominate the consulships and the two praefectures at Rome into the 390s. Ausonius here is a pivotal figure in the episode, for he was nominally still pagan in his religious sympathies. Under Gratian he was perhaps the most influential political figure in the west, even though he was not of an old Roman senatorial family. Ausonius was probably of Greek descent on his father's side and from an aspiring (but none-too-wealthy) landholding family in Gaul on his mother's. Ausonius also married well (M. K. Hopkins). Ausonius held the consulship in 379, while his aged father, Julius Ausonius, was given a praefecture; his son, Decimius Hilarianus Hesperius, also held the praefecture; and his son-in-law was made proconsular in Africa (Arnheim:98–100).

It is sometimes suggested that Ausonius' writings, especially during the reign of Valentinian I (Gratian's father), reflect Christian ideas and sympathies. Yet he was also an intimate and sometimes political patron of Aurelius Symmachus, and in 389 he tried to dissuade Paulinus of Nola from renouncing public life for the monastery (cf. Coster:187–193). It is rather surprising, then, that one should hear so little of Ausonius in the debate over the altar of Victory. Presumably, his political influence had diminished significantly after the death of Gratian, but Ambrose did not shy from the fray. It suggests, therefore, that while Gratian was still alive, Ausonius was forced to refrain from taking a public stand in the debate because of his ties to both sides. No matter how important he had become as imperial office-holder and power-broker, as a provincial he was not on the inside of the old pagan social circle, seen most clearly in the priestly colleges at Rome.

Ausonius had been the court-tutor of Gratian at Treves. There, in 369 he had first met Aurelius Symmachus, who had been sent as senatorial delegate to the imperial court, to mark Valentinian's *decennalia*. Ausonius was the teacher and intimate correspondent of the aristocratic Campanian governor Meropius Pontius Paulinus, later renowned as the Christian bishop and ascetic, Paulinus of Nola (Arnheim:184). In turn Paulinus was a close confident of the Christian Anicius Auchenius Bassus, also a proconsul of Campania. Paulinus' son would later hold the same office, while Bassus' son of the same name was later consul of Rome for 408 (his father having held the urban praefecture in 382).[21] It should be noticed, then, that the leading offices of Campania alternated between these powerful Christian families and the equally powerful pagans associated closely with the Symmachus circle (Nicomachus Flavianus and Caecina Decius Albinus). Both were leading patrons in the Campanian region and had important connections in Rome itself. Hence, the same kind of analysis can be hinted for the internal connections of the Christian circle of Bassus and Paulinus as that described above for Symmachus and the old pagans.

Unfortunately some of the more telling prosopographic links are missing on the Christian side. It is clear, however, that the circle of Christian matrons around Marcella, Paula, and Melania were pivotal in consolidating the Christian power base both in Campania and in Rome.[22] A daughter of Auchenius Bassus (probably Tyrrania Anicia Juliana) was married to Q. Clodius Hermogenianus Olybrius, who held the proconsulship of Africa and praetorian praefecture under Theodosius (Seeck:xci; cf. Arnheim:183). His parents were a notable Christian couple—the poetess Betitia Faltonia Proba (Clark, 1986:124–147) and Clodius Celsinus Adelphius, corrector of Campania. They, in turn, were related by both filiation and marriage to Sextus Claudius Petronius Probus (also proconsul of Africa) and his wife Anicia Faltonia Proba, likewise both Christians (cf. Arnheim:110–111). This Sextus Petronius Probus was an important correspondent of Aurelius Symmachus and was praetorian praefect of Africa and the entire western praefecture in 383 under Gratian, with whom he had served as consul in 371 under Valentinian. Before that Sextus Petronius Probus was prefect of Gaul (366) at the time when Ausonius was brought to Valentinian's court at Treves.[23] In turn, their son Anicius Hermogenianus Olybrius was married to Anicia Juliana, a granddaughter of

Anicius Auchenius Bassus. All of these individuals could claim the title of *clarissimus/a*.

This set of intermarriages shows the interconnectedness of the Christian circle of the aristocracy (cf. Clark, 1979:64–66). Although they were close to the pagan circle, indeed part of a larger social stratum of the clarissimate perpetuated through numerous mixed marriages, there was a tendency to foster internal cohesiveness within each circle through multiple linkages. It helps to understand how the brokerage of power was beginning to flow, especially given the number of Christian connections to Africa, and thence to Numidia, Mauretania, and Gaul. The Anicii were an important link for the diffusion of Christianity among the aristocracy, though interestingly enough with a different slant on public service and marriage than the circle of Jerome and Paula. Anicius Auchenius Bassus (the father or son) also dedicated a memorial inscription at Ostia to Monica, the mother of Augustine, who died in 387 (cf. Brown, 1972:170). Bassus and Paulinus may have been related through the earlier proconsul of Campania, Anicius Paulinus, though Pontius Paulinus' family (like Ausonius and Melania the Elder) originally came from Gaul and Spain. Paulinus had first encountered Ausonius at Bordeaux. In any case, Bassus and Paulinus and their families were known as prominent patrons of several Campanian towns (Arnheim:182–183).

In part, the resolution regarding the Altar of Victory may have resulted from a policy (reacting against Julian) of Valentinian I, his heirs (Gratian, Valentinian II, and Theodosius I), and his provincial advisers (especially Maximinus) to weaken the hold of these old Roman aristocratic families and their hereditary pontifical offices on the Senate. They ceased exclusive control of important posts in the western provinces (Arnheim:95), and provincial aristocrats gained considerable ground (cf. Chastagnol:162). No wonder, then, that the Symmachus circle should be found favoring the claims of the "interloper" Eugenius, a moderate Christian, after the death of Valentinian II (A. H. M. Jones, 1964:1.161–169). Symmachus' son-in-law Nicomachus served as urban praefect to Eugenius for 392/3. The more fanatical Christians who supported Theodosius I feared Eugenius would turn out to be another Julian. The feelings ran high on both sides.

By this time, more of the provincial aristocrats had strong leanings toward Christianity. But there was support at Rome and in Campania as well, as in the Christian representatives of the equally famous houses of the Caeionii and Anicii. As with Paulinus, they likewise had ties to important Christian leaders in the provinces, especially Africa (Brown, 1972:177–178). While one branch of the *gens Caeionii* remained staunchly pagan in the Symmachus circle (see Fig. 1 above: Caeionius Rufius

Volusianus and Caecina Decius Albinus), another branch became powerful supporters of Christianity. Indeed, there are clear and important links to the families of Auchenius Bassus and Paulinus of Nola. From this line come some of the most prominent Christian women patrons who show up among the supporters of Jerome and Rufinus (cf. Clark, 1985; and her article in this volume). Marcella, Paula, and Julia Eustochium continued support for Jerome from the time that he left Rome (384) until his death.[24] Other Christian members of the family (e.g., Paula's son, Julius Toxotius the younger) remained in Rome and helped them maintain friendly ties with Paulinus of Nola (cf. Kelly:91–101, 273–280). Melania the Elder, originally from Campania, returned from Jerusalem to stay with Paulinus of Nola. Melania's son, Valerius Publicola, who served as consular of Campania, married Albina, the niece of Symmachus' colleague Caeionius Rufius Volusianus (noted above). In 383 (while Jerome was in Rome and Symmachus was preparing his *relatio* concerning the altar) Albina gave birth to Melania the younger (cf. Clark, 1984). It is significant, to be sure, that much of the Christian influence came through the aristocratic widows who saw asceticism as a new avenue of social expression (cf. Clark, 1986:175–193). Still, the appearance of prominent Christians within certain lines of these noble families did not automatically translate into a wholesale acceptance or rejection (Brown, 1972:175).[25]

The religious affiliations were rooted deeply in traditional social relationships reinforced by strong ties within certain cliquish circles. Local geographical connections, as seen in Campania, Gaul, or Africa, were also important and need further investigation in this light. It would seem, then, that Ausonius, the social climber, stood in the middle between these competing networks of power and influence on the western emperor. One can hardly conclude that the debate over the altar was waged on the theological and philosophical fronts alone (cf. Brown, 1972:164–165; MacMullen, 1988:77). Thus, what is needed is a fuller recognition of these interlocking (and sometimes competing) social networks and some way to measure the role of social ties in the shaping of the new order under the Christian emperors. But one must start by recognizing the role of religious groups in mediating social ties or forming social networks.

Networks of Influence and Religious Diffusion

Though there were surely changes in the Roman social structure between the time of Cicero or the younger Pliny and that of Symmachus, the operation of these cliquish webs of power and influence remain a factor in the politics (cf. MacMullen, 1986a:517–523; cf. Arnheim:103–104). One difference for the post-Constantinian period, however, is the greater prominence of Christians as actors in the social and political drama, causing an added dimension or layer of political influence to be operative. Nonetheless, it would be inappropriate to assume that the Christians brought a new or contrasting mode of social organization into the picture. Indeed, it is possible to see such influences from the religious side even in the earlier periods, especially when one considers the diffusion of the various "eastern" religions into the hellenized Roman world. Two examples will illustrate the point.

1. Politics, Patronage, and the Isis Cult at Pompeii

Turning again to the first century and its politics, one may notice the patterns of social influence in civic elections at Pompeii. Factionalism and electioneering were rife at Pompeii in its heyday. They are attested by the surviving layers of placards and graffiti on regular public billboards reused from year to year. But almost any blank wall that could command public attention and whose rights could be obtained would do as well. The main targets were the offices of duovir and aedile, held by decurions, two men each, for one year at a time. What developed was a common shorthand for campaigning for election and voicing one's support, called *programmata* (Franklin:17–19). Important dignitaries, of course, named their favorites, but so did clients, neighborhood groups, clubs, guilds, taverns, baths, or brothels. Almost any identifiable group whose support could be wheedled, cajoled, bartered for political favors, or purchased outright was susceptible. Indeed, to have one's support solicited was itself a small measure of success in the public arena of Pompeian political life. Still, there was an expectation of return; political debts had to be paid off (Franklin:87–92). Within this environment a particularly interesting group of relations deals with political support by various individuals and groups associated with the cult of Isis (Tran Tam Tinh:181–185). In the election of 79 CE, for example, "all the worshipers of Isis" supported Cn. Helvius Sabinus for aedile; however, one leading Isiac priest, Popidius Natalis, supported the opposing slate. The reason seems simple enough; the candidate was his patron, C. Cuspius Pansa.[26] Yet another of the programmata shows Cuspius Pansa (or his father of the same name) being supported for election by a guild of "Isiac bakers," and he is known from other sources as a devotee of Isis.

What is intriguing is the range of social relationships, here translated into public political support, that were mediated through contacts in the Isis cult. Another important figure was L. Popidius Ampliatus, the brother of the younger Pansa's running mate, L. Popidius Secundus, on the aedile-slate for 79.[27] The *gens Popidii* was one of the most prominent among the local Pompeian nobility. Quite a number of them show up as decurions, as civic benefactors, and as candidates in the annual elections over the years. L. Popidius Ampliatus himself stood for election as aedile in 75. In 79 Ampliatus naturally threw his own weight as former aedile behind his brother. But there is also evidence that through his various contacts he supported Pansa as well. Some of Ampliatus' clients, such as L. Vetutius Placidus and a certain Montanus,[28] painted programmata on their houses for Pansa. This same L. Vetutius Placidus also had a second patron, L. Julius Polybius (a duovir in 73), who likewise supported Pansa.[29] A further connection exists here in that a candidate for duovir for 79, C. Gavius Rufus, who is linked in the slate with Cuspius Pansa, had been on the aedile-slate of 73 linked to Julius Polybius. A number of subtle links exist among these political supporters. Nonetheless, both Montanus and Julius Polybius, in an unusual move, chose to call a split slate by supporting Cn. Helvius Sabinus as the second aedile in 79, instead of Popidius Secundus.[30] Interestingly enough, their mixed alignments for 79 match those seen in *programmata* of the Isis temple.

In discussing these patterns, Franklin (111) notes that clients were expected to support their own patrons when standing for election, but that there was more variability when it came to support for a third party favored by the patron, even the patron's own brother. Rather than a lack of control or continuity (as Franklin suggests) in these patron-client relationships, whether the client was an individual or a group, it suggests that competing lines of influence or social contact were at work. The social relationships were not merely dyadic, but were more highly layered and complex than a monovalent hierarchical structure of patronage would suppose. The system of public benefactions and private patronage created a tentacular network of relationships woven through individuals and groups (Jongman:285–329). Here, as just one key example of the complexity, one may look again at the mediating influence of the religious associations enacted through the Isis cult for diffusing such social contacts.

In addition to the lateral homogeneity already seen in Symmachus' circle of old pagans, in this case one may note the role of clientellage and religious affiliations in vertical social relations as well. A good example is the case of Numerius Popidius Ampliatus, a freedman of the prominent L. Popidius Ampliatus noted above. Numerius Ampliatus, his wife Cor(n)elia Celsa, and his son, Numerius Popidius Celsinus, became significant benefactors of the Temple of Isis at Pompeii.[31] The sign over the gateway attests to their prominence, since their beneficence rebuilt the temple after it had been damaged in the earthquake of 62.[32] As a freedman, however, the father's participation could only carry him so far, were it not for the social contacts it represented. Instead, his benefaction to rebuild the Iseum was made in the name of the son, Numerius Celsinus.

Numerius Ampliatus thereby made it possible for the younger Numerius to be enrolled in the Pompeian decurionate, even though the boy was only six. In all likelihood, part of the funds came from subventions by his patrons, the Popidii, who fostered such public beneficence by their freedmen to increase their own networks of influence in the civic arena. It was quite common to sponsor the upward mobility of one's clients in order to create a network or pyramid of social, economic, and political tentacles (D'Arms, 1981:133–148). In Pompeii a significant number of Greek cognomina show up in the lower levels of the decurionate through this process (Jongman:319–329). What is significant here is that a *collegium* or "foreign cult" should be the vehicle for these networks (cf. Treggiari:162–204). Normally, ex-slaves were prohibited from the decurionate; however, the benefaction earned a formal grant of *dignitas* for the son. It had a reciprocal benefit, too, in that it accrued not only to the status of the patron, the freedman-client, and his family but also to the public stature and acceptance of the Isis cult as a fixture in the social life of Pompeii. A private act of benefaction to the Isis temple was rewarded with public honors and status (White, 1990:30–31). It is in this context, too, that one must also consider the role of electioneering by groups or individuals attached to the Isis temple.

2. *Synagogues and Sympathizers*

Another way in which these networks facilitated diffusion may be seen in the case of Jewish synagogue communities in urban centers of the East. Thus group attachments, such as suggested by the "Synagogue of the Augustasians" at Rome, might have derived similarly from webs of clientellage (cf. Treggiari:205–206). One often finds a number of sympathizers in the Jewish community for whom a clear sense of conversion is not demonstrable. Such is the case for the prominent city councillors and decurions of Sardis who were donors to the synagogue. One sees it also in the decurions and other non-Jewish participants who were listed as *theoseboi* ("godfearers") in the roster of the Jewish social agency at Aphrodisias (White, 1990:99, 88–90 respectively). Nor does it suffice any longer to consider these "godfearers" as second-class adherents (or "semi-proselytes") to Judaism.

Something of the social dynamics at work here may be seen in the case of a donation of property made by the patroness Julia Severa to the Jewish community at Acmonia, Phrygia in the later first century CE.[33] Julia Severa was a prominent member of the local nobility; she was a priestess of the local imperial cult, *agonothetis*, and a municipal archontess. She was married to L. Servenius Capito, a local decurion.[34] It seems that this aspiring family was descended from Italian colonists on the patrilineal side and from local Galatian royalty on the matrilineal. On the basis of these claims, their son, L. Servenius Cornutus, was admitted to the Senate under Nero. Another descendent of Julia's, C. Julius Severus, was admitted to the tribunate under Hadrian.[35] The status and social mobility of these local decurions under Rome was the result of "a nexus of leading families pushing their wealthiest and most promising members into the Senate" (Levick:107).

In this regard the religious affiliations with the local imperial cult were clearly to their advantage (Price:65–68). But then, why should Julia Severa have made a donation to the Jewish community for the building of their synagogue? Clearly, she was not a convert to Judaism, nor does it seem that the honors accorded her by the Jews (in the inscription on the building) should have been the prime motivating factor. The relationships reflected in the synagogue inscription may hold the key. The honorific indicates that the private building, which had originally been built by Julia Severa, was renovated for Jewish religious usage by three named leaders of the synagogue, two archisynagogoi and an archon. The names of these leaders suggest, moreover, that they were likely freedmen or clients of Julia's family (White, 1990:81–82). The two archisynagogoi bear the names Publius Tyronnius Clados and Lucius son of Lucius. The latter may offer an obvious familial connection to Julia's husband over several generations. For the former, a certain Tyronnius Rapo is also attested in connection with the family and especially her municipal archonship.[36]

In other words, the synagogue building project commemorated in the honorific was the result of two interconnected acts of patronage and the social relations they reflected. The first was the donation of an existing private edifice by Julia to her Jewish clients, who held leading positions in the synagogue. The second was from these synagogue leaders to the Jewish congregation in donating the funds for the renovation project proper. Thus, the three synagogue leaders also possessed some measure of wealth and social standing at least within their own social circles. At the same time they had some line of access to the patroness. Through the interlocking acts of patronage they were able to solidify their social position and that of the Jewish community within the local environment. By the same token, the honors paid to Julia Severa by layers of dependents further enhanced her position in the local pyramid of Acmonian society. In this case, then, the status owing to contacts or attachments also worked up and down the social ladder. Ultimately, even the lowest members of the Jewish community had "ties" into the aristocracy through the social makeup of the synagogue. To be sure, few could expect to approach Julia Severa alone, but they had friends. Although these ties were filtered through several tiers of intermediate relationships, their "voice" in the stratified social din was a significant achievement for such outsiders.

Needs, Attractions, and Recruitment in Religious Groups

The last case returns the discussion to the issue of how Jewish and Christian groups, or any new cult for that matter, were established and attracted adherents as they made their way into the Roman urban settings. Traditionally, much attention has focused on the way in which the Christian message of immortal life through Jesus Christ offered a more satisfying and compelling response to the religious needs of the age than could its competitors (White, 1985:115–117). So, the background is typically portrayed: the civic religion of Greece and Rome was dominated by meaningless rituals, while the numerous "foreign" cults (including Judaism) attest to, but could only partially meet, the deeper needs of people for personal piety and salvation (cf. MacMullen, 1981:52–55; Price:247). Usually, then, conversion is understood in terms of psychic reorientation through intellectual assent and commitment to propositions and beliefs that satisfy such needs.

Recent studies of religious recruitment, both ancient and modern, raise some questions with this picture (cf. MacMullen, 1985:76–82; 1984:4–8; Frischer:46–47). But, then, so should some of the evidence of religious diffusion noted above. What appears as expansion and recruitment often results not from psychological appeal as much as gaining access to certain social networks (MacMullen, 1981:116–127; White, 1985:115–120). Thus, recent work by Rodney Stark, William Sims Bainbridge, and others points to certain inadequacies of a model of religious conversion or recruitment based solely on *ideological appeal* in response to some sense of *need or deprivation*, whether psychic or social (Stark and Bainbridge, 1980:1376–1378; cf. White, 1985:124). Instead, they argue that social bonds are often determinative of ideological attachment: "faith constitutes conformity to the religious outlook of one's intimates—membership spreads through social networks" (Stark and Bainbridge, 1980:1377). Even if *deprivation-appeal* factors are operative in religious propagandizing, nonetheless new recruits will not be retained unless they are socially bonded into the group. Similarly, strong social bonds and intact social networks tend to reinforce existing commitments (1394). Their analysis of contemporary sect-cult recruitment patterns shows that recruitment of social "isolates," that is individuals who are themselves unattached to local networks, have little impact on overall success in diffusion. This point is especially important since such social "isolates" or "outsiders" would seem to be the most likely candidates for *deprivation-appeal* recruitment (1379; cf. Stark and

Roberts:53–67). Recruitment to new religious groups often moves through preexisting social networks, especially extended family units. These are particularly efficient because of the multiplicity of social contacts that can be accessed (Stark and Bainbridge, 1980:1387, 1392). Here one begins to gain a sense of the importance of matrices or overlapping webs of social interaction.

In the context of the extended family structures of the Roman world, such insights become even more significant. Among the social structures that one finds most often are the economy of "friendship" and "kinship" and the popularity of clubs and collegial groups, often with religious overtones. But one of the most important social structures both for the maintenance of the traditional religions and for the profusion of new cults was the operation of patronage and clientellism (MacMullen, 1981:111, 125, 129; White, 1990:143–147). A metaphoric sense that interpersonal relations are key to understanding the social structures is easy to come by. What is needed, then, is a more complete sense of the dynamics of social networks in terms of theoretical orientation and thence in historical application.

NOTES

1 Sallust, *BJ* 63.6; *Catalina* 23.6; cf. Gelzer (1975):37; Wood:84–96; Habicht, 1990:16–34.

2 Cicero, *De officiis* 2.55. Cf. Taylor:39–46. For Cicero's reliance on political electioneering, see the treatise ascribed to his brother Quintus called *Handbook on Electioneering* (*Commentariolum petitionis*, in *Epistuale Ciceronis*, Tuebner ed. III.1:562–577) and Taylor:64–67. Also on electioneering see below the discussion of Pompeii by Jongman:289–310.

3 Pliny, *Epp.* 2.4.2; 6.32.2. Cf. Seneca, *De beneficiis* 2.21.5–6; Martial *Epigr.* 4.67. (Cf. Duncan-Jones, 1974:28).

4 Lucretius, *De rerum natura* 2.11–14 (my translation).
certare ingenio, contendere nobilitate,
noctes atque dies niti praestante labore
ad summas emergere opes rerumque potiri.
o miseras hominum mentes, o pectora caeca!

5 Tacitus, *Annals* 2.85: *ea superstione infecta*; 15.44: *exitiabilis superstitio rursum erumpebat . . . eius mali* (the former of Jews, the latter of Christians); cf. Pliny, *Ep.* 10.96.9: *superstitionis istius contagio pervagata est.*

6 Pliny, *Ep.* 10.96.9; Origen, *Contra Celsum* 3.49, 55; Tertullian, *Ad Scapulam* 5; cf. *Apologia* 2, 37.

7 Tacitus, *Hist.* 5.5: *. . . unde auctae Iudaeorum res, et quia apud ipsos fides obstinata, misericordia in promptu, sed adversus omnis alios hostile odium. . . . Transgressi in morem eorum idem usurpant, nec quicquam prius imbuuntur quam contemnere deos, exuere patriam, parentes liberos fratres vilia habere.*

8 These same areas of social bonds and relationships are outlined and elaborated in Cicero, *De officiis* 1.51–58 in terms of moral categories of rights and justice (cf. Wood:143–173). Compare Juvenal *Sat.* 8.1., cf. Arnheim:103.

⁹ Symmachus, *Ep.* 1.68 (Titianus), 61 (Bassus). Cf. CIL X.6656, VI.1679; Seeck:xciii, cvi; Arnheim:119.

¹⁰ CIL VI.1778–1780, = ILS 1259–61, trans. in Lefkowitz and Fant, 1982:279 (no. 264a). Cf. Ammianus Marcellinus, *Res Gestae* 27,9,8; A. H. M. Jones, 1971 [=*PLRE*] I.722.

¹¹ Jerome, *Ep.* 107.5.

¹² CIL VI.1717; cf. Arnheim:119–121 (with further discussions of Christians within the family of Fabius Titianus also interconnected to Paula).

¹³ CIL X.1700; cf. Arnheim:79–80.

¹⁴ CIL VI.1739; Ammianus Marcellinus 14.6.1; cf. Arnheim:88–89.

¹⁵ CIL VI:1782.

¹⁶ CIL VI.1698; cf. Arnheim:83.

¹⁷ Jerome, *Ep.* 24.

¹⁸ CIL VI.512, 846.

¹⁹ CIL X.1.

²⁰ Symmachus, *Rel.* 3.14, my translation.

²¹ Bassus, a Christian and Symmachus' immediate predecessor as urban praefect, was also suspected of embezzlement while in the office; cf. Symmachus, *Rel.* 23.4–7; 26.2; 34.7.

²² Cf. Jerome, *Ep.* 30.14. See further discussion below.

²³ CIL VI.1756; Symmachus, *Epp.* I.56–61; Arnheim:196; M. K. Hopkins, 1961:243.

²⁴ Marcella, the niece of Caeionius Rufius Volusianus Lampadius, was an older aristocratic widow who had become interested in Christian asceticism after meeting Peter of Alexandria during his stay in Rome (ca. 373–378; cf. Jerome, *Epp.* 47, 127). Together with her mother (Albina) and sister (Asella) she had formed a Christian conventicle for piety and study in her home on the Aventine (Jerome, *Epp.* 47.3, 24). Significantly this circle included a number of prominent matrons and widows: Principia (*Ep.* 127), Lea (*Ep.* 23), Marcellina and Felicitas (*Ep.* 45.7), and Paula and Julia (*Epp.* 127.5, 46.1).

²⁵ Cf. Jerome, *Ep.* 108; 107.3; *Vita Melaniae Junioris* I.12, II.19–23 (cf. Clark, 1985).

²⁶ CIL IV.787: *Cn. Helvium / Sabinum aed(ilem) Isiaci / universi rog(ant)*; CIL IV.1011: *Cuspium Pansam aed(ilem) / Popidius Natalis cliens cum Isiacis rog(at)*. Cf. Franklin:22, 103–104.

²⁷ CIL X.847–848; IV.7418; cf. Franklin:105–107.

²⁸ CIL IV.7289, 7850 respectively.

²⁹ CIL IV.7955; cf. Franklin:106–107.

³⁰ CIL IV.7849 and 7850/7928 respectively.

³¹ CIL X.847–848.

³² CIL X.846: *N. Popidius N(umerii) f(ilius) Celsinus / aedem Isidis terrae motu conlapsam / a fundamento p(ecunia) s(ua) restituit. Hunc decuriones ob liberalitem, / cum esset annorum sex, ordini suo gratis adlegerunt.*
(cf. White, 1990:31, with translation).

³³ CIJ II.766 (= *Monumentis Asiae Minoris Antiquae* [MAMA] VI.264); cf. Brooten, 1982:144, 158.

³⁴ MAMA VI.153, 263, 265.

³⁵ IGRR III.173.

³⁶ Cf. IGRR IV.655.

SOCIAL NETWORKS:
THEORETICAL ORIENTATION
AND HISTORICAL APPLICATIONS

L. Michael White
Oberlin College

ABSTRACT

Network theory developed out of structural-functionalist approaches in social anthropology. Rather than serving as a theory of society, it attempts to offer methods and models for analyzing social relationships within a given society. This study gives an overview of the basic elements of network analysis in terms of two sets of factors: interactional dynamics and morphological structures. Then it probes some lines of application to the historical contexts of the Roman and early Christian environment. One such area of application lies in the way group identity might be affected by the totality of relationships both of those within the group and of group members to those outside. A second area of application comes from the current interest in patronage systems in the Roman social order. Patronage serves both as a network structure and as a cultural ideal for relationships in the Roman environment. Observing this fundamental social dynamic should offer new insights into the arena of the early Christians' activity.

Network Theory and Structural-Functionalism

Network theory belongs to the field of micro-sociological rather than macro-sociological analysis. It is neither a theory of any one society as a whole nor a theory of human societies in general, but is rather a method or tool for analyzing social relationships which are the constituent parts of larger societal groupings. As Jeremy Boissevain (1974:25) says, "It offers a concept or social dimension intermediate between relationship and social system (or society), between local level and national level." It recognizes both the significance and the latent power of collectivity—kinship structures, clubs, "old boy" systems, and other intermediate social units—within a larger societal framework.

Network theory developed out of the school of micro-sociology known as structural-functionalism and is closely related to functionalist approaches in social anthropology, as employed in the work of A. R. Radcliffe-Brown (190). Structural-functionalism focuses on the patterns or structures of interrelationship between individuals and social units in a given cultural context with special attention to the way such relational structures function in maintaining the whole society. Yet, criticisms of structural-functionalism have arisen because it tends to focus on individuals while assuming a rather static societal framework with little notion of change. Such elements are especially important within complex urban settings, where factors like social or geographical mobility or cultural diversity are in view (Mitchell, 1969a:5–9; Barnes, 1969:52–53). Thus, the notion of networks came to be more than a metaphor for complex social relations; it offers a method for analyzing the links within those complex relational structures. Hence it is also dependent on the analysis of dynamics of role and status for individuals within a social grouping (as in Bates, 1956), though its focus is not on individuals themselves but on their ties to others within the same group (Mitchell, 1969a:1, 10).

One of the pioneering studies was by Elizabeth Bott (1957) in applying anthropological field technique to the analysis of roles within familial structures in London to develop a notion of kinship relations as social networks in that context (cf. Mitchell, 1969a:5). Bott was able to demonstrate a connection between the actualized social relations and the ideological concepts operative within a particular social environment (Bott, 1957:212–214; cf. 1975:248–249). In other words, the role and status of individuals is constrained by the networks in which and through which the individuals operate. "The behaviour of people in any one role relationship may be traced to the effects of the behaviour of other people, to whom they are linked . . . in some other relationship" (Mitchell, 1969a:46).

As an illustration, one need only reflect on the types of relations in a given academic environment. Most faculty find their anchor location in a specific departmental affiliation, but there are numerous other modes of linkage: extradepartmental caucuses or committees (Women's studies, African-American studies, junior faculty, etc.), faculty senates or review committees, a specialized interdepartmental research or curricular group (archaeologists, classicists, medievalists, literary theorists, environmental scientists), a sexual harassment support group, the "power table" at the faculty club, the noon-hour athletes (whether the aerobicizers, squash players, or runners), and the list goes on. An individual might find him- or herself linked in different ways to a wide array of others depending on these subgroups. Some are consciously cultivated, others are happenstance, while still others are simply givens that must be accepted. But the full array of these relations, or the different weight attached to some of them, will have an impact on the way that individual operates within the larger academic setting. One's colleagues within a department need not be one's closest friends in other arenas in order for the ties to have some effects on attitudes and actions. Loyalties to department might well influence decisions in other arenas, and vice versa. In the case of the field of religion studies, there will be further variations that have profound effects both on actions and interactions depending on whether one is in a Divinity School, a Liberal Arts department, or a Graduate School research program. Oh, by the way, watch out what you say in the sauna; important business is often conducted there, too. But then so it was in the baths of Rome, the gardens of Pompeii, or the porticoes of Athens.

These networks only represent the professional sphere, and the same individual might have an equal number of extramural attachments through family, old friends, neighbors, religious groups, civic clubs, bridge clubs, the odd Tupperware party, or other social contacts. Then, there are more distant, but no less significant, relations with colleagues in the same field but at other institutions who constitute widening circles of professional context for one's work: editorial boards, program units at annual meetings, research clusters, former students, and, of course, one's mentors and classmates from graduate school days, to name but a few. While the intensity of the attachment might be higher than that with local colleagues, the lack of proximity or day-to-day contact will mean that the synapses of relationship will behave in slightly different ways.

The complexity of these overlapping networks or matrices is multiplied when one factors in those familial units where both members of a couple are professionals, though it will have a rather different impact if they are, say, both faculty (but one in the humanities and the other in the natural sciences), or by contrast one a faculty member and the other a downtown attorney, a public school teacher, an artist, or a free-lance writer. Each set of relations will have a bearing, though the weight may vary according to the investment of the parties involved. But it is also the effect of balancing the entire matrix, the total package of relations, that provides a constraining and structuring effect through these interlocking networks.

Network Analysis

Network analysis arises from the notion of society as process rather than as a static, self-regulating system (Boissevain, 1974:26). It is modeled after message transmission in a closed communication system, but where the messages are in fact social transactions or exchanges that are determined by the status and weight of relations between the parties. Thus, it focuses on individual actors by examining relations in action for a specific network in a specific social context. A person's network forms a social environment from and through which pressure is exerted in either direction to influence behavior. The network environment is partly ascribed or inherited (by virtue of position in society) and partly achieved or constructed (either consciously or accidentally). What gives network analysis its quantitative dimension (as opposed to a metaphor of dyadic relationships) is the ability to evaluate connectedness, that is the weight and influence among different relationships in a person's social environment (Boissevain, 1974:27-28).

Two interrelated sets of factors are part of the analysis. The first involves the *interactional dynamics* of the network; the second is its *morphological structure* (Boissevain, 1974:33; cf. Mitchell, 1969a:14). Once again, by analogy to an electronic communications system, the first, *interactional dynamics*, would be reflected by the number, type, and force of impulses sent to different nodes or stations within the system. The analyst wants to evaluate how well or how quickly, by what paths, and with what effect those messages are received. Continuing the analogy, the second, *morphological structure*, would be represented by a diagram of the structure of the circuitry itself. The two levels of analysis are mutually informative for understanding the connectedness of an individual to others in his/her social environment. The first measures the impulses of connectedness while the second maps the structures of connectedness.

Interactional Dynamics

In any given network there are four main interactional dynamics that may be analyzed. First, is the *multiplexity* (or structural diversity) of role relations of individuals within a network. Characteristically, such analysis begins by viewing one individual (often designated *EGO, ALPHA*, or the like) as the anchor point around which the other relational actors are positioned. It also identifies the kinds of ties that link the actors. Multiplexity refers to the different types of links that an EGO can have with another individual actor (e.g., a brother-in-law who is also a business partner and a former fraternity buddy), thus producing a more emotionally weighted, and hence stronger, net of bonds.

Second, having plotted the relations of these actors according to the types of linkages that exist, one may then calculate what kind of exchanges can therefore be anticipated. This is called the *transactional content* and gives one of the means of relative weighting among relationships (Boissevain, 1974:33). Because these relationships also supply certain norms and expectations they provide a symbolic or normative value, as in kinship or friendship ties (cf. Mitchell, 1969a:20).

The case of Aurelius Symmachus (discussed above) is once again illustrative. The circle of pagan supporters is but a part of Symmachus' total network, which included numerous other pagan and Christian correspondents, professional acquaintances, clients, and friends. One sees that he was connected to each other key figure in this inner circle through multiplex and transactionally intense links. Indeed, the circle is marked by the overlay of simultaneous links: kinships, friends/intimates of parents and/or wives, intermarriage, neighbors (both in Rome and in the resorts of Campania), professional/career associations, and participation in religious clubs and offices. Because of their social class, these ties are also relatively equitable (hence reciprocal), though there are some subtle lines of patronal influence from the likes of the elder Praetextatus to Symmachus or Symmachus to his son-in-law. Thus, these interactional dynamics help to understand why certain behaviors or stances would be "normal" within the framework of that social circle.

The final two interactional criteria deal with the flow of exchanges among actors in the network. They include *direction* and either *frequency* or *duration* of interactions. These factors serve as measures or indicators of importance, symmetry, and equity/inequity in the relationship (Boissevain, 1974:34). Thus, kinship ties will tend to have a reciprocal flow (where familial norms work equally on both parties), while inequitable patron-client relations will tend to be more unidirectional or differentiated in terms of expectations and returns (Mitchell, 1969a:25).

Morphological Structures

The analysis of structures of connectedness are concerned with the size, density, and clustering of actors within segments of a network. While these attributes are easier to measure in small, tightly circumscribed (hence partial) networks, they are also operative in larger network segments of a complex society (Boissevain, 1974:35). Also, while an EGO is usually identified with an individual actor, EGO might also serve as appellation for a small group within a larger, complex social framework (Mitchell, 1969a:14; cf. Laumann and Pappi:18).

The *size* of a person's primary network of contacts might range very large, since it reflects all the other individuals an EGO might access, but these will tend to break down into smaller segments or subgroups. Hence some contacts might be made directly while others will be indirect, through another member of the network. Measuring the size seeks to take into account all such possible links in a ratio with the actual or active links in any given situation. This process also produces an awareness of second order zones of networks (cf. Boissevain, 1974:45–47).

Density measures the degree to which members of EGO's network are also in contact with one another independent of EGO. It indicates the potential communications within the network; therefore, it is very influential on both the form and content of transactions that actually occur (Boissevain, 1974:37–39). This is an important measure, since different networks of the same size might have different configurations owing to the density (or interconnectedness) and the dynamics that might accrue.

Finally, the *degree* of connection (or compactness) measures the average number of links each person has with others in the same network. It serves as a correlative index that likewise shows the strength of connections within a given network. Here, assuming one has a rather complete profile of the actors, one may begin to quantify the measures (cf. Boissevain 1974:39–40):

> DENSITY (D) = no. of actual links (Na) *divided by* no. of persons (N), figured as a percentage using the formula $D = 100 \times Na + 1/2\,N\,(N-1)\,\%$.
>
> DEGREE (d) = $(Na \times 2) \div N$

While density and degree measure the interconnectedness of a network around an EGO, *centrality* seeks to locate EGO more precisely within the active field of the environment. Thus, while a given EGO might be the subjective center of analysis, that might not accurately reflect his/her objective position within the network. Here the perspective of analysis shifts in an important way, since it becomes clearer that one is concerned with more than the individual alone, hence less an EGO-centric analysis. The more central a person is in a network, the more links go through him/her, and the more influential he/she will be in bringing about communication. Conversely, the higher the density or degree of a given network, that is the more links there are between members, the less EGOcentric it is. Thus, the higher the general accessibility among members of the network, the less EGO is able to monopolize or dominate the flow of communication. For EGO centrality is inversely related to density (Boissevain 1974:41). A close correlate of this notion is the measure of reachability (or just *reach*), which similarly seeks to calculate the number of steps required for EGO to communicate (directly or through intermediates) with all members of a network. Reach is directly related to the degree of compactness in a network, but not necessarily to its density (Mitchell, 1969a:15–17). When contacts are so mediated, certain actors in the network will serve as "gateways" or "brokers" of contact, and thus become indispensable in communications among the various segments (Mitchell, 1969a:38; Boissevain, 1974:147–157).

A morphological characteristic that occurs in very complex social systems is the tendency for *clusters* or network segments to develop within a larger network (Boissevain, 1974:43; cf. Barnes, 1969:64). Clusters are smaller networks unto themselves which have a relatively higher internal density (i.e., interconnectedness among members of the cluster) than the density of the surrounding network contacts. Clusters may have fewer pathways or contacts to other areas of the larger network, and hence are relatively isolated from the rest. Such clusters are often made up or effectively recruited out of the different activity fields of an EGO, and the actions of EGO may vary sharply between these activity fields so long as they remain relatively isolated. The inconsistency of actions of EGO between clusters is predicated on the influence of expectations and messages operative within each. A good example is a person who is a member of a professional group with one set of political or moral objectives and a religious group with a different set. The individual will tend to behave according to the norms and expectations of each group so long as he/she is with the members of that cluster. The inconsistency is abated because the members of the respective groups, though still part of EGO's total network, have few if any other links to one another. EGO, however, will be required to reconcile or balance on a personal level the inconsistencies in norms and expectations among the groups. Hence higher overall density is more likely to force greater consistency of activity norms. Likewise, the higher number of contacts will transform individual cases of reconciliation into a larger social rationalization (Boissevain, 1974:43–44). This notion will become extremely important in the applications which follow below.

Historical Application

If one thinks of social environment as a kind of cultural ecosystem of human relations, then network theory can be used to provide understanding in two ways. As a metaphor for structuring human interaction, it helps to see the role of coalition dynamics as intermediate structural stages between the level of the individual and the level of society as such. As a method of analyzing, and even quantifying, social linkages it can help to evaluate the particular types of structures and influences in a given social system or environment. Yet, part of any given cultural ecosystem is the construct of cultural symbols and norms which are determinative for and reflective of the actions and values of such interactive relationships. One of the great advantages of network theory is that it does not presuppose any one social or cultural symbol system. Rather it derives both the nature and the normative value of different types of relationships from the specific social context being studied. Both as social metaphor and as analytical method are there potential applications to social historical analysis.

While initial forays (as suggested in the previous chapter) would suggest intuitively that network analysis can be used, the application to specific historical studies must be handled with care. For the methods of network analysis come largely from anthropological fieldwork and empirical social observation. It might seem at first that one faces insurmountable difficulties of application when attempting to apply these methods to the fragmentary evidence of ancient historical settings. Two aspects of historical research require special caution in this regard. The first is the inevitable necessity of historical reconstruction and conjecture to fill out the record of ancient periods. This process is often necessary whether one is dealing with archaeological remains (such as lacunae in papyri or damaged inscriptions) or with literary sources whose authorship or historical credibility is questioned. The difficulty lies in properly balancing the weight of reconstructed "data" (with varying degrees of probability and conjecture) to be used in the place of empirical observations.

The second is closely related but in some ways is a reverse tendency from the first. It arises from the tendency to derive predictive and prescriptive implications for human social behaviors from theoretical models in the social sciences as a way of filling in (that is "reconstructing") the aforementioned gaps in history. While, in certain cases one is able to generalize on human social situations in this way, not all theoretical models claim this same probative value. The crucial element is often the ability to transfer the structures of a theoretical model deduced from empirical data and analysis on one society or cultural context to serve as predictors of similar or analogous structures in a different society or cultural context operating at a different time. While cross-cultural analogies often pose salient questions to ask of the historical data, they do not always offer answers.

Such problems have been addressed in discussions of using historical observations drawn from N. D. Fustel de Coulanges (1873) or Marc Bloch (1961) in doing anthropology of contemporary Mediterranean cultures (Davis:239–258; cf. Gilmore:175–205). Davis (240) contrasts this traditional approach of "historic landscaping" to the focus on "social process," as in the functionalist schools of Evans-Pritchard and Radcliffe-Brown (245, cf. Evans-Pritchard:173–175). The difficulty often lies in the use of so-called historical facts (generally treated uncritically) to establish either causalities or "survivals" in the particular contemporary society being studied (Davis:248–254). At times this has led to misplaced propositions regarding the universal nature, character, and structure of certain social concepts or institutions among otherwise unrelated preindustrial societies. A good example is the discussion of hospitality by a disciple of Evans-Pritchard, Julian Pitt-Rivers (1968). In this study, hospitality is treated as a "natural law" generated from social necessity and structural continuity; however, Pitt-Rivers fails to consider, among the hodgepodge of examples adduced, that individual cultural values, norms, and symbols serve as differential criteria of development of the social action in individual societies (cf. Davis:253–254).

Several sociological and anthropological approaches have profitably found application in historical work on facets or phases of the Graeco-Roman period, in some cases including early Jewish and Christian contexts (cf. Carney). Among them we may mention those of Karl Polanyi and Louis Gernet (Humphreys:31–106), Mary Douglas and Claude Levi-Strauss (Rykwert; Malina, 1981; 1986), and Robert Redfield (Sjoberg; Snyder:9). It is all the more important then to test and reassess the "data" for historical periods with an eye toward theoretical issues but without being slavish to one theoretical model (cf. Smith; Gager:9–14; Kee, 1980:22–29). In this way the historian can provide fresh insight to the period under consideration but also offer more nuanced or critically evaluated social data to be used in further empirical studies. Historical studies must then be seen as test cases for, rather than necessary conclusions from, such social science models. Here, insights drawn from the operation of social networks within the framework of Roman cultural norms may ultimately help to shed light on the culture itself and hence on the applicability of other anthropological categories or models. Such an approach is employed by Gabriel Herman (1987:32–34) in adapting the work of Pitt-Rivers (1973) on kinship structures to the operations of ritualized friendship patterns in classical Greece. Network analysis of Greek kinship-friendship linkages might further refine such a picture.

To take up but one concrete example, we may consider some implications of network theory on observing changes in societal norms or mores and the impact at the level of cultural change, particularly as applied to the later Roman world. One of the key postulations (noted above) regarding the structural characteristics of social networks holds that a high rate of *density* within a given network or network segment ("cluster") will tend to reinforce consistency of behavior among its members (cf. Boissevain, 1974:43–44). Thus, by derivation it may be assumed that so long as that density is maintained at a fairly constant rate there will be less likelihood of deviation (or at least less tolerance of deviation) from those established behavioral norms. If, on the other hand, the rate of density is altered sharply (either in absolute or relative terms) one might expect tensions to arise over the maintenance of these norms. One such case might occur if a particular network segment or cluster should find itself progressively marginalized from the rest of the social system. The result is a higher internal density while interlinkages with other segments of the overall network system are reduced. Such a shift may well incline the subgroup represented by the segment to undergo an inordinate experience of alienation and a concomitant sense of reorientation toward internally defined norms. Indeed, such is often seen in the formation of a sectarian group, where the group's religious ideology comes to be focused inwardly as the degree of separation from the larger environment increases (so see Stark and Bainbridge, 1980:1380; Bainbridge). The reverse is also true. When a sectarian group (by definition, then, with a high internal density) begins to experience more individual connections to outsiders, there will tend to be for those individuals a higher conflict or tension over the discordant norms and expectations of the discrete network subsets in which they operate. The ultimate result may be a wholesale acculturation of the cluster to the norms of the larger network system as distinctive sectarian norms and constraints are resolved, reconciled, or reinterpreted (cf. White, 1988:22–24).

More study needs to be devoted to social structures during processes of social transition. Indeed, the bulk of network theory is predicated on analysis of relatively small, self-contained social groupings with little change. But what happens when there is substantial influx of new population groups, and especially when these new groups also import different cultural norms or symbol systems? Such was indeed the case in both the Hellenistic and Roman periods just as it has been in the U.S. during the nineteenth century and more recently since the end of World War II. So, what happens when a religious sect, largely of Jewish ethnic origins and highly committed to an apocalyptic worldview, finds itself living in and attempting to recruit from the population of a cosmopolitan Roman city?

For me, then, two issues arise from network theory in social contexts where network clusters develop (even partially) from differentiated social groupings, especially where religious and cultural pluralism are involved. First, the correlation of internal density with external interlinkages within network clusters may serve as a symptom of cultural assimilation. As in the example above of sect formation, high internal density with low external interlinkages will tend to produce separation. High density with high interlinkages will tend to produce acculturation, where the cluster still retains its group identity. High interlinkages with low or declining density will tend to produce assimilation, so that group identity may itself diminish. In matters of religious group formation, this set of observations may further explain why sects and cults will tend to behave differently within and toward their respective host cultures (cf. White, 1988:17). It will also have implications on the nature of recruitment (or "conversion") to such religious groups (cf. Stark and Bainbridge, 1980:1377).

The second implication has to do with the symbol systems themselves in contexts of high cultural pluralism. I return to the situation of an individual who finds him/herself operating in distinct network clusters where the norms and expectations are radically different. If this individual is the sole "gateway" for interlinkage between the two groups he/she will often experience dissonance of behavior and expectations between the two arenas of activity. To the extent that the two arenas are isolated from one another (hence no other interlinkages) the individual will be able to cope with this dissonance by adopting a personal reconciliation of the different norms. However, as more interlinkages occur between other members, then new explanations and reconciliations will be required. In this case, one individual's success in reconciling the two sets of norms and expectations may provide a model for others and further gateways for interlinkage are opened. The process of reconciliation of the norms will further offer a path of harmonization at the ideological level, and hence both personal and ideological acculturation of the network cluster to the larger network system. Nor should we assume *a priori* that harmonization will always work in the direction of acculturation away from the sectarian ideology. Depending upon the cultural context and the circumstances it is conceivable that the experience of individuals in the dense cluster will serve as a model for others in the larger network system, in which case harmonization will tend to re-import these features back into the larger cultural framework. The beginnings of the Jesus movement as a sect (or several sects) alongside other sects within Palestinian Judaism might offer examples of both tendencies.

For emphasis, I would repeat that in the case just suggested both the cluster and the larger network system are assumed to be operating within the same basic symbol system or worldview. A further step may be envisioned in this process of social transformation when the members of the network cluster are operating with a different symbol system, as is generally suggested for the early movement of Jews and Christians into the Roman urban environment. Now, when interlinkages occur and reconciliation or harmonization follows, the added impact that must be considered is at the level of the two sets of cultural symbols themselves. Thus, the process of harmonization between network segments may involve both the discarding of certain cultural symbols and the synthesis of new ones out of the existing stock. The result may go to the level of a cultural worldview shift, even though some of the basics symbols and social structures will closely resemble that which went before. Perhaps, there is a clue here for the so-called "christianization" of the Roman world (White, 1988:23–24). We have typically seen this process as ideological conversion out of the religious "syncretism" of the Hellenistic-Roman age, but network theory suggests that there are some hitherto unexplored social dynamics. What is needed then is further historical analysis of the particulars of the Roman social world as well as further testing of the theoretical models. A good example comes in the suggestions regarding processes of social mobility and political action in contexts of class and status differentiation, typical of the Roman world (Laumann and Pappi:256–267; cf. MacMullen, 1974; D'Arms, 1981).

Looking To Networks Past

As a field technique from social anthropology, one characteristic of network analysis is its attention to the personal profiles of individuals and their interlinkages within the social environment under investigation (cf. Boswell, for example). This feature of network analysis may be particularly amenable to social history application since it offers similarities to and affinities for historical prosopography. It may also offer new means of analyzing prosopographic data beyond the level of generating stemmas or family trees, as suggested for the Symmachus Circle in the preceding chapter. In this vein there are already prosopographic social history studies of groups or individuals and their connections, as in the case of the Arval Brotherhood (Sheid:293–330; Syme, 1980:70–84), the correspondence of Abinnaeus (Bell et al.:22–33), or the social origins of the western aristocracy in the later empire (Arnheim).

Perhaps the most readily discernible network structures from the Roman world are the familial organization of the extended household and the operation of patronage. Indeed, patronage may be seen both as a kind of "friendship" structure, as Aristotle conceived it, or as kind of quasi-kinship structure. It is akin both to patterns of godparenthood (a kind of ritualized fictive kinship) and to the political structures of a hierarchical syndicate organization (best known perhaps through the *mafiosa*). These, too, suggest network dynamics that might be used as analogies for asking certain questions of the cultural norms behind such structures.

For example, Davis (223) suggests that godparenthood in Christian areas of the Mediterranean is often part of a system of familial alliances (like marriage, under the authority of the Church) whereby corporate kinship groups are brought into permanent relation to each other. Godparenthood becomes thereby an achieved relationship, linkage, and alliance between individuals and family clusters. In these contexts values relating to personal identity, such as honor and shame, tend to be subordinated to social norms expressed in relational terms of stratification. Hence, honor and shame must be analyzed as norms of behavior operating within a very specific cultural network structure (Davis:89–101). That patronage has highly symbolized meaning within a given, historical cultural system is further attested by the fact that godparenthood (i.e., the *Godfather*, like the *Patron* or *Don*) is used as the designation for the larger set of social relationships beyond such familial alliances. When in the Roman world the gods are addressed as benefactors of humankind or as protectors of

Emperor or city, the patronage model has been extended into a symbolic sphere. (See the articles below by Hendrix and Stoops.)

In many respects, the Roman system of patronage (from Latin *patrocinium*) served all these functions. As its Latin derivation suggests, it too originated within the household structure under patriarchal authority (*patria potestas*) of the *pater familias*. The development of Roman patronage was also influenced by the Greek system of civic benefaction (*euergesia*), but in later usage the terms became virtually interchangeable. One difference is that Aristotle had defined benefaction as a subspecies of friendship between unequals, whereas by later Hellenistic and Roman times it also came to have these familial connotations as well.

In typical Latin usage by the later Republic *amicitia* became a polite circumlocution for "client" (*cliens*) in order to avoid calling attention to the inevitable reality of inferiority in the relationship. Both Hellenistic monarchs and Roman emperors used the language of friendship in a similar fashion as expression of statecraft in order to create political dependencies among conquered territories (Herman, 1980/1:103–149; Gruen: I.54–55; Badian, 1958). Ultimately, it has been argued, the change to imperial rule under Augustus and his successors witnessed the wholesale appropriation of a system of patronage networks, rising to a pinnacle in the emperor himself, both as structure and as ideology (Syme 1939:369–388; Ste. Croix; Gelzer [1975]:62–139; Mattingly). Recent studies of the dynamics of Roman patronage and its technical vocabulary have demonstrated its formal characteristics both in structuring social relations (Treggiari; D'Arms, 1981) and in creating a symbolic ideal (Saller:7–40; cf. Wallace-Hadrill).

Some studies have already begun to analyze the elements of Roman patronage structures as they appear within New Testament and early Christian sources. Peter Marshall (1987) has profitably used the technical language of "friendship" to analyze the social conventions and social relations between Paul and his Corinthian congregation. In particular, he observes correctly that the intentional ambiguities of the technical vocabulary allow for nuances of meaning to be played out between the ideal of friendship as "true brotherly affection" on one side and "patronage" and loyalty exchange on the other. Letters, hospitality, and "friendship" language, reflect patterns of relations. Similarly, Dale Martin (1990) has recently shown how much of the vocabulary of "slavery" as used by Paul is also derived from a well-established technical usage from the environment. In this usage, slavery is selfconsciously used to reflect social status, where such status is a measure of concrete social relationships. Thus, both studies suggest further lines of potential analysis using network insights to draw out some of the implications of these structured social relationships and the cultural ideals that they embody.

What often makes patronage systems, such as those seen throughout the Roman environment, susceptible to network analysis is a two-fold recognition. First is the awareness that patronage relations involve real individuals who can, depending on the nature of the extant sources, be identified through prosopography as actors. Of course, the greater the detail that can be assembled, the more complete will be the picture. But such is the task of social description. Second is the recognition that patronage (and even public benefaction), because it is modeled on reciprocity and obligation, constitutes a mechanism for structuring social exchange (Gelner; Eisenstadt and Roniger). It has been recognized that the basis of patronage is a dyadic relationship between unequals that produces bonds of uneven exchange—loyalty in exchange for largess (Landé). Still, it is possible to see direct application in complex group situations (Wolf), where layers or multiple lines of patronage constitute a basic dynamic of the network, as I have tried to sketch out in the article above. Many of the studies that follow demonstrate the pivotal role that patronage relations played in the environment, and they offer further insight to application of network analysis to the historical situation.

PART II

MAPPING SOCIAL NETWORKS IN THE ENVIRONMENT

BENEFACTOR/PATRON NETWORKS IN THE URBAN ENVIRONMENT: EVIDENCE FROM THESSALONICA

Holland Hendrix
Union Theological Seminary

ABSTRACT

Network analysis provides a useful means of evaluating both the structures and the dynamics of social relations in Graeco-Roman society. In so doing it may also offer further insights on the development of Christianity, particularly the extent to which it did or did not adapt socially to organizational patterns in the environment. The present study, therefore, focuses network analysis on two related and sometimes overlapping types of social relationships (benefaction and patronage). The location is Thessalonica, a chief city of Macedonia (Greece) under the early Roman Empire and a center for early Christian activity. Four cases of non-Christian benefactor/patron relations known from epigraphic or literary remains are discussed in detail. Analysis of these four cases shows that in Roman Thessalonica there developed specific hierarchies of benefaction structures that operated as networks between individuals, groups and/or institutions, and the Roman imperial power. Significantly, the inscriptions also show religious elements in linking these networks of social relations to the divine realm. Finally, the dynamic qualities of these network relations serve to promote the individual actors within them by connecting them to larger spheres of influence and power. At the same time one can also see that the networks themselves may be enhanced beyond the local limits, but not without certain costs.

Introduction

Social historians of early Christianity should consider the behavior of Christians both as social groups and as individuals in society. This requires a thorough appreciation of the kinds of social organizations and more discrete social networks operating in Graeco-Roman societies. A number of scholars have contributed to our understanding of Graeco-Roman social organizations and the extent to which early Christians did or did not adapt socially according to organizational patterns in their environments. It is important to continue this line of inquiry. The present study, however, focuses on two related types of social networks among Thessalonicans: benefactor-beneficiary and patron-client. Although the objects of my scrutiny are non-Christian networks, I hope that the theoretical models and analytical methods employed may be of use to students of early Christianity. It is my further hope that elucidating particular networks in an ancient Greek urban environment will contribute to our understanding of less visible social processes in Graeco-Roman antiquity.

In using the terms benefactor-beneficiary and patron-client to describe particular types of human interaction, constant attention must be paid to the entire range of evidence from the locale under study. This is all the more necessary when the locale is a Greek city undergoing transformations in response to increased Roman domination.

Generally speaking, the use of the term "benefactor" (*euergetes*) and other associated terms such as "good will" (*eunoia*), "commitment to the good" (*philagathia*), and "manifest excellence" (*arete*) reflects corporate activity. A durable corporate group with fixed structural properties grants corporate honors and amenities to one who has benefited the group. Patron-client terminology generally reflects a more individualized phenomenon in which one party is bound to another through specific transactions or the assumption of particular obligations.[1]

This general categorization should in no way be construed as written in stone. In fact, many stones from Thessalonica say quite the contrary. L. Canuleius Zosimus in the mid-second or mid-third century CE fondly memorialized his deceased wife, a freedwoman, as "benefactor" (*IT* 451). So also the Thessalonican philosopher Sosivius honored his apparent patron, the procurator Septemius Aurelius Paulinus, as "benefactor" (*IT* 145). The fact that ambiguities existed should prompt us to consider in more detail the distinctiveness and interpenetration of these categories of relationships as well as the terms used to designate them.

Certainly we can no longer presume that Romans necessarily transplanted intact their highly developed system of patron-client relations, or that Roman imperialism was generated by expanding *patrocinium* on an international political scale.[2] To be sure, Roman and Greek "clients" of Roman patrons were operating in Greece during the late Republican and early Imperial times, and as Roman domination spread, so Roman patronage networks became more firmly embedded in the social fabric of the Greek East. But in the process, there appears to have been a mutual domestication of the Greek benefactor-beneficiary phenomenon and Roman patron-client relationships. Disentangling the threads in this complex development is not our purpose here, but that it is complex should be borne in mind. In the present study, distinctions will be made between corporate and individual activity. However, as will be seen, distinctions cannot always be made on the basis of terminology. Thessalonican "clients" used the language of benefactor-beneficiary relations in speaking and writing publicly about their patrons.

Network analysis concentrates on how various connections between people influence their behavior in specific situations. The structure of the connections (who is connected to whom in how many ways) is as important as the nature of the connections (kinship, friendship, creditor-debtor, employer-employee, etc.).[3] One can study benefactor/patron relationships from a variety of network analytical perspectives. Benefactor/patron relationships may be viewed as one connection interrelating individuals also connected in other ways.[4] When adequate information is available on the interconnectedness of individuals, such an approach is particularly useful in analyzing conflicts involving competing loyalties (Boissevain 1974: 148–49).

Benefactor/patron relationships may also be viewed as partial networks themselves. From this perspective, benefactor-beneficiary and patron-client relationships involve processes of social exchange articulated through interconnected individuals comprising a social network. Network connectedness not only includes specific benefactors and their beneficiaries or patrons and their clients but also extends to third parties that are attached to one or both actor(s) and that are potentially interconnected through the benefactor-beneficiary or patron-client relationships. An example of such a network is the "friends of friends" phenomenon (Boissevain, 1974: 148–49), in which one or more individuals may mediate or influence encounters with previously unconnected others. Insofar as the connection is utilized to promote the interests of those previously unconnected, the mediator serves as a "broker" in facilitating exchange between the two parties.[5]

An analysis of benefactor/patron relationships as partial networks is the task of the present study. Adopting this perspective as opposed to the more inclusive one that assesses patronage networks as one facet of multifaceted networks reflects three essential concerns. First, network analysis is based on data gathered in field observation. Some connections between individuals may become apparent only through extensive direct questioning. For Graeco-Roman Thessalonica, such basic data-gathering techniques are obviously impossible. Second, the evidence, largely epigraphic, does not lend itself to anything approaching exhaustive network description. Prosopographical research is helpful in delineating some connections (kinship, patronage, commercial, etc.) but is of limited utility in ascertaining network density, multiplexity, frequency, and so on. Third, networks are most visible in crisis situations involving mobilized loyalties. Except in cases of sepulchral, some votive, and occasionally honorific inscriptions, epigraphic evidence is seldom directly expressive of conflicts and crises.

In limiting ourselves to benefactor/patron relationships as networks, we might pose a number of fundamental questions. What connections are visible in benefactor/patron relationships? How are the connections interrelated (what structural properties are apparent)? What are the dynamic features of the connections? Before addressing these questions to the evidence of networks in which Thessalonicans were involved, we should survey briefly developments in benefactor/patron patterns in the Greek East as they pertained to transformations in the phenomenon at Thessalonica.

Greek Benefactors and the Coming of Rome

A Greek benefactor in the Classical and Hellenistic periods was someone who was honored for an important public or private service.[6] Such service may have involved fulfilling in exemplary fashion the liturgies (those duties involving expenses) of a particular office. Dedicated professional or unusual personal service could also motivate honors. Individuals benefiting from the service might honor their benefactor with a crown to be presented on a formal occasion, perhaps a statue to be displayed conspicuously and crowned periodically, an inscribed testimonial to the benefactor's generosity and excellence together with a record of the honors accorded him or her, and any other amenities that it was in the power of the group or individual to grant.

If the benefactor were a foreigner and the beneficiaries had some power in the assembly, then citizenship might be granted with all its privileges as well as other honors appropriate for benefactors. In fact, it would appear that the peculiar honors and ceremonies that came to be associated with benefactors in general were derived historically from grants of proxeny (citizenship status) to non-native individuals who made distinctive contributions to their host communities.[7] In a later period when particular Romans were perceived as benefiting Greek communities or individuals, they were honored in ways typical of the foreign benefactor traditions. Monuments and inscriptions attested to their generous benefaction. (See Hendrix 1984.)

In the Hellenistic kingdoms, the functions and honors of the Classical Greek benefactor were appropriated by leaders claiming royal authority. This was accompanied by an escalating emphasis on Alexander's divine status. The title "benefactor" and "*soter*" (savior) became personalized and regularized epithets of an increasingly divinized Hellenistic royalty (as, for example, with Ptolemy Savior or Eumenes Benefactor).[8] Among Roman leaders of the second century BCE one finds the same peculiar coordination of savior/benefactor and royalty that had become characteristic in the Hellenistic East. As Roman governor-generals assumed leadership in the East, they were perceived and perceived themselves as the equals of Hellenistic kings and so rightful claimants to the full stature of Alexander's heirs.[9]

This claim was realized fully with the rule of Augustus. When one listens carefully to acknowledgments of Augustus' divine governance, what strain of royal practical theology predominates?

> Decree of the Greek Assembly in the province of Asia, on motion of the High Priest Apollonios, son of Menophilos, of Aizanoi: Whereas Providence that orders all our lives has in her display of concern and generosity in our behalf adorned our lives with the highest good, Augustus, whom she has filled with *arete* for the benefit of humanity, and has in her beneficence granted us and those who will come after us [a Savior] who has made war to cease and who shall put everything [in peaceful] order; and whereas Caesar, [when he was manifest], transcended the expectations of [all who had anticipated the good news], not only by surpassing the benefits conferred by his predecessors but by leaving no expectation of surpassing him to those who would come after him, with the result that the birthday of our god signalled the beginning of good news for the world because of him . . . .[10]

The good news, a gospel for the world, is the divine grant of *arete* manifested in the unsurpassed benefactions of Augustus.

Four Cases Of Benefaction At Thessalonica

This oppressive summary is intended to highlight an extremely important development in benefactor/patron patterns in the Greek East. In the Classical and early Hellenistic periods benefactors were for the most part inhabitants of various *poleis*. With the insinuation of Roman power into the area, networks of benefaction were expanded and new patron-client networks forged in order to maximize benefits from Roman powers. The banality of this observation invites the equally banal conclusion that this phenomenon merely reflected the changed political-economic realities of the times. But such a simplistic economic reduction precisely misses the point. To what extent were benefactor/patron networks principal *agents* in changes involving economic, social, and religious realities? With this question added to our agenda, we may consider four cases of benefactor/patron networks as reflected in inscriptions from Roman Thessalonica.

CASE I. *"The Youths and a Gymnasiarch"*

οἱ νέοι

Ἀθηναγόρας Ἀπολλοδώρου, Πύρρος Κλειτομάχο[υ],
Νεικόστρατος Ν[ε]ικομάχου, Διογένης Ἐπιγένου,
Στράτων Ξένωνος, Ν[ε]ικήρατος Ἀνδροκλέους

5   εἶπαν·
ἐπεὶ Παράμονος Ἀντιγόνου αἱρεθεὶς γυμνασίαρ[χος]
εἰς τὸ ᵛ τρίτον ᵛ καὶ ᵛ πεντηκοστὸν ᵛ ἔτος πολλὴν π[ροση]-
νέγκατο προθυμίαν [ε]ἰ̣ς [τ]ὸ̣ π̣ρ̣ο̣σ̣τατῆσαι τῆς ἀρχῆς εὐ[σχη]-
μόνως, ἔν τε τοῖς χορηγουμένοις ἅπασιν ἐκτενῆ π̣[αρα-
10   σκευάζων ἑαυτὸν καὶ τὰς ἠθισμένας τειμὰς Γ - - -⁵⁻⁶- - -
τοῖς τε θεοῖς καὶ Ῥωμαίοις εὐεργέταις ἐπαύξων· π̣[ρονο]-
ούμενος δὲ καὶ τῆς εὐταξίας τῆς ἐν τῶι τόπωι κ[αὶ κα]-
θόλου στοχαζό[μ]ενος ἐμ πᾶσι τοῦ πρέποντος, οὐ τ[ὴν δα]-
π⟨ά⟩νην τὴν προσήκουσαν παραλέλοιπεν, ἀλλὰ τ[ὸν]
15   χρόνον τῆς ἀρχῆς ΤΗΣ ΑΣ τιθεὶς τὸ ἄλε[ιμμα δι]-
ατε⟨τέ⟩λεκεν· δίκαιον δέ ἐστιν τοὺς φιλοδόξῳ προα[ιρέ]-
σει χρωμένους τῶν καθηκουσῶν τιμῶν τυγχάνε[ιν],
ἵνα καὶ ἕτεροι, θεωροῦντες τὰς γινομένας τιμὰς
ὑπὸ τῶν νέων, τῶν ὁμοίων ζηλωταὶ γίνωνται·
20   ἔδοξεν τοῖς ἀπὸ τοῦ γυμνασίου ἐπαινέσαι τ[ε]
τὸν Παράμονον ἐπὶ τῆι προαιρέσει καὶ στεφανῶσ[αι]
θαλλοῦ στεφάνωι καὶ εἰκόνι χαλκῇ καὶ γραπτῆι τ[ε]-
λείαι, τὸ δὲ ψήφισμα ἀναγραφὲν εἰστήλην λιθίν̣η̣[ν]
τεθῆναι προφανὲς ἐν τῶι γυ[μ]νασίωι, χορηγηθέ[ν]-
25   τος ὑπὸ τῶν ταμιῶν κατὰ τὸ παρὸν τοῦ τε εἰς τὴ̣[ν]
γραπτὴν εἰκόνα καὶ στήλην ἀναλώματος.

                intervallum

ἐπέχε ἱροτονήθη ᵛ ἔτους γ´ ᵛ καὶ ᵛᵛ υ´,   vacat
[Ὑπ]ερβερταίου ᵛᵛ δεκάτηι [[Ε]] ἀπιόντος.   vacat

                vacat

Translation:

The Youths

Athenagoras son of Apollodoros, Pyrros son of Kleitomacho[s],
Neikostratos son of Neikomachos, Diogenes son of Epigenos,
Straton son of Xenon, Neikeratos son of Androkles
5   made the motion:
Whereas Paramonos son of Antigonos, elected gymnasiar[ch]
for the year 53 has e[ngag]ed very
eagerly in the oversight of the office with [grace and]
dignity, zealously offering himself among those who provide
         for public expenses
10   and increasing the customary honors G - - - - - -

for the gods and Roman benefactors; (and) being c[on]-
cerned with good order in the place a[nd gen]-
erally endeavoring after that which is most proper
   in all things, he has not
neglected t[he] attendant [ex]pense, but rather
15 has [com]pleted his term of office - - - - TES - - - - - - -
   having given the oil;
and it is good that those who aspire to public re[cog]-
nition obtain the appropriate honors
so that others also when they consider the honors bestowed
by The Youths might strive for similar honors;
20 be it resolved by those from the gymnasium to commend
Paramonos for his aspiration (to public recognition) and
   to honor him with a
crown and with a bronze likeness, life-size and painted,
and the (honorific) decree engraved on a stone stele
is to be given a conspicuous place in the gymnasium; ex-
25 penses for the painted likeness and the stele are to be
met by the presiding treasurers.

(vacant space)

Sanctioned (by vote) in the year 3 and 50, (vacant)
on the tenth day from the end of Hyperbertaios ("E" erased).

(vacant)[11]

A youth organization of the city issued this honorific decree commending the gymnasiarch Paramonos. The inscription bears a date equivalent to September 95 BCE.[12] The provisions of the decree imitate civic declarations granting honors to benefactors.[13] Though rather modest, the tributes are quite typical of those awarded by other Greek cities to their patrons.

Apparently, Thessalonican gymnasiarchs of this period were responsible not only for underwriting expenses of the gymnasium programs but also for contributing honors on behalf of its affiliates to the gods and Roman benefactors.[14] As will become clear in the next case to be presented, this reference is certainly to the civic cults of the gods and of Roman benefactors at Thessalonica. Since the decree mentions no other deities consecrated by the gymnasium (Heracles, Apollo, Hermes, etc.), one might conclude that the gods and Roman benefactors were the cultic patrons to whom the Youths were devoted.

The precise nature of the honors that Paramonos increased to the gods and Roman benefactors (lines 10–11) is obscured by the ambiguous qualifier "customary."[15]

CASE II. "The Youths and a Prince"

vacat

[ᵛ ἔτους ᵛ . ᵛ καὶ ᵛ . ᵛ καὶ ᵛ]ᵛ Σεβαστοῦ. ᵛ
[κατὰ · τὸ · δόξαν · τῇ · βουλῇ? ·] καὶ · τοῖς · νέοις · Π · Κερ-
[- - - - - - -ᶜ⁻¹⁶- - - - - - - - κατ]ὰ διαθήκην · ἱερέως · καὶ ἀγω-
[νοθέτου Αὐτοκρά]τορος · Καίσαρος · θεοῦ · υἱοῦ · Σεβαστοῦ
5 [Γ · Ἐιουλείου · Ῥοιμη]τάλκου · δυνάστου · ἀνταγωνοθε-
[τοῦντος · ? Ἡλιοδώ]ρου · τοῦ · Ἡλιοδώρου · ἱερέως · θεῶν
[- - - -ᶜ⁻⁸- - - το]ῦ Φ[ίλ]ωνος · Ῥώμης δὲ καὶ Ῥωμαίων εὐεργετᾶ
- - - -ᶜ⁻⁷- - νος · το[ῦ] · Διονυσίου · πολειταρχούντων
- -ᶜ⁻⁴- δώρου · τοῦ[· Ν]εικάνδρου · Ἀσκληπιοδώρου · τοῦ
10 Ἀσκληπιοδώρου · [Σω]σιπάτρου · τοῦ · Εἰσιδώρου · Ζωίλου
τοῦ · Ζωίλου · τοῦ · Λυσιπόνου · Ἀθηνογένους · τοῦ
Πλουσίας · γυμνασιαρχοῦντος · Μενελάου
τοῦ · Ἀντιγόνο[υ ·] ἐφηβαρχοῦντος Νεικολάου
τοῦ · Ἐπιμένο[υ]ς · ταμίου · τῆς πόλεως · Γ · Ἀγιλ-
15 ληίου Ποτείτου · ἀρχιτ[έ]κτονος · Λ · Εἰουλείου · Φύρμου (!),

intervallum

ταμιευόντων ᵛ τῶν
νέων [[- - - - - -ᶜ⁻¹³- - - - - Υ]]
Τ Μεμμίου Ζωσίμου
- - - -

Translation:

[In the year - and -] of Augustus.
[Decreed by the *boule*?] and by the *neoi*, P(ublius) Cer-
[- - - - - - - - - - - - - - - b]y a bequest, in the time of priest and ago-
[nothete of Impera]tor Caesar Augustus son of god
5 [G(aius) Julius Rhoime]talces, prince, and (in the time of)
vice-agonothe[te]
[Heliodo]ros son of Heliodoros, and of priest of (the) gods
[- - - - - - - - so]n of Philon, and of (priest) of Roma and Roman benefactors
- - - - - - nos so[n] of Dionysios; in the term of politarchs
- - - - doros son of [N]eikandros, Asklepiodoros son of
10 Asklepiodoros, [So]sipatros son of Isidoros, Zoilos
son of Zoilos (and) of Lysiponos, Athenogenes son of
Plousia; in the term of gymnasiarch Menelaos
son of Antigono[s]; in the term of ephebarch Neikolaos
son of Epimenes, of city treasurer G(aius) Agil-
15 lius Potitus, of archit[e]ct L(ucius) Julius Firmus,

(vacant space)

presiding treasurer of the
neoi [[Deina - - - - - - [son] of]]
T. Memmius Zosimos[16]

This inscription seems to record the dedication by the Youths and another civic body (the *boule*?) of a building made possible by a testamentary bequest. The dating of the dedication includes both specification of the "Augustan year" and naming of the current priest and agonothete of the Imperator Caesar Augustus son of god, the priest of (the) gods and of Roma and Roman benefactors. In the dedication's closing, the presiding politarchs, gymnasiarch, ephebarch, city treasurer, architect, and treasurer of the Youths are indicated.[17]

If L. Robert is correct in identifying Rhoimetalces (line 5) as a Thracian prince of the early first century CE, the inscription provides some evidence that the "priest and agonothete of the Imperator" at Thessalonica could be an honorary office held by a non-resident.[18] The designation of a "vice-agonothete" in line 6 suggests that at least some of the duties (and expenditures?) of the priest and agonothete may have been undertaken by a local assistant of the honorand.[19]

Gaius Julius Rhoimetalces' tenure as Thessalonican priest and agonothete of the Imperator Caesar Augustus son of god is not so surprising as it might at first seem. Prince Rhoimetalces had opposed his father's attempts to destabilize Augustus' settlement of East Macedonian and Thracian affairs.[20] In 18 CE, he was confirmed by Tiberius as co-ruler of the area (Tacitus, *Annals* 2.66). Although Rhoimetalces' governance did not escape Roman criticism, his later assumption of the title "king" presumably had Imperial endorsement. An association with Thessalonica appears to have been formalized during the earlier years of Rhoimetalces' rule; in the inscription the priest and agonothete is designated "prince."

CASE III: *"Damon and the Proconsul"*

A Thessalonican dedicated a statue of Metellus to Zeus Olympios at Olympia probably during or shortly after the Roman's service as proconsul in 143 BCE. The inscription on the base reads as follows.

Δάμων Νικάνορος Μακεδὼν ἀπὸ
Θεσσαλονίκης ᵛ Κόϊντον Καικέλιον
Κοΐντου Μέτελλον, στρατηγὸν ὕπατον
Ῥωμαίων, ᵛᵛᵛᵛ Διὶ Ὀλυμπίωι
ἀρετῆς ἕνεκεν καὶ εὐνοίας ἧς ἔχων διατε-
λεῖ εἴς τε αὐτὸν καὶ τὴν πατρίδα καὶ τοὺς λοιποὺς
Μακεδόνας ᵛ καὶ τοὺς ἄλλους Ἕλληνας.

vacat

Translation:

> Damon son of Nikanor, Macedonian from
> Thessalonica; (dedicated this) for Quintus Caecilius
> son of Quintus Metellus, pronconsul
> of the Romans; to Zeus Olympios
> on account of his *arete* and goodwill which he continues to manifest
> to myself and to the home city (=Thessalonica) and the rest of the
> Macedonians and the other Greeks.[21]

CASE IV. *"A Poet and his Patron"*

In 13 or 11 BCE, the Thessalonican poet Antipater followed his patron, the Roman magistrate L. Calpurnius Piso, to Asia Minor.[22] On his departure, he composed the following poetic prayer to Apollo.

> Φοῖβε Κεφαλλήνων λιμενοσκόπε θῖνα Πανόρμου
> ναίων τρηχείης ἀντιπέρην Ἰθάκης,
> δός με δι' εὐπλώτοιο πρὸς Ἀσίδα κύματος ἐλθεῖν
> Πείσωνος δολιχῆι νηὶ συνεσπόμενον,
> 5 καὶ τὸν ἐμὸν Βασιλῆα τὸν ἄλκιμον εὖ μὲν ἐκείνωι
> ἵλαον εὖ δ' ὕμνοις ἄρτισον ἡμετέροις.

Translation:

> Phoebus, the Cephallenians' harbor-watchman,
> dweller on Panormus' beach, opposite craggy
> Ithaca, grant me to go with fair sailing
> through the waves to the Asian land in the
> wake of Piso's long vessel. And dispose
> my valiant sovereign to gracious favor
> towards him, gracious also to my songs.[23]

Analysis of the Cases

To return to the questions asked at the outset: (1) What connections are visible in these benefactor-beneficiary, patron-client relationships? (2) How are the connections interrelated (what structural properties are apparent)? (3) What are the dynamic features of the connections?

The choice of these questions was influenced by network analytical studies of Jeremy Boissevain. Boissevain distinguishes the structure from the inherent dynamism of conflict groups (Boissevain 1974:8; cf. Mitchell 1973: 33–34). In analyzing networks he elaborates the distinction between structural criteria (size of network, density, degree, centrality, and clusters) and interactional criteria (multiplexity, transactional content, directional flow, frequency, and duration of interaction) (Boissevain, 1974: 28–45). The evidence to be considered does not yield information sufficient for a systematic deployment of Boissevain's criteria. However, the choice of questions represents more than a metaphorical application of the distinction between structural and dynamic features. As Boissevain observes, "structural criteria are statements about the theoretical possibility of a person to transact" while "interactional criteria are indicators of the possible importance of various links" (Boissevain, 1974: 45). By asking who is connected to whom and how the connections are interrelated, one attempts to establish what possibilities exist for transaction. Identifying the dynamic features may suggest the possible importance of various connections.

(1) Who is connected to whom?

In the inscription for the gymnasiarch (Case I), a particular group of named Youths took the initiative for granting corporate honors to Paramonos. Two complexes of connections may be manifest here. There is the obvious connection between Paramonos and the Youth organization. Paramonos, as gymnasiarch, went beyond the call of duty in governing and funding the activities of the Youths. Another more discrete connection may have existed between the gymnasiarch and those who moved that he be publicly honored. Since they are not designated as officers or seniors of the organization, their initiative may have been more than "conventional." They could have been recipients of specific benefits that called for reciprocal recognition. A third connection existed between Paramonos and "the gods and Roman benefactors." As gymnasiarch, Paramonos was responsible for the honorific interrelation between the Youths and "the gods and Roman benefactors." He was the mediator in satisfying the organization's honorific responsibility to its divine patrons. A fourth connection is stated in the honorific. Paramonos is represented as a model patron for others in the *polis*. Publication of honors to Paramonos was intended explicitly as a recruitment device for other potential patrons. The transaction between Paramonos and the Youths was extended as an open-ended invitation for connection to the Youth organization: ". . . it is good that those who aspire to public recognition obtain the appropriate honors so that others also when they consider the honors bestowed by the Youths might strive for similar honors" (lines 16–19).

As priest and agonothete of Imperator Caesar Augustus, C. Julius Rhoimetalces (Case II) was officially connected to the city of Thessalonica. The priesthood was a civic office, and in the case of Rhoimetalces' tenure probably represented an honor bestowed by the city.[24] Rhoimetalces was connected by the priesthood to the Imperator Caesar Augustus, civic honors for whom he officially mediated. He was also connected to Augustus as a Thracian "prince" (the title is included in the inscription). It was Augustus who designated him as dynastic successor and secured his continuance. As "prince," Rhoimetalces was also, of course, connected to the Thracians. Direct connections to the others cited in the inscriptions (the Youths, politarchs, etc.) are not explicit.

In Damon's honorific for Metellus (Case III), he was acting as a private citizen of Thessalonica. The proconsul Metellus is portrayed as the personal benefactor of Damon and as displaying goodwill to Thessalonica, Macedonia in general, and all the Greeks. Damon's honorific activity also engages Zeus Olympios as an object of the honoree's apparent gratitude.

Antipater's poetic prayer (Case IV) enjoined Apollo to grant safe passage for himself and by implication his patron in whose "wake" he followed. The poet also connects himself through Apollo to "his valiant Sovereign" Augustus who is, in turn, connected to Piso. A number of transactions are reflected in the prayer. The poet is a supplicant before Apollo on behalf of himself and his patron. Insofar as the invocation seeks divine protection and promotion of Piso, it involves an honor for the Roman as well. The poem's audience includes Piso, of course, and its composition represents a discharge of Antipater's duties as artist/client. But the ultimate benefactor is Apollo, whose gifts are to be realized through the Emperor's goodwill to Piso and Piso's continued patronage of the poet.

(2) How are the connections interrelated?

The gymnasiarch inscription (Case I) reflects a hierarchy of benefaction. A group within the Youths initiates honors ultimately decreed by the organization for its chief officer, Paramonos. Among those beneficent activities for which Paramonos is honored, pride of place is given to his "increasing the honors to the gods and Roman benefactors." A hierarchy of benefaction extends from those initiating honors to the organization as a whole to Paramonos to the gods and Roman benefactors. It is noteworthy that at Thessalonica in 95 BCE, Roman benefactors had already become conventionally associated with the civic cult of "the gods" as honorands of gymnasium activities.

A somewhat similar hierarchy of benefaction is operating in the case of Rhoimetalces (Case II). The city honored the Thracian prince with its most distinguished priesthood. Rhoimetalces was, in turn, the official mediator of the city's honors for the Imperator Caesar Augustus son of god. Notable is the respective status of the Thessalonican priesthoods. In every extant instance in which the "priest and agonothete of the Imperator" is mentioned, he is listed first in what appears to be a strict observance of protocol. The Imperator's priest and agonothete assumes priority; the priest of "the gods" is cited next, followed by the priest of Roma and Roman benefactors. Whereas in 95 BCE honors to Roman benefactors were associated with "the gods" of Thessalonica, by the early first century, the structure of civic honorific activity had become increasingly differentiated. The emperor emerged at the apex of the hierarchy, superseding even local patron deities.

Through his honorific activity, Damon of Thessalonica (Case III) insinuates himself into a pan-hellenic hierarchy of benefaction. There are three levels of benefaction at work here. According to the dedication, the proconsul Metellus was Damon's personal, Thessalonica's civic, and all the Greeks' pan-hellenic benefactor. Appropriate to the expansiveness of Metellus's purported goodwill, honors for his *arete* are directed to Zeus Olympios, executor of Greek interests.[25]

Antipater's prayer (Case IV) explicates a hierarchy of benefaction in which the god is invoked to protect and bless the immediate source of human benefaction, that is, the patron and, in turn, the patron's source of power, which in this case was the Roman emperor. Hymnic honor to the god on the devotee's behalf involved a prayer for the good disposition of the ruling hierarchy responsible for the devotee's continued well-being.

(3) What are the dynamic features of the connections?

What can these examples tell us about the operation of benefactor-beneficiary and patron-client networks in affecting particular sorts of human and corporate behavior? In all but one of our cases, the task is hampered immeasurably by a paucity of evidence for the subsequent activity of actors in the networks analyzed. Added to this is the difficulty that the actors even when identified are inaccessible for direct questioning.

The most that can be said in the case of the Youths is that their activity was designed to *expand* connections to insure the continued well-being of their association. This was achieved by promoting the association's elected leader in a public display of honors. One might infer (but it is only inference) that this promoted the interests of the gymnasiarch outside his connectedness to the Youths. In return for his investment as governor of the Youths and augmentor of their honors to the gods and Roman benefactors, Paramonos was repaid with increased public visibility, which no doubt enhanced his attractiveness as a broker for other parties. This might have led to positions and transactions involving more than honorific payoffs. One may also infer that the cluster initiating the honors reinforced their connectedness to Paramonos and might have stood to gain from whatever benefits accrued to the former gymnasiarch. Although the corporate activity of the Youths was directed to the polis, the increase in honors to the gods and Roman benefactors may have been intended, in part, to expand the association's connections with Roman benefactors. Increasing honors to Romans was one way in which Greeks sought to stimulate Roman obligation and benefaction. So, for example, the early cult of Roma at Smyrna was generated in lieu of Roman benefactors attached to the city and may have been designed, in part, to attract the beneficence of individual Romans (see Wardman).

In the case of Rhoimetalces, the "friends of friends" phenomenon comes to the fore. Presumably, in assuming a position of such civic distinction, the dynast would have been recognized as a "citizen," perhaps worthy of other civic benefactor honors. Such an opportunity to extend or consolidate his sphere of influence might have been an attractive enticement for the dynast. From Thessalonica's perspective, it also should have proved an advantageous policy. Since at least Antony's time, Thracian rulers had been important allies of Roman interests. And although under C. Julius Rhoimetalces, Roman affairs had suffered some reverses in Thrace, the prince had been supported firmly by Tiberius and his magistrates, as exemplified in the dynast's assumption of a royal title. By the honorific extension of its office of priest and agonothete of the Emperor to Rhoimetalces, Thessalonica forged an important link to Imperial benefaction. It not only secured the attention of a regional power instrumental in the execution of Imperial policies but also further consolidated patronage ties that were connected directly to the emperor. A "friend of Caesar" was now officially a "friend of the city."[26]

Thessalonica's honorific embrace of Rhoimetalces reflected the increasing expansion of a hierarchy of benefaction. Provincial magistrates and other influential Romans continued to be honored together with the goddess Roma. But the cultivation of Roman patronage now necessarily extended beyond honors for magistrates and local Roman magnates. Through its differentiation of honors to the emperor, the city expressed its esteem and solicitation of commitment directly to the supreme ruler. With the honorific involvement of Rhoimetalces, yet another important avenue of influence was established. A benefactor perhaps in his own right, the Thracian client/ruler may have been a valuable mediator for the city's interests in the Imperial establishment.

In what amounts to a publication of Damon's special connectedness to Metellus, this Thessalonican may have been promoting himself as "a good friend to have." By broadcasting his success as a client of Metellus, Damon projects himself as a potential broker on behalf of those connected to him. The pan-hellenic hyperbole of the honorific may reflect at least one successful Thessalonican's ambition in garnering pan-hellenic connections through his distinctive access to Roman power.

In discharging his obligations as artist/client of Piso, Antipater also projects himself into Piso's extended network, which includes the emperor.[27] Apollo is enjoined not only to dispose the emperor to graciousness towards Piso but also (potentially) towards the poet's work. The subtle aspiration expressed by Antipater is that the emperor's patronage might extend to the poet and not just through the mediating link of Piso. That Piso proved to be an effective connection for Antipater is suggested by the poet's ultimate association with the royal household. For a time, at least, he was in the circle of poets attached to Gaius Julius (Julia's and Agrippa's son and adopted son of Augustus).[28]

From this specific analysis a number of general observations may be made. In delineating what structural possibilities existed for transaction in the four partial networks considered, we observed the operation of hierarchies of benefaction. Human benefactors and patrons constituted one dimension of a network of benefaction that interrelated divine and human spheres of mutual interest. In the case of the two "corporate" examples, at the top of the network were those deities who were kept interested in promoting the well-being of the corporate group or city through a variety of honorific conventions. An important aspect of these honors was appropriate recognition of those human agencies who bore the burden of corporate or civic well-being. The human benefactor/patron was a mediator of divine power and at the same time a facilitator of appropriate response to the divine and human spheres.[29] We detected a similar hierarchy of benefaction operating in individual honorifics as well. Benefaction and honors were articulated reciprocally through a network extending from divine persona through the benefactor/patron to the beneficiary/client. The evidence permits the further observation that among Thessalonicans of the first centuries BCE and CE Romans were associated with deities as important instruments of benefaction.

It is essential that students of religion employing network analytical methods extend networks to include divine referents where appropriate. Benefactor-beneficiary and patron-client networks are interpretive abstractions descriptive of social realities as they were actually engaged and perceived by Greeks and Romans. Even when we encounter individual honorific expressions, they are not subjectively autonomous but are attempts to relate the individual to other humans and to divine persona. Analyzing particular networks of benefaction can point us not only to *what* people in the Graeco-Roman world believed, but also, and perhaps more importantly, to *how* they believed what they did (see Geertz 1971). How did they relate themselves and others to what they held to be divine realities? And how, in turn, was the divine mediated in socially meaningful ways?

Conclusions

On the basis of the networks analyzed, four general observations may be made about the possible importance of connections for interpreting interaction in the networks as well as behavior outside of these networks. First, in each of the cases except that involving Rhoimetalces, the honorific behavior itself manifested and reinforced the connectedness of benefactor-beneficiary and patron-client. The honorific activities were transactions in more encompassing exchanges. Furthermore, the activity of the Youths reinforced the connectedness of members of the corporate group in the expression and fulfillment of their mutual obligations to their benefactor.

Second, dynamic features of the networks are apparent in attempts to promote persons in the network. So Antipater links Apollo to Piso in promoting the patron in the poet's effective network and links Apollo and Augustus in promoting the patron in Piso's extended network. Antipater's behavior established the possibility of transactions between previously unconnected personae of his network and reinforced transactions between already connected personae in a way that would be beneficial to the poet. The activity of those Youths who nominated Paramonos for honors may reflect a similar phenomenon. The discrete cluster of Youths responsible for the motion may have been operating as an "action-set" (Boissevain 1974: 186–91) in promoting the interests of one to whom they were closely (or potentially closely) connected. In commending Paramonos to the Youths, the action-set may have been furthering their own interests through the promotion of Paramonos.

Third, if one of the reasons for Damon s honorific was the publication of his connection with Metellus, another dynamic feature of the network is manifest. The network is activated (in this instance through publicity) to promote the interests of the person outside the network. As was noted in the analysis of the gymnasiarch inscription, the honors accruing to Paramonos probably had a positive effect on his interests outside the network. In this instance behavior in the network influenced behavior outside the network.

Finally, another example of behavior in the network influencing behavior outside the network is a dynamic feature exhibited in all the cases studied: network expansion. In their publication of Paramonos' honors, the Youths explicitly solicited connection to the corporate group, and in their emphasis on the gymnasiarch's increase in honors to the gods and Roman benefactors, they may have been attempting to attract expanded Roman beneficence. Thessalonica's grant of its most distinguished priesthood to a Thracian prince represented an expansion of the city's connections with a locally powerful dynast and potentially the Imperial court itself. Rhoimetalces' acceptance afforded an expansion of his ties with the most important urban center in Macedonia. If Damon's honorific was intended to memorialize the pan-hellenic scale of Metallus' benefaction, it may also have been calculated to focus attention on the Thessalonican as a link to so important a benefactor. Antipater's prayer reflects his ambition to extend his effective network to include the emperor.

The general observations on the structural and dynamic features of benefactor-beneficiary and patron-client relationships involving Thessalonicans invite at least two conclusions. The social effect of the relationships is both static and dynamic. Benefactor-beneficiary and patron-client networks are operative in establishing and reinforcing the mutual status of the persons involved. Balanced discharge of the obligations (expected behavior) of benefactor-beneficiary and patron-client maintains and reinforces their respective powers.[30] But at the same time the networks permit mobility in the hierarchy of benefaction, mobility that normally has ramifications in social fields other than the network. So, for example, a benefactor (Piso) may serve as broker in effectively connecting a beneficiary (Antipater) with one of the benefactor's patrons (Augustus). Or a beneficiary (the Youths or a cluster therein) may be called upon by the benefactor (Paramonos) to support interests other than those of the corporation. In essence, benefactor-beneficiary and patron-client networks represent stable mechanisms or, in less functional terms, structured processes for change, a fact long recognized by social anthropologists studying factions (cf. Wolf). What may be of particular import to historians of religion, however, is that the dynamic aspects of these relationships can work against conventional social barriers, as, for example, in the case of proxeny grants to foreigners, Greek honors to Romans, civic or individual honors to women as benefactors, and so on.

This leads to a second conclusion that may be of some value in understanding the religious history of Thessalonica and perhaps other Graeco-Roman settlements. A curious fact of Thessalonican religious history is that by the mid-second century CE the previously important and ubiquitous cult of "the gods" disappears from the public and private record. Boissevain has observed (1974),

> Patterns emerge, or emerged in the past . . . because persons make similar decisions in the face of similar influences . . . people decide their course of action on the basis of what is best for themselves, and not only, as structural-functionalists would have us believe, on the basis of the accepted and sanctioned norms of behavior.

The evidence analyzed in this study manifests a peculiarly consistent expansion of benefactor-beneficiary and patron-client networks including civic, corporate, and individual spheres towards Roman benefaction. Greek locals obviously continued to contribute to civic and individual causes, but the evidence suggests a decisive, asymmetrical shift toward Romans (*vis-à-vis* Greek benefactors) as sources of benefaction.[31] If benefactor/patron networks expanding in the direction of Roman interests generated action-sets, coalitions, and factions as one might expect, these may have been influential in transforming civic religious institutions to cultivate augmented Roman attention. Networks operating according to hierarchies of benefaction were expanding away from local referents, human and divine. And in the process "the gods" of Thessalonica were increasingly less active divine personae in the patronage of the city.

Although this does not constitute a sufficient explanation for the demise of the cult of the gods at Thessalonica, an essential dynamic has been identified that, correlated with other developments, might account for the abandonment of what had been a significant civic religious institution. Concentrating solely on evidence of the cult and other civic cults and religious movements in the city and elsewhere foreshortens the analytical perspective. Analysis of the dynamic features of other social processes operating in the urban environment (as, for example, benefactor/patron networks) establishes a more inclusive field in which to observe the interaction of social, economic, religious, and political interests. If an examination of benefactor/patron networks enhances our understanding of transformations in particular Graeco-Roman religious complexes, it should prove to be a useful approach in the study of early Christianity.

NOTES

[1] Although one sometimes finds "benefactor" in non-corporate honorific contexts at Thessalonica, of the six epigraphic attestations of *patron* (primarily from the 3rd century CE; *IT* nos. 187, 190, 297 [probably denoting "uncle"], 405, 658, 811), only two manifest corporate activity (*IT* nos. 187, 190). Both involve one individual honoring another with the permission of the "assembly and people" of Thessalonica; the phrase "patron and benefactor" is applied to the honorand.

[2] On this, see most recently Gruen (I, 158) as opposed to, for example, Badian (1968) and Bowersock (1964). See also MacMullen (1977: 74–6, 106–7, 112–13, 124–25). The kind of detailed study called for here is exemplified in the work of Rawson (1977: 340–57). Saller (1982) is a sound treatment from the Roman perspective, but his analysis of patronage in the provinces is limited to North Africa.

[3] For an analysis of clientage networks as compared to the operation of other networks see Trouwborst (111–23).

[4] As in, for example, Boissevain (1974: 207–33) and in the study by Elizabeth Clark in this volume.

5 Boissevain distinguishes "patrons" from "brokers": patrons dispense "first order resources" controlled directly by them whereas brokers dispense second order resources as contacts to other persons controlling resources. In the present study, emphasis is placed on patrons and clients who may also operate as brokers in their own networks.

6 The most extensive discussion of the benefactor phenomenon in Graeco-Roman antiquity is that of Frederick Danker. See also E. Skaard and A. D. Nock (1972, II: 720-35).

7 On Greek proxeny conventions, see M. B. Walbank.

8 This follows the summary observation of A. Henrichs in a compact footnote to his study of Democritus and Prodicus (110 n. 65).

9 On this trend. see E. Rawson.

10 Letter of Paulus Fabius Maximus and Decrees by Asians on the Provincial Calendar; for the translation followed here, critical editions and discussions, see Danker (215-22).

11 Text and restorations follow Edson, IT 4; author's translation.

12 For the date and its official significance as the last month of the Macedonian year, see Edson, IT 4.

13 On youth organizations' imitation of civic conventions (at Athens), see J. H. Oliver (1977).

14 These are only vaguely alluded to in lines 9 and 14 (provision of oil is specified in line 15). Other costs might have included gymnastic equipment (scrapers, etc.), sponsoring cultural events, and financing athletic contests (involving purchase of prizes to be awarded and room and board for the participants). For a discussion of duties known to have been assumed by gymnasiarchs in Greek cities, see H. Marrou (173-75, 543-44).

15 Possible honors alluded to here are discussed in Hendrix (1984: 268-71).

16 This follows the reading of L. Robert (1974a: 212-15) and not that of Edson, IT 133 (author's translation). Robert identifies Rhoimetalces as Prince (later King) Gaius Julius Rhoimetalces, son of the Thracian King Rhescuporis, which demands an early first century date for the inscription (after 18-19 CE).

17 The prominence given by the engraver to the Youth's treasurer's name and title supports Robert's suggestion that the dedication may have been for a construction associated with the gymnasium.

18 In Tacitus' account of events in 21 CE (*Annals* 3.38), Rhoimetalces is besieged at Philippopolis (about 100 miles north/northwest of Philippi). This may have been at least one of the Thracian ruler's principal residences.

19 For a discussion of this unusual term, see Robert (1974: 212 and notes 198-99).

20 An exceptionally lucid account of the events leading up to the demise of Rhoimetalces' father is given by Bowersock (1964: 58-9 and Appendix II, 152-55). The complex genealogy of the Macedonian and Odrysian dynasties in Thrace is discussed also by Robert (1974a: 215).

21 *IT* 1031; author's translation.

22 Information regarding Antipater's career is derived solely from his compositions surviving in the *Anthologia Graeca*. The most extensive study of the poet is that of C. Cichorius (325-32) . See also the valuable summary of Gow in A. S. F. Gow and D. L. Page (II: 19-21). That Antipater was an artist/client of Piso at least for part of his career is strongly suggested by *Anthologia Palatina* (=AP) 9.428 (=Gow and Page #1), *AP* 9 .93 (=Gow and Page #31), *AP* 10.25 (=Gow and Page #40), *AP* 6.335 (=Gow and Page #41), *AP* 9.552 (=Gow and Page #42), *AP* 6.249 (=Gow and Page #45), and *Anthologia Planudea* 184 (=Gow and Page #30).

23 Text and translation follow Page (I: 36-7) . The work is to be dated either to the period in which Piso was assuming administrative duties in Asia Minor (13 BCE) or to

the time of an otherwise unattested Asian tour undertaken after his victories in Thrace (11 BCE).

24 On the civic nature of the priesthood, see Hendrix (1984: 134–35, 312).

25 Damon's choice of Olympia might also reflect his sensitivity to Metellus' publicity of his particular attachment to Jupiter. On his return to Rome after the defeat of Andriscus, for example, he constructed temples for Jupiter *Stator* and Juno *Regina*. See J. R. Fears' discussion of the episode (736–826, 758–59).

26 Though such technical language is not to be found in evidence of Rhoimetalces' relationship to the city, its use in analogy is quite warranted. If the dynast were granted such civic distinction, he should have been regarded as a "public friend" or "friend of the city." As client/prince and later king, with Tiberius' endorsement, Rhoimetalces in theory, if not in fact, could have been counted among the *amici* of the emperor. On the denomination of benefactors as public friends, see Walbank and sources in Danker (30, 65, and 90).

27 Mary Noble (5) has summarized the distinction between "effective" and "extended" networks as follows: "The effective network is made up of those people known to ego who also are known to each other. The extended network includes people who are known to ego but not to other members of ego's network and who in turn know other people."

28 See especially *AP* 9.59 and 9.297 (=Gow and Page nos. 46 and 47).

29 In the Greek polis, this interrelation between the divine and human spheres was manifested in any number of ways. Benefactors' honors were usually sanctioned by the city's patron deity or deities. So, for example, the honorific crown granted a benefactor might be dedicated in the temple of the city's principal deity and an inscription declaring the honors would be installed in the temple precincts. A city's benefactors were honored periodically in concert with honors for the patron deities of the city. Divine patronage of the city was realized, at least in part, by the tangible benefactions of its human patrons.

30 An asymmetrical discharge, of course, may enhance the power of one over the other. So, for example, Smyrna's honors for Roma may have constituted a projection of obligation to which the Smyrneans hoped individual Romans might respond. See further Boissevain (1974: 33, 215–19).

31 One relatively well-preserved inscription (*IT* 7) records local benefactor honors for Parnassos dated to 60 BCE. The date may be significant. In 60 BCE, the Macedonian proconsul C. Antonius Hybrida was called to Rome to answer charges of misadministration (extortion) and *maiestas*.

ORACLES AND THEIR SOCIETY: SOCIAL REALITIES AS REFLECTED IN THE ORACLES OF CLAROS AND DIDYMA

Thomas L. Robinson
Union Theological Seminary

ABSTRACT

This study explores the relevance of primary historical data for developing social description of religious practices in the Greek east under the Roman empire. The main sources and methods are archaeological. The focus is an examination of two famous oracle sanctuaries. Located on the Aegean coast of Asia Minor (Turkey) less than eighty kilometers apart, the sanctuaries of Claros and Didyma were both dedicated to Apollo. Yet the epigraphic remains reflect sharp differences both in oracular expressions and in their clientele. Analysis shows that these differences increased during the Roman period and were determined by the social contexts in which each sanctuary operated. It suggests, therefore, that such longstanding religious traditions and institutions were dependent upon local social networks of interaction that may be glimpsed through their propagation.

Introduction

Along the western coast of Asia Minor, less than eighty kilometers apart, stood Apollo's oracular sanctuaries at Didyma and Claros. Both of these sites claimed very ancient origins, indeed, in the case of Didyma, commonly known also as Branchidae, a few inscriptions record oracles from as early as the sixth century BCE. For both sanctuaries, however, the Roman imperial period, especially the century of the Antonines, was a time of prosperity and influence; for Claros it seems to have been the time when the oracle first achieved status as a major sanctuary with international renown. Throughout antiquity, of course, the archetypical oracle of Apollo was Delphi. Its wealth, fame, and authority were unrivaled, and a large number of traditional oracles circulated in its name.[1] In spite of the periods of substantial influence and fame that Claros and Didyma enjoyed, they never rivaled Delphi in the popular consciousness. One result of their lesser status is that Didyma and Claros appear far less often in ancient literary texts that cite putative oracles of Apollo or that offer discussions of oracles. We are more dependent for our knowledge of oracles from these sites on epigraphical and archaeological materials than is the case with Delphi. This study, with its limited compass, will offer some introductory observations concerning these sanctuaries and the oracles that have come down to us from them.[2] We will concentrate on texts from the imperial period inasmuch as the majority of our witnesses for the oracles of Didyma and practically all of our texts from Claros derive from that period.

In any attempt to see these sanctuaries in their interactions with the societies they served, a constant limiting factor is the extremely narrow range of our knowledge of the day-to-day functioning of these oracles. Little is known through literary descriptions, and a high percentage of inscriptional texts has been lost or badly damaged. Even where substantial epigraphical evidence is available, the range of phenomena that inscriptions reveal has often been substantially affected by changing customs concerning what was thought important or proper to inscribe on stone and whether the people involved had sufficient wealth to pay for a permanent stone record of an oracle. The combination of chance, shifting customs, and expense necessarily skews our vision of these oracles as we depend on epigraphical evidence. At the same time, however, for those things that the inscriptions do reveal to us, the permanence of the stones provides us with substantial confidence that we are dealing with trustworthy witnesses to the activity of the oracle.

The Sanctuary of Didyma and Its Neighbors

The ruins of Didyma are some of the most impressive of ancient remains along the western coast of Asia Minor. They lie about sixteen kilometers south of the site of Miletus. Didyma was connected with Miletus by a Sacred Way and was part of Milesian territory and under Milesian control throughout its history.[3] The temple of Didyma has been under study and excavation for more than a century and detailed information is available about its remains. They were first explored in the last century by the French scholars Rayet and Thomas (1880–85) and then especially Bernard Haussoullier (1902), who produced a still useful study of the history of Didyma and Miletus.

Shortly after the beginning of the twentieth century German archaeologists under the direction of Theodor Wiegand (1908, 1911, 1925) began work at Didyma as a continuation of their excavations at Miletus. This long term work eventually produced a detailed description of the site (Wiegand, 1941) and a study of some 615 inscriptions of Didyma.[4] Since 1962 new German excavations have been undertaken, and a large number of new studies have come forth.[5]

Since guides to the archaeological remains of Didyma are readily available, we may simply repeat the observation made long ago by Rayet that the Didyma sanctuary is not a temple in the ordinary sense, but quite specifically an oracle, a sanctuary built around a sacred spring where the god was believed to speak. Its architecture is externally similar to an ordinary temple, but internally quite different from other sanctuaries. With its *naiskos* inside an *adyton* open to the sky, it was oriented entirely toward the oracular activity of the god (Rayet-Thomas:2.57). Remarkably little, however, is known about the process of prophecy or even the functions of cult personnel. The titles of numerous functionaries are known from inscriptions—*prophētēs, hydrophoros, tamias, hypochrēstēs, grammateus, paraphylax, neōkoros*—but the inscriptions are almost totally silent about what they did.[6] Most prominent in the inscriptions are the prophets, but it is not clear what prophetic function they actually fulfilled.[7] When one reads the records of these aristocratic gentlemen of Miletus, deeply involved in the politics and trade of that city, who each held the post of prophet for one year and whose clearest responsibility was to finance numerous activities associated with the sanctuary, it is difficult to imagine them having more than a rather formal function in relation to the process of inspiration and divination.

In 1979 an inscription was discovered that indicates clearly for the first time the functioning of the office of prophetess at about the beginning of the first century CE.[8] The lack of inscriptions at this point indicates that the position did not carry the status for aristocratic women that, for example, the position of *Hydrophoros* of Artemis did.[9] The cultic function for the prophetess in this period is unknown, though a much later description of the prophetic process at Didyma in the work of Iamblichus, *On the Mysteries*, gives prominence to the role of the inspired prophetess.[10] Iamblichus, however, seems rather uncertain about the process of inspiration, since he describes her as receiving the god by either holding a staff, or being seated on an "axis" seat, or dipping her feet or the hem of her garment into the water of the spring or by breathing the vapor of the water. The statement is highly suggestive, but it does not allow us to see how, in fact, the sanctuary's personnel produced some of the lengthy, carefully crafted oracles in epic verse that are extant.

Of the history of Didyma in the Roman imperial period little is known. Work on the Hellenistic temple, which was begun under the patronage of Seleucus I in the early third century BCE but was never ultimately finished, continued off and on throughout the period, providing employment for countless skilled and unskilled workers and a focus for the benefactions of the wealthy.[11] Trajan was responsible for the construction of a new Sacred Way from the Didymeion to Miletus c. 100 CE.[12] Hadrian permitted himself to be named prophet when he visited Didyma in 129 (*Did II* 356, 495). More than 230 years later the emperor Julian repaired the Sacred Way and with pride wrote that he himself also held the office of prophet.[13] As to the ongoing life of the sanctuary in the intervening decades we are left primarily with the inscriptions recording honors for officials and occasionally oracles given by the god.

The Sanctuary of Claros and Its Contacts

The oracular sanctuary at Claros was considerably smaller than Didyma and attained its greatest stature only in the Roman imperial period. It is situated near the northern coast of the Gulf of Ephesus about thirteen kilometers south of old Colophon, which until the third century BCE was its mother city. It lay ca. two kilometers north of the coastal city of Notion, which after the destruction of old Colophon by Lysimachus came to be called Colophon-on-the-Sea and became the governing city for Claros.[14] The site is in a valley watered by a small stream called the Halesos or Ales, which floods yearly and over the centuries buried the remains of Claros under about four meters of earth. The temple itself was only uncovered through a new series of excavations led by Louis and Jeanne Robert throughout the decade of the 1950s (See Robert, 1954b; Picard). They discovered a Doric temple that was built primarily in the early Hellenistic period but was finally completed only under Hadrian, whose name as dedicant is on the architrave. From the early imperial period the temple contained colossal statues of a seated Apollo between standing figures of Artemis and Leto.

Two particular features of the site are of special interest. First is the underground portion of the temple where the oracle itself was located and second is the approximately 300 inscriptions that were found at the site. These recorded delegations sent from cities to visit the sanctuary, and they also list the cultic officials of Claros—the priests, *thespiodes* ("singers of prophecies"), prophets, and scribes.

The underground portions of the temple consisted first of two narrow passageways beginning from steep steps on either side of the pronaos. These went through a series of right-angle turns, met underneath the temple, and divided again to enter a chamber beneath the cella from opposite sides. The chamber was equipped with benches and an omphalos, and beyond it a low, narrow doorway led to a second smaller chamber where was located a well from which sacred water could be drawn to inspire the god's spokesman. According to Robert's reconstruction (1967:311–312) of the procedure, it was probably the *thespiode* who entered that second chamber, drank the water, and pronounced the god's words. The prophet, he suggested, sat on a small seat that has been found cut into the stone beside the doorway to the innermost chamber and there wrote down the inspired words. The oracles were given only at night on certain days of the month, after preparatory sacrificial rites were carried out by the priest. The inscriptions also record that sometimes mystery rites for inquirers were associated with the oracular procedure, but no details are given except to suggest that the initiated inquirer could enter the oracular chambers along with the cult personnel.[15] Clearly the elaborate rites were organized to be as impressive and appropriately mysterious as possible. They thereby maintained the power and attractiveness of the mantic process for the society it served. The most direct evidence of the oracle's procedure, however, is the nature of the oracular texts themselves, and these indicate that oracles were rendered in a variety of manners ranging from short fixed oracles apparently chosen by lot to long complex compositions that surely required considerable reflection and effort to produce. As was the case with Didyma, we simply do not know fully by what methods the officials at Claros believed that they received the words of Apollo.

One of the more remarkable features of the buildings at Claros is the great number of inscriptions that cover much of the propylaea, much of the exposed marble surface of the temple (including four of the five steps of the stylobate and the spaces between the flutes of columns), and even extend to the surfaces of statue bases and exedras. All of these 300 or so inscriptions record delegations sent to Claros by cities that wished to consult the oracle, but not a single text of an oracle has been found among them. Unfortunately, only about a fourth of these texts have been published in full and the conclusions that can be drawn from them are therefore limited.[16] At least two observations, however, can be made that are very important for understanding the development of the oracle at Claros.

The first, made by Robert on the basis of his own lists of the numerous unpublished as well as published inscriptions, concerns the areas of surrounding society that Claros chose to serve. He noted that Claros drew very little of its clientele from the old Greek cities of the coast of Asia Minor and Greece proper but rather cultivated primarily the more recently Hellenized regions of the interior of Asia Minor and Thrace. Among the inscriptions were delegations from the Macedonian and Thracian region,[17] Bithynia,[18] Paphlagonia and Pontus,[19] Lycaonia and Cappadocia,[20] Pisidia,[21] Caria,[22] Lydia and Phrygia,[23] a few from Ionia and Aeolia,[24] and a few from Crete.[25] Only one delegation from a city in Greece itself is found among the inscriptions, and that is the refounded Roman colony of Corinth. Interestingly enough, Pausanias (2.2.8) mentions a statue of Clarian Apollo at Corinth. Thus the inscriptions reveal the intensive activity of Claros with reference to numerous cities on the margin, so to speak, of the Greek world. Claros evidently worked to build official ties with these cities that would be manifested in the public delegations recorded in these inscriptions that covered the sanctuary. What private consultations were made by individual citizens of the cities, for the most part we do not know.

Several of the cities, especially Laodicea, Iconium, Heraclea, Tabai, and Chios, sent delegations on a regular basis year after year to consult the oracle. The inscriptions also indicate that these delegations regularly included a choir of young people who would sing an anthem to Apollo especially composed for the occasion. The earliest of the inscriptions that have been published come from the early second century CE, and the latest from the early third century. Those limits mark the period of Claros' greatest activity and prosperity.

A second observation based on these inscriptions has to do with the cultic officials of the sanctuary. Most of the inscriptions begin by giving a date according to the prytanis (chief magistrate) of Colophon; they then list the cultic officials of Claros before giving the names of those who made up the delegation to the oracle. The development of a chronology of these inscriptions is made possible by the fact that for most of the years that the records were being inscribed, the prytanis of Colophon was Apollo himself, that is, the financial responsibilities that the prytanis would have had to bear were paid out of the revenues of the temple. The earliest of these prytanies of Apollo that appears in an inscription is the forty-sixth (before 115 CE) and the latest (after 205) is the one hundred twenty-second. Interspersed are numerous years in which some leading citizen was prytanis, and these must be taken into account in working out an absolute chronology. Enough of the prytanies are exactly datable, however, to provide a fairly secure frame.[26] Using such information one can place chronologically the activity of various cultic officials and to some extent follow their careers as they appear in inscriptions.[27]

The point to be noted here has to do with the period around 132 CE. Before that time the published inscriptions list either the prophet of Apollo alone or the priest and prophet as the cultic officials of Claros. During this period the office of priest was held for a long period—in one case it is described as being for life—and the office of prophet was held for one year.[28] A change came, however, about the year 132, shortly after completion of the sanctuary under Hadrian. An inscription from the sixty-third prytanis of Apollo is the earliest published and clearly datable delegation inscription recording the office of *thespiode*, the "singer of prophecies."[29] From that point on, the inscriptions consistently record the *thespiode* as one of the leading oracular officials. Like the priest, the *thespiode* regularly held office for many years. Their rank may be indicated by the fact that the inscriptions usually give the names of these men in the order priest, *thespiode*, prophet, scribe.

Whether the office of *thespiode* was created new or perhaps elevated from a subordinate position, the introduction of a second office alongside the priest, held for a long term by a single man, very likely had considerable impact on the functioning of the oracle and contributed to its success in the later second century. Two men working together for a number of years directed the oracle along with a rotating series of yearly prophets and scribes. For example, the inscriptions show that Gn. Julius Reginus Alexander held the office of *thespiode* for about twenty-five years from c. 150 to c. 175. during about the first ten years of that period the priest was Ti. Claudius Rufus, who retired to serve at least one year as prophet in 160–61. The next long-term priest was C. Julius Zotichus who served from c. 165 to c. 178. After Alexander retired (or died) as *thespiode* his successor was Ti. Claudius Ardys, who served until at least c. 190. This stability of the officials over a considerable period of time provided a context in which policies could be planned and carried out for the promotion of the Clarian sanctuary. Relationships with various cities could be cultivated. The fame and glory of Clarian Apollo could be propagated. The voluminous inscriptions engulfing the sanctuary bear witness to their success, as we shall see below.

The Oracular Texts as Social Evidence

If we turn our attention to the inscriptional evidence for oracles of Didyma and Claros, some common characteristics are readily apparent. First, the vast majority of the oracles that have been preserved from both Didyma and Claros deal in some way with religious matters. In fact, it is probable that all of them included some treatment of cult or cultic personnel, though in some cases such matters were subordinate.[30] Second, there is, so far as I can see, not a single prediction of any specific event among these inscriptions. There are promises of blessings to be received if the recipient supplicates some specified god, as well as other such anticipations of the future, but the inscriptions, at least, give no support to the idea, popular in antiquity, that the god could, in remarkable and often enigmatic ways, foretell the specific events that were to come.

More interesting than these general observations, however, are the distinctions that separate the late Didymaean oracular inscriptions from the Clarian ones. Two facts are sufficient to alert us to the differences. First, whereas almost all of the extant Didymaean oracular inscriptions record responses evidently given to individuals or, occasionally, private groups, all except perhaps two of the Clarian inscriptions record oracles given to official delegations from cities. Second, whereas the great majority of the Didymaean texts were preserved in Didyma itself or in Miletus, none of the Clarian oracles proper were found at Claros, but rather they were scattered in the various cities that had received them. Are we to conclude from these quite distinct contrasts that Apollo spoke at Claros primarily to the cities of Asia Minor, while at Didyma he limited his recipients to individuals? Such a hypothesis might deserve some consideration, but a far readier explanation of the phenomena lies to hand in the differing social structures and customs of Claros and Didyma in propagating oracular activity.

The Didymaean Oracular Inscriptions

If we begin with the Didymaean evidence, we may note first that those oracles that we know through inscriptions were given to a very limited class of inquirers. The great majority were given to cultic officials: prophets and treasurers of the Didymaean oracle, priestesses of Demeter and Athena, etc. If we divide the inscriptions that come from Didyma itself from those that derive from Miletus, the situation comes more clearly into focus.

Inscriptions from Didyma proper

In the corpus of Didymaean inscriptions several distinct groups of texts were identified. The largest of these groups was the series of "prophet-inscriptions," in which the yearly prophet would record his tenure in office (*Did II* 202–306a). The position as prophet of Apollo was evidently the most elevated office in Miletus and Didyma and was likewise a very expensive office.[31] Only the wealthy, prominent families of Miletus supplied candidates for this honor, and the inscriptions that the prophets left behind often ring with aristocratic family pride, sometimes tracing ancestors back for centuries.[32] A second, much smaller group of inscriptions honors the treasurers (*tamiai*) of the sanctuary, a subordinate financial office often held by less aristocratic members of Milesian society, who usually could not hope to attain to the office of prophet, or occasionally held as a preliminary office by one who would later become prophet.[33]

All records of oracles that survive from Didyma itself and that are not too fragmentary to be identified with certainty are records from these two groups of officials. One of the most common adjectives used throughout their inscriptions to describe these men is "pious," *eusebēs*, and oracles evidently came to be recorded in their inscriptions in order to confirm that quality either explicitly or implicitly. Already in the late second century BCE a former treasurer who was also construction supervisor for the temple recorded an oracle that had directed his sacrifices to Poseidon under the appropriate epithets, "securer" and "savior" (*Did II* 229 II). Among the prophet-inscriptions, through the second century CE the texts that deal with oracles only refer to an oracle without actually quoting it. From the first century BCE to the second, perhaps third, century CE we have four inscriptions in which prophets referred to oracles that Apollo had given, bearing witness to their piety or calling them to their task.[34] After about the year 200 CE some prophets began recording the text of oracles that they had received. The pattern is most clearly visible in *Did II* 277 from sometime in the third century. In that inscription the prophet Titus Flavius Ulpianus first recorded his illustrious family and then stated that the god had often borne witnesses to him and had, because of his piety, addressed him in an oracle. He then quoted the flowery seven-verse oracle of praise and evidently went on to quote a second oracle, but that portion of the stone has been lost.[35] Other texts, like the Damianos inscription (*Did II* 504), record oracles that do not explicitly glorify the official but indirectly display his piety in his concern for the proper worship of the gods.[36]

Inscriptions from Miletus

Several of the inscriptions from Miletus fit a similar pattern, but in these the cultic officials are not part of the service of Apollo. In other words, these texts show even more clearly the connections of the Didyma sanctuary to the larger fabric of Milesian society. The most striking example is the long, carefully composed oracle praising Satorneila, the aristocratic priestess of Athena Polias at Miletus, from about 200 CE.[37] Somewhat earlier, Alexandra, the priestess of Demeter Thesmophoros, recorded two lengthy oracles, which emphasized the importance of the cult she led and reflected her piety.[38] The social status of these two cases should be noted. The few Milesian texts that have been preserved from earlier periods do not generally come from aristocratic sources. Later, however, the local Milesian aristocracy had become more central to the fame of the oracular institution.

In looking at these inscriptions we can observe that a standardized question-formula was in use at Didyma that lent itself to rather elaborate inquiries. The formula runs as follows: "Someone asks, since (*epei*) such and such is the case, whether (*ei*) . . . [the question]."[39] In this formula the *epei* clause allowed for considerable expansion to describe the circumstances or pious interests that had led the inquirer to come to the god. These clauses thus bring into the inquiry procedure an autobiographical element. It provides us interesting insights into the concerns of these inquirers, just as it also served to publicize their piety and their status when the inscriptions were displayed.

The inscriptional evidence leaves two great gaps: oracles given to people who did not have the money necessary to erect an inscription (or who simply did not care to spend their resources that way), and oracles given to cities that sent official delegations to the god.[40] To summarize these observations, the oracles of Didyma that have survived in inscriptions from the imperial period come primarily from a very limited range of oracles given to what surely was a tiny segment of the clientele of so large and famous a sanctuary. They can be used in a positive manner to illuminate *some* of the possibilities for Didymaean oracles. In them we get glimpses of Apollo as he settles labor disputes, establishes cult sites and altars, authorizes cultic epithets, explains dreams and mysterious phenomena, gives assurance to the worried, enforces vows, praises the piety of prophets and priests, interprets philosophically the significance of the gods and of religion, and encourages conservative reform of the cult. We have oracles of a single verse and others that are lengthy, carefully composed, and philosophically sophisticated, in keeping with popular theories of religion of the day. Still, it must be surmised that the sanctuary as a public institution operated under the aegis of a clearly defined social matrix within the environs of Didyma and Miletus. A final case study will yield further evidence in this regard.

Aelianus Poplas: A Prominent Prophet of Didymaean Apollo

Even within the limited number of these oracular inscriptions, however, some recent studies have been able to make connections with oracles preserved in literary texts in order to illuminate the social context that they reflect. The literary texts under consideration come from the surviving excerpts of a collection of oracles and other materials that were gathered by a Christian living during the reign of the emperor Zeno (474–91 CE). The collection is known by the name of "Theosophy."[41] The intent of the compiler was to show that the pagan witnesses agree with the aim of Christian scripture and doctrine (*Theos.* 1–7). The collection is quite diverse in character, but in the midst of its section on oracles is a pair of pagan oracles, both of which were reportedly given to the same man, identified by the name Poplas.

The introductions to these oracles are of interest in establishing their social context and may be translated as follows:

> To a certain man named Poplas, who asked whether it was profitable to send to the emperor concerning money for public benefactions, he (Apollo)

answered as follows: (In a four-verse oracle Apollo approved an embassy to Rome.) (*Theos.* 22)

The next text in the series is introduced in this way:

> On another occasion, when Poplas was distressed because affairs were going against him, and his property was diminishing, and he was not well physically, and when he sought to learn from whom he might be able to obtain aid, he (Apollo) replied as follows:
>
> *Propitiate the bright eye of life-giving Zeus.*
> (*Theos.* 23)

The rarity of the name Poplas combined with the description of Poplas' life situation enabled L. Robert (1968) through a prosopographical study to identify the man mentioned in these texts with an individual known as Aelianus Poplas, who appears repeatedly in the inscriptions of Didyma. In one inscription from the early third century set up by a woman to commemorate her period of service as a *Hydrophoros* in the cult of Artemis Pythia, the woman identified herself as related to Aelianus Poplas and proceeded to list *his* offices: treasurer at Didyma, chief president, president of the city senate, president of the Didymeia games, prophet, "Wreath-bearer" (the office by which the year at Miletus was designated), president of the festal assembly (the Didymeia), and twice chief priest of the Augusti.[42] Hence, the connection to the imperial cult becomes clearer. This same Poplas is also listed in another inscription as the uncle of another prophet, and indeed as one of numerous prophets that a single prominent family had produced (*Did II* 179, 277). It appears from one fragmentary inscription that he volunteered to take on the financial responsibilities of prophet, and his name appears on a Milesian coin bearing the portrait of Julia Maesa, the grandmother and sponsor of Elagabalus (218–22), and on others with the image of Caracalla (211–17).[43]

The study of the name Poplas done by Robert is confirmed by the perfect mesh between the situation implied in the *Theosophy* and what the inscriptions reveal about Aelianus Poplas. The inquiry of *Theosophy* 22, "whether it was profitable to send to the emperor concerning money for public benefactions (*eis philotimias*)" is completely understandable for one who was "twice chief priest of the Augusti" in a large city such as Miletus. The practice of prominent citizens referring matters both great and small to the emperor was a growing phenomenon throughout the second and third centuries, as the control of Rome became more and more directly involved in the life of provincial cities.[44] Especially was this practice important for a priest of the Augusti whose responsibilities to pay for civic benefactions might often involve the need for imperial approval or an imperial grant of money for public works.

A second century example of such a consultation comes from an inscription of Apamea in Phrygia honoring a certain Manneius Ruso for his services to the city. One of his services was that he had gone on an embassy to the Augusti and obtained for the chief priests the right to make certain benefactions, which consisted of a specified number and type of gladiatorial exhibitions.[45] Also in 145 CE Antoninus Pius wrote to Ephesus about a dispute between the city and one of its leading citizens Vedius Antoninus over a benefaction (*philotimia*) that Vedius had performed for the city.[46] Another inscription from the time of Poplas' career records Caracalla's ruling on a dispute between Philadelphia and Sardis as to which city had the right to the *philotimia* of a certain Julianus, a Philadelphian living at Sardis.[47] For patricians of Aelianus Poplas' standing, the stakes involved in obtaining imperial patronage were very high in terms of both financial and social position within the city aristocracy.[48] It was in this context that Poplas, a man who served as both prophet of Apollo and priest of the Augusti, consulted the oracle about the advisability of taking a request for money for benefactions directly to the emperor. Although such an embassy could always fetch both opportunities and dangers, the god advised him to proceed.

Again, the following oracle in *Theosophy* 23 fits the same situation. The introduction to the oracle envisions Poplas as a man of property who had suffered reverses in public affairs, who saw his property diminishing, and who, perhaps understandably in such a situation, had also become physically ill. Here, in this literary text, one sees another side of ancient *philotimia*, the "endangered" benefactor (Danker:318). The expense of numerous offices and liturgies was able to cripple financially even a very wealthy individual, especially if such burdens were accompanied by economic or political reverses of other sorts.[49] In discussing the prophet inscription from Didyma, Albert Rehm (*Did II* p. 324) noted that in those inscriptions one could follow the rise and decline of various families, changes that often evidently followed changing financial situations in a trade city like Miletus.

In an unaccustomed condition of fiscal difficulty, Poplas went to Apollo to learn "from whom he might be able to obtain aid." It is likely that Poplas hoped for some quite practical guidance on where to turn for financial aid in his difficulties. Apollo responded, however, in a typically oracular manner by prescribing a cultic action for the inquirer, a response that involved less risk of the oracle being proved false: "Appease the bright eye of life-giving Zeus."[50] Whether we may imagine that Poplas was satisfied with this response or not, it is significant that these texts show us a prominent citizen, who served at one point as part of the cultic personnel of the oracle, himself trusting the god for guidance in a time of personal difficulty. This fact shows that whatever the method by which the oracles were produced within the sanctuary, it was not in a manner that completely undermined the confidence in the oracle of those who were directly involved with it.

The Civic Oracles from Claros

The pattern of preservation of Clarian inscriptions is, as we have noted, in many respects the reverse of that with the Didymaean. Since in the second and third centuries hundreds of lists of delegations to the oracle were inscribed in Clarian buildings, the names of chief officials were recorded numerous times, and they developed no custom of erecting special inscriptions to record their tenure. That does not mean, however, that Claros never provided oracles, like those from Didyma, praising the piety or work of a cultic official. From the late second century, for example, we have an inscription from Stobi in Macedonia in which a woman honors her grandmother, Claudia Prisca, who had been priestess of Artemis Lochia for sixty years, "and whose purity was attested by Clarian Apollo."[51] Many other such oracles for priests and priestesses may well have been rendered, but no record remains. It hints, nonetheless, at similar networks of social relations for the prominent local citizens who provided contact with the distant oracular sanctuary.

The circumstance that caused most of the inscriptional records of Clarian oracles to be preserved is the service that Claros rendered to cities of Asia Minor in periods of crisis, especially during epidemics and famines. Three-fourths of the inscriptions can probably be best interpreted as dealing with such situations. The most notable example of such a crisis was the plague that struck the empire after the Parthian campaign of Lucius Verus in 162–166. It was a widely destructive epidemic that the soldiers had brought back with them and that broke out in many localities for years to come.[52] The four longest of the oracular inscriptions (those from the cities of Caesarea Trocetta, Pergamum, Hierapolis, and Callipolis) may have been written for cities suffering the ravages of that plague.[53] It is not possible to be confident about limiting the connection to that single epidemic, however, since a great deal of uncertainty encumbers an evaluation of the extent and intensity of the plague (Gilliam:248–49). The statements of the oracles are usually quite general and could apply to any important local epidemic. Sometimes the oracles speak of damage to crops and point to problems of famine as well as disease and may well deal with crises other than "the plague." (See also Magie:1.663; 2.1534n.9.) In any case these inscriptions show us that numerous cities of Asia Minor looked to Clarian Apollo for guidance to any action that might cause the gods to minimize or cut short such disasters. When answers were given, they erected copies of the oracles they received in the city *agorai*, indicating their gratitude to the god.

An element of propaganda is also apparent in these oracular activities. In each case the petitioning city was ordered to perform distinct public rites. At Caesarea Trocetta houses were to be sprinkled with sulfured water, embodying the Nymphs; at Callipolis there were to be offerings to the chthonic deities; at Hierapolis, sacrifices to Gaia, Aether, and other powers; and at Pergamum, four choirs of Ephebes were to sing hymns at special sacrifices to Zeus, Athena, Dionysus, and Asclepius. In addition, three of the cities (Trocetta, Callipolis, and Hierapolis) were ordered to set up statues of the god wielding his bow, to drive harm away. Both Hierapolis and Callipolis were commanded to erect these statues at the gates of their cities so that the city would stand under Apollo's protection. For Hierapolis it is specified that the image is to be of Clarian Apollo.

The Hierapolis oracle also points to at least two other aspects of Clarian propaganda. The god phrased his response in such a way as to identify Apollo of Claros with Apollo Careios, who apparently had an oracle in Hierapolis.[54] He also complained that he had not received sacrifices from the Hierapolitans, and commanded them to send choirs of youths and maidens to Colophon in order to sing hymns and offer sacrifices to the god.[55] It seems clear that the officials of Claros wished to establish closer ties with the city of Hierapolis, which, quite unlike its neighboring city of Laodicea, had not regularly sent delegations to Claros.[56] The oracle here functions as an explicit means of drawing Hierapolis into the orbit of the Clarian sanctuary.

Another element of propaganda is apparent in the very length of these oracles. The stones are often damaged at the end of the texts, but we can see that several of them were at least thirty verses long. As we have already noted at Didyma, such a length constituted a break with the traditional brevity of oracles before the imperial period, and corresponds to the elevation of the *thespiode* under Hadrian. In addition to their impressive length, two of the texts (those from Caesarea Trocetta and Callipolis) also displayed poetic virtuosity by moving through a complex series of poetic meters, rather than simply using the traditional dactylic hexameter. We may safely assume that such oracles were not merely dashed off as a versification of some incoherent trance utterances. Nor were they composed on an impromptu basis. They represent a considerable investment of effort, in terms of professional artistry, on the part of Clarian officials. Here, then, the new office of *thespiode* became important. They also suggest that the named representatives of petitioning cities, who secured the oracle and who had the oracles inscribed as votives, likewise went to considerable expense. Thus, these texts reflect a variety of means to add to the glory of the god Apollo through his oracle at Claros and to bring other cities into closer dependence.

As one might expect, these civic oracles strongly emphasize the public cult. The commands of the god relate to public action—statues to be erected, hectacombs offered, choirs organized and sent on journey. One sees less of the individual piety that is so central to the inscriptions from Didyma. However, it must be noted that the persons named (usually one or two) often set up the inscriptions themselves to commemorate their own actions in securing the oracle on behalf of the city. In addition to paying for the inscriptions, the statues, and the labor, it is not unlikely that these individuals also sponsored as liturgies the public rites dictated by the oracle and sanctioned by the city council.

At Caesarea Trocetta, one of the dedicants, a Paphlagonian, is designated as priest of Apollo for his city, even though he is a foreigner by birth and has no clear cultic function. At Callipolis, the two are called archons and treasurers. Are these the familiar civic offices or are they special roles related to some local Apolline cult? At Pergamum, the two "delegates" (who had actually gone as initiates into the *adyton* to receive the oracle) are clearly being honored by the city council with its Neocorate status in the imperial cult. In other words, by virtue of the contact with the sanctuary at Claros, such delegates also merited public honors and status akin to that of benefactors back home. One should also be aware of potential links to the imperial cult (Price:150, 187, 254). Thus, it may be, finally, that Claros, lacking the official local institutions and offices seen between Didyma and Miletus, fostered similar (though less exclusive) contacts by offering city officials the opportunity to show their own form of piety and public beneficence in the name of Apollo. As the fame of Apollo spread, so did theirs. The officials of the sanctuary at Claros seem to have been conscious of the propagandistic value of the impressive oracles that it delivered to cities near and far in times of crisis.[57]

One other indication of Clarian tendencies comes from the remarkable series of six nearly identical Latin inscriptions from widely scattered localities in the western empire. They read: *Dis deabusque secondum interpretationem oraculi Clari Apollinis*, "to the gods and goddesses according to the interpretation of the oracle of Clarian Apollo."[58] Exactly how these inscriptions came to be erected in such widely scattered locations has been cause for considerable dispute, but it seems clear that they represent commands by the Clarian god that dedications "to the gods and goddesses" as a group be set up in many parts of the Latin world, and that these be specifically linked to Apollo of Claros.[59] Just as Claros' Greek clientele came primarily from the "margins" of the Greek world, so too as

Claros developed the recognition of Apollo in the Latin world it concentrated on the widely extended frontiers of the Roman empire. Here the role of propaganda and a tendency toward a piety that stresses the unity of all deities appear to merge (cf. Robinson, 1981:313–323).

Conclusion

The limiting factors of custom and chance have determined that the stones from antiquity preserve for us fairly narrow segments of the oracular activity of Claros and Didyma, each segment quite different from the other. Within their limited range, however, the texts show that in the imperial period both of these sanctuaries were building on and developing beyond the oracular traditions of past centuries. They show that the cultic officials who composed these oracles consciously incorporated the trends of religious thought of the times as well as the needs of their recipients. They also illustrate, especially at Claros, an active program of religious propaganda, building the renown of the god by responding in an impressive way to the needs of cities of Asia Minor in times of crisis. The officials of these sanctuaries saw no strict limits on the kinds of material that the god could incorporate into his oracles, and while surely most of their responses were brief replies to quite ordinary questions, they were also quite ready to expand at length their responses to questions they thought worthy. In both cases, the success and the operation of the oracular sanctuary depended on active participation in the social structures of local aristocratic networks.

NOTES

[1] Studies of the full corpus of Delphic responses are provided by Parke and Wormell; Fontenrose.

[2] A more detailed discussion with a corpus of oracular texts from both sanctuaries is found in Robinson, 1981.

[3] A Milesian tradition recorded by Pausanias (7.2.6) traces the oracle back to a Carian sanctuary before the Ionian immigration.

[4] Wiegand, 1958 (by A. Rehm), here abbreviated *Did II*. This work must now be supplemented by the many more recently discovered inscriptions described in excavation reports in the *Mitteilungen des deutschen archäologischen Institues, Istanbuler Abteilung (MDAI[I])*.

[5] See, for example, Günther, 1971; Fehr; Tuchelt, 1973, 1976; Voigtlaender; Haselberger.

[6] *Did II*, 323–25; Günther, 1971:115–19.

[7] *Did II*, 202–306a.

[8] The prophetess Tryphosa was mentioned in an inscription erected in Didyma by her great-granddaughter, who was *Hydrophoros* of Artemis Pythia in Miletus

(Günther, 1980:170–76 [no. 5]). Earlier known inscriptional evidence for the office of prophetess was limited to a very fragmentary inscription (*Did II* 272, cf. p. 323).

9 *Did II* 307–88 record the numerous *Hydrophoroi* inscriptions known to Rehm.

10 Iambl. *Myst*. 3.11, 123, 127; cf. B. Haussoullier, 1920:268–77 and Günther 1971:119–23.

11 Tuchelt, 1973:107–15. Cf. Strabo 14.1.5; Pausanias 7.5.4.

12 *Did II* 55–57; Tuchelt, 1973:108, and no. 1 d-g; Haussoullier, 1902:281–87.

13 Haussoullier, 1902:xxx-xxxi, 287–90; *Did II*, p. 323. Cf. Julian *Ep*. 451b.

14 Akurgal:133–34, cf. plan p. 230.

15 Cf. *IGRom* 4.1586: . . . *hoitines myēthentes embateusan*. A very similar phrase is used in 4.360. Macridy published several texts that state that an inquirer *epetelese kai mystēria* (1912:50–52 [nos. 15, 16, 20]; cf. p. 46 [no. 2]). All of these texts date from the second century CE. Cf. Dibelius:84–89.

16 The largest number are available in the following: Macridy, 1905:164–71; 1912:46–56; Robert, 1954b:116–20, 203–16, 327–29, 380–83; 1959:190; 1969:299–303; 1974:74–80.

17 Stobi, Charax, Thasos, Aenus, Perinthus, Plotinopolis, Deultum, Odessos, Dionysopolis, Marcianopolis, the Chersonesus, Philippopolis, and, to the north, Olbiopolis.

18 Apamea, Caesarea Germanica, Nicea, Nicomedia, Creteia-Flaviopolis, and Prusias ad Hypium.

19 Neoclaudiopolis, Amisus, Amaseia, and Neocaesarea.

20 Iconium, Hyde, and Caesarea.

21 Apollonia, Antioch, and Sagalassus.

22 Tabai, Heraclea, Sebastopolis, Bargasa, and Aphrodisias.

23 Thyateira, Laodicea ad Lycum, Julia, Acmonia, Meiros, Aezani, and Parium.

24 Cyme, Phocaea, and Chios.

25 Lappa, Hierapytna, and Cydonia.

26 Thus, for example, Apollo's prytany no. 63 came in 132–33 CE, no. 70 in 144–45, no. 79 in 155–56, no. 83 in 160–61, no. 93 in 177–78, no 101 in 185–86, etc. Robert, 1954a:210–16.

27 With their extensive lists of names these inscriptions offer also a mine of prosopographical data for the cities in question. The process of coordinating the information from Claros with local records from the various cities has been started by the work of the Roberts (1954a) on Tabai, Heraclea, and Sebastopolis.

28 As an example, note the form of an inscription from the early Hadrianic period listing a delegation from Heraclea: "In the 51st prytany of Apollo, on the 30th of the month Artemision, when Artemidorus the son of Alexander was *priest*, Atimetus II was *prophet*, and Hephaestion the son of Herophilus and Soteles the son of Pothoumenos were *scribes*, the youths who sang the anthem were T. Statilius (*et al.*) . . . ." Macridy, 1912:53 (no. 25); Robert, 1954a:203 (no. 132).

29 "To Good Fortune. From the free and autonomous city of Amisus, ally of the Romans. In the 63rd prytany of Apollo, when M. Ulpius Artemidorus was *priest*, when Asclepidus the son of Demophilus of Patroxenidus of the Heraclidae of Ardys was *thespiode*, when Hermias the son of Attalus was *prophet*, when Attalus II and Hermogenes the son of Dadeus were *scribes*. Chrispus son of Tryphon and P. Publius Callicles came as ambassadors, who when they had been initiated, entered (the adyton). In the 163rd year of the freedom (of Amisus = 132 CE)." *IGRom* 4.1546; Macridy, 1905:170. Cf. note 15 above. It is, of course, possible that the office might be able to be dated somewhat earlier on the basis of some unpublished text.

30 One notable inquiry dealt with the resolution of a labor dispute, but the oracle also included instructions to offer sacrifices to Athena and Heracles.

31 Rehm notes that one often was the chief officer of Miletus, the *Stephanephoros*, some ten years before he became prophet. The prophet was required to pay for certain

festivals and sometimes provided gifts of money to the citizenry as well as other monetary endowments. *Did II*, p. 324.

32 Note, for example, *Did II* 259, which provides an extensive family tree. These inscriptions provide an excellent example of the great importance of *philotimia* in ancient society as a motivation for large expenditures of private funds for public benefits. Cf. Brown, 1978:31–32.

33 *Did II* 389–423. Often these are, unlike the prophet inscriptions, on limestone rather than marble.

34 *Did II* 229, 282, 280, 243.

35 Cf. also *Did II* 278, an oracle for Ulpius Athenagoras.

36 See also *Did II* 499. *Did II* 217 (Appendix no. 6), an oracle concerning worship with hymns, was recorded in the house of the prophets and probably also belongs to this group, although no prophet's name has been preserved on the surviving stone.

37 Text in Herrmann, 1971:291–98.

38 *Did II* 496 A-B.

39 This formula is found in between ten and twelve of the late oracles from Didyma.

40 Habicht, 1969:23–26 (no. 2); Lechat:518–19 report now lost inscriptions of oracles given to the cities of Pergamum and Cyzicus. It should be noted, however, that both cities are still relatively close, and both had major institutions of the Imperial cult.

41 The extant portions of the Theosophy are best preserved in a manuscript now in Tübingen, and thus the work is often called the "Tübingen Theosophy." The critical edition is by Hartmut Erbse (1941).

42 *Did II* 363. *Syngenēs Ailianou Popla, tamiou, archiprytanidos, boularchou, agonothetou, prophētou, stephanēphorou, panēgyriarchou, dis archiereōs tōn sebastōn.*

43 The Julia Maesa coin reads *epi arch(iprytanidos) Ali(ianou) Popla. Sammlung Consul Eduard Friedrich Weber Hamburg* (Catal. Hirsch, XXI, 1908). On the Caracalla coins cf. Robert, 1968:575–76.

44 Peter Brown (1978:31–32) notes that already Plutarch "with complete justification" had complained of the way prominent citizens (*hoi prōtoi*) tended to invite the rulers' decisions on every sort of matter and thus forced them to rule more than they wished. Plut. *Praec. ger. reipub.* 814F-815A. Cf. Magie: 1.596–99.

45 *IGRom* 4791, line 13–17 (*Presbeusanta pros tous sebastous*).

46 *SIG*³ 850. Cf. Robert, 1968:582.

47 *SIG*³ 883.

48 Peter Brown (1978:47) very vividly describes the pressures that were building in the city aristocracies in the early third century as "a governing class, which had been committed for generations to competition in power, honor, and reputation, regrouped itself in an age where the rewards of such competition, for the successful few, appeared greater than ever before."

49 Cf. Plut. *De vitand*. 830E. Robert, 1968:585.

50 On the meaning of this and similar Didymaean oracles cf. Robinson, 1981:228–48.

51 (. . . . *martyrētheisan te epi hagneia hypo tou Klariou Apollōnos.*) Wiseman:153.

52 Gilliam:225–251; cf. Lucian, *Alexander* 36.

53 Buresch:21–29, 81–86; *IGRom* 4.360; West, 1967:183–187.

54 West:183–87 (lines 16–17). The oracle urged the Hierapolitans to worship Apollo Careios, and then used the first person pronoun and spoke of their descent from Mopsos, the legendary founder of Claros.

55 West:183–87 (lines 22–25). This illustrates the meaning of phrases found in several inscriptions of delegations at Claros that list the names of "those who hymned the gods according to the oracle." Cf. Robert, 1969:300 (no 8.).

56 Robert, 1969:303. Robert shows that among the surviving delegation inscriptions from Claros, twenty-five are extant from Laodicea, whereas none appears from Hierapolis.

⁵⁷ It has already been noted above that the oracle of Glycon in Abonuteichos had its own distinctive manner of responding to the crises of 166. It provided an oracle of one verse that could be copied by anyone and posted at the door of their house in order to protect the inhabitants from plague (Lucian, *Alex.* 36).

⁵⁸ These come from Sardinia, Dalmatia, Numidia, Britain, and from Volubilis and Banasa in Morocco.

⁵⁹ All of the dedications are anonymous except the one from Housesteads in Britain, which adds the phrase, *Coh(ors) I Tungrorum,* "the first cohort of the Tungrians (set this up)."

ELITE NETWORKS AND HERESY ACCUSATIONS: TOWARDS A SOCIAL DESCRIPTION OF THE ORIGENIST CONTROVERSY

Elizabeth A. Clark
Duke University

ABSTRACT

As a theologian and writer Origen of Alexandria was without peer in early Christianity, and his work exerted great influence for centuries. Nonetheless, Origen's name came to be associated with "heretical" ideas. Ultimately, a rancorous theological debate erupted and engulfed many of the leading figures of the day, both East and West. Two of the chief combatants were Jerome and Rufinus, each of whom managed to sway many to his own side in the debate. Analysis of the factions and progress of the debate, however, reveals that dispassionate reason and theological abstraction were not the driving forces. Rather, social description shows that much of the conflict stemmed from personal ties and loyalties revolving around Jerome and Rufinus. This social historical account when combined with network analysis reveals new insights into both the battle lines and the personal dynamics that propelled the Origenist controversy.

The Origenist Controversy and its Social Dynamics*

One night in A.D. 397, the Roman nobleman Macarius had a dream. Macarius, who had been attempting (without apparent success) to compose a refutation of astrological determinism through an appeal to God's benevolence, saw a ship approaching across distant seas which would, God promised, solve his difficulties with the *mathematici*. Macarius later realized that his dream had portended Rufinus' arrival from Palestine and translation, at his request, of Origen's *On First Principles*.[1] Jerome, Rufinus' chief antagonist in the Origenist controversy, took a different and dimmer view: the trireme carrying that vast treasure of Egyptian and Eastern teaching[2] might better have sunk *en route*, for although it had come to Rome to "solve the puzzle of the *mathematici*," it had in fact "unloosed the faith of Christians."[3]

As is well known, Origen's *Peri Archōn* entertained a variety of theories that fourth-century Christians found reprehensible. As catalogued by Jerome, they were: that within the Godhead, the Son was subordinated to the Father and the Holy Spirit to both;[4] that rational creatures fell from a heavenly, incorporeal pre-existence to acquire bodies, identified with the "coats of skins" of Genesis 3:21;[5] that the devil could resume his angelic status and be saved:[6] that demons could be transformed into humans, and *vice versa*;[7] that since bodily substance was destined to pass away, there would be no physical resurrection;[8] that a succession of worlds may have already existed and may exist in the future;[9] that hellfire is not external to us, but the pangs of guilty conscience;[10] that Christ may come again to suffer for the demons;[11] and that allegorical exegesis is preferable to literal for those of advanced spirituality.[12]

Of these theories, Jerome was most disturbed by the alleged denial of physical resurrection and the fall of rational creatures into bodies.[13] His partner in attack, bishop Epiphanius of Salamis, worried that Origen's allegorical exegesis undercut the historicity of Biblical events. (His empirical line of argument has been advanced by the *simpliciores* of all ages: "I have seen the waters of the Gihon with my own eyes and have drunk real water from the Euphrates."[14]) Other teachings of the *Peri Archōn* either seemed less threatening to orthodoxy or had been resolved by Church decree after Origen's day.

When charged with Origenism, Rufinus' first response was to affirm Nicene doctrine[15]—a totally irrelevant affirmation, Jerome scathingly snapped.[16] Rufinus next confessed his belief in a bodily resurrection.[17] He refused to pronounce on the origin of souls, however, asserting (correctly) that since the Church had not declared any one opinion as orthodox to the exclusion of others, Christians were entitled to continue debate.[18] As a further defense, Rufinus claimed that dubious theological motifs in Origen's books had been inserted there by heretics,[19] and that Jerome himself had earlier engaged in extensive translation of and commentary upon Origen's works.[20] Had not Jerome deceived his readers, who expected on the basis of his extravagant encomia to encounter Origen in the heavenly halls after they died?[21]

Students of early Christianity can readily guess that other, non-theological issues lay only slightly beneath the surface of the controversy. Not surprisingly, only portions of Jerome's and Rufinus' diatribes on these subjects actually concern Origen. We hear much, for example, about a struggle over ecclesiastical jurisdiction: had Epiphanius of Salamis overstepped his rights when he ordained Jerome's brother Paulinianus in Palestine, allegedly within the territory of John of Jerusalem?[22] A second disputed question was who had authored the famous *Apology* for Origen, the blessed martyr Pamphilus (as Rufinus claimed) or the wretched Arian, Eusebius of Caesarea (a view Jerome found attractive).[23]

A third point concerned correct principles of translation. Jerome and Rufinus each thought his own style of translation to be correct, if not always literal, and each wished to impugn the translating abilities of the other.[24] Jerome's agenda was to fault Rufinus for altering the *Peri Archōn* in the direction of orthodoxy[25] and to ridicule the barbaric yet pretentious style of his opponent.[26] Rufinus countered that Jerome, in his earlier translations of Origen's works, had sometimes proceeded in less than literal fashion.[27] More nastily, he insinuated that Jerome's study of Hebrew and subsequent translation of the Hebrew Scriptures into Latin was a covert condemnation of the Septuagint, an attempt to sneak "Jewish" views into the purity of Christian teaching.[28]

Fourth, Rufinus, assumed the role of Tertullian *redivivus* and challenged Jerome's constant citation of secular literature: Cicero, Virgil, and Horace had nothing to do with Christian truth.[29] Jerome's snide rejoinder was to claim that Rufinus' writings made obvious that *he* had never studied literature at all.[30]

Last, the quarrel over asceticism resurfaced. Rufinus pounced upon the "Manichean" tone of Jerome's *Epistle* 22 to the virgin Eustochium and his *Against Jovinian*.[31] (Rufinus delights to remind his readers that Jerome had been so transported by ascetic enthusiasm that he had blasphemously called Paula, the mother of the letter's recipient, "the mother-in-law of God."[32]) Jerome's response was to question Rufinus' ascetic rigor, comparing his wealth to that of Croesus and Sardanapolus,[33] and hinting that the soft life prevailed in Rufinus' and Melania the Elder's Jerusalem monasteries.[34]

Yet a third issue lies even more deeply imbedded in the dispute than this second layer of extra-theological ones. The principals in the controversy, who had known each other for many years, each had his coterie of admirers well in line before the controversy ever erupted. If there is anything surprising about the way the conflict developed, it is the degree to which the factions lined up precisely on the basis of old friendship and association. Only a few "switch" characters can be noted in the entire complex drama, Theophilus of Alexandria being the most important. In fact, the multifaceted relations to be examined (kinship, marriage, hospitality proffered and received, religious mentorship, gift-giving, and literary and financial patronage) illuminate the developing antagonisms with less recourse to the theological debate than we might heretofore have imagined.

Two points need underscoring before we unravel the web. First, although contemporary social scientists assume that network description proceeds through direct observation, interviews, and questionnaires, the literature from the Origenist controversy is so abundant that a scholar working fifteen centuries later need not despair at ferreting out the relationships through which the controversy evolved. Second, the amenability of the controversy to network analysis in no way dampens its high drama: there is friendship gone awry, jealousy, betrayal, larceny, bribery, vanity, and sheer pigheadedness. Above all soars Origen's genius, triumphant over prejudice and calumny.

Network Analysis

Network description is often employed by social scientists when structural/functionalist analysis appears inadequate for their particular purposes (Mitchell, 1969a:1; 1973:9, 15; Boissevain, 1974: 4–7; Noble: 4; Eisenstadt and Roniger: 47). While structuralist/ functionalist methods are standardly employed to examine small, localized societies, some researchers deem them less helpful in examining either relations *within* groups or the operations of complex and/or urban communities (Mitchell 1969a:9). In addition, sociologists and anthropologists often criticize the structuralist/functionalist approach for its assumption of a static social model which insufficiently accounts for the process of change.[35] An approach was sought that better lent itself to the consideration of societies and relationships characterized by hierarchy, asymmetry, and inequality, without reverting to an individualistic, psychological analysis. The examination of networks was the result of this quest, and social scientists agree that the method has proven especially fruitful in the study of friendships, disputes, and patronage[36]—precisely the topics relevant to an examination of the Origenist controversy.

The determining concept of network theory is that "the variations in behaviour of people in any one role relationship may be traced to the effects of the behaviour of other people, to whom they are linked in one, two or more steps, in some other quite different relationship" (Mitchell, 1969a:46). Structures of relationships, in other words, quite apart from issues of content or motivation, may be determinative for the behavior of persons. Who is linked to whom and how, and which persons are linked to each other through third parties, are thus decisive questions for social network analysts.

The study of networks has been applied to religious groups by Rodney Stark and others. Modifying the earlier thesis that "explains recruitment to religious cults and sects on the basis of a congruence between the ideology of a group and the deprivations of those who join," Stark and his associates argue that the key factor in religious recruitment is the "interpersonal bonds between members and potential recruits" (Stark and Bainbridge, 1980:1376). Faith, then, "constitutes conformity to the religious outlook of one's intimates . . ." (*Ibid.* 1377), and recruitment moves through these pre-existent bonds (*Ibid.* 1379). For example, Stark describes a Doomsday group in which 75% of the core group of sixty adults were linked by kinship, clearly the basis of their successful recruitment (*Ibid.*

1382–83). The Mormons' success in gaining new members can be shown to depend heavily on the links of potential recruits with Mormon friends and relatives (*Ibid*. 1386–89). And in a study of the Amanda commune cited by Stark, interpersonal ties were claimed to be "more effective than ideology in sustaining commitment" (*Ibid*. 1383–85, 1391). Moreover, Stark notes studies which suggest that conventional religious groups also rely on network influences to increase and sustain membership (*Ibid*. 1389–90).

Four concepts used by network analysts will be especially helpful in our investigation. The first is the measurement of density in a network, i.e., "the number of links that actually exist expressed as a proportion of the maximum number of links that could possibly exist" (Mitchell, 1969a:35). Dense networks, in which many persons are connected with each other, make probable that actions by individual members of the network are as strongly conditioned by other relationships existing in the network as by the alleged matter at hand.

A second concept to be employed is the uniplexity or multiplexity of ties, i.e., whether individuals are linked with each other in one role or in many (Barnes, 1972:13; Mitchell, 1969a:17–18, 24–25, 35; Boissevain, 1974:30–39; Mitchell, 1974:288–89; Niemeijer:46–49). The greater the multiplexity of ties, the stronger the likelihood that a person's action in a certain situation is conditioned by the variety of roles he plays in others' lives, not just by the immediate role in which he acts.

Third, network researchers speak of "brokers" and "gatekeepers," persons who provide access between the more and the less powerful persons in a network (Barnes, 1972:10; Mitchell, 1969a:38; Boissevain, 1974:ch. 6; Mayer:114). In the case of the Origenist controversy, we will see that the liaison persons do not always mediate between those of unequal status, but often operate in a "horizontal" plane between persons of roughly equal power who, because of geographic separation, are dependent on intermediaries to carry messages, literature, and information for them. Much of the history of the Origenist controversy, I posit, rests on the success or failure (mostly failure) with which these "go-betweens" performed their tasks.

A fourth concept, "the strength of weak ties," has less direct application to our analysis, but provides some suggestive links with the notion of "brokers" or "go-betweens." According to Mark Granovetter, the prime advocate of the "strength of weak ties" theory, "weak ties" (the relations between acquaintances, as contrasted with those of friends) are essential to relations *between* groups (Granovetter, 1973:1360, 1376; 1983:201), for "weak ties" often serve as the bridges connecting clusters of friends (Granovetter, 1973:1364–68, 1378; 1983:202, 219). Granovetter's theory seems not applicable at first glance, both because the "Gesellschaft" type of relations it seems designed to explain (*Ibid.* 203–204, 209) is foreign to the material under investigation, and, more importantly, because Jerome's and Rufinus' clusters are composed chiefly of "strong-tied relations," where the principle of "transitivity" holds—the friends of friends tend to be one's own friends as well (*Ibid.* 218). Yet there is a second-level meaning to "weak ties": if ties are seen from the viewpoint of the larger social structure, not from that of individual relationships, they appear as the links that join the parts of a social system. And as intermediary links, the "weak ties" much resemble "brokerage" relationships. Thus our examination of the success or failure of these intermediaries can be understood as an illustration of Granovetter's theory. These concepts will be illustrated by the historical material pertaining to the controversy, to which we must now turn.

The Networks of Jerome and Rufinus

A thumbnail sketch of the conflict between Jerome and Rufinus might go as follows:[37] the first round of dispute occurred in the mid-390s in Palestine, when Epiphanius of Salamis charged John of Jerusalem with Origenism, and Rufinus aligned himself with John. Jerome, who rallied to Epiphanius' side, translated his admonitory letter to John for private consumption, but (according to Jerome) Rufinus' allies bribed someone for a copy and misused it to promote controversy.[38] Jerome began composing a fiercely anti-Origenistic tract against John, but abandoned it when he and Rufinus patched up their relationship just before Rufinus' departure for the West in 397.[39] When Rufinus arrived in Italy, Macarius prevailed upon him to translate Origen's *On First Principles* into Latin, as described above. An uproar resulted among Jerome's Roman friends, who sent Jerome a copy of the translation and requested that he act. Now under attack, Rufinus defended his theological orthodoxy in a statement to Pope Anastasius and a treatise, the *Apology against Jerome*. Before Jerome had the text of Rufinus' *Apology* in hand, he wrote two books against Rufinus on the basis of reports reaching Palestine; a third book followed after Jerome had obtained a copy of Rufinus' *Apology*. Only through the intervention of other parties and the passage of time did the controversy abate.

Rufinus continued to translate Origen's writings to the time of his death in about 410. Jerome, however, who could not relinquish a grudge, continued to slander Rufinus, dubbing him with nicknames such as "Grunnius Corocotta Porcellius"—"Porky the Grunter."[40] Such a summary, however, is misleading, for it concentrates too exclusively on the theological debate and vastly underestimates the role of networks in the controversy's development. A more complete account will require a description of the relationships obtaining among the members of Jerome's and Rufinus' groups.

In their early years, Rufinus and Jerome had been best of friends, perhaps fellow students in Rome. Jerome then departed for Gaul, but did not forget Rufinus: at Rufinus' request, he had two treatises of Hilary copied out for him.[41] After Jerome's return to Italy, the two probably mingled in the religious community at Aquileia, which included the priest Chromatius (Kelly: 30–33; Murphy, 1945: 19–27). Here Rufinus was baptized by Chromatius.[42] In 371 or 372, their paths diverged. Jerome went to Antioch, Rufinus to Egypt.[43] One of Jerome's first extant letters is addressed to Rufinus in Egypt: he yearns to kiss Rufinus, who "so often in the past joined me in error or in wisdom."[44] Ironically, in light of later events, Jerome closes with the sentiment, "the friendship which can come to an end has never been genuine."[45] In this letter, Jerome reports that among the people with him in Syria was Hylas, "the servant of the holy Melanium."[46] This mention establishes that Jerome had at least second-hand knowledge of Melania the Elder from the early 370s. Later, he describes her as a second Thecla.[47] Likewise, in his *Chronicle* for 377, Jerome calls Rufinus a model monk.[48]

Rufinus' Circle

Soon after his departure from Aquileia, whether in Rome or in Egypt, Rufinus met Melania. Visiting Nitria, they met some of the "Tall Brothers," monks who later would suffer for their allegedly Origenistic views.[49] During Melania and Rufinus' Egyptian sojourn, the Arian-sympathizing emperor Valens ordered a persecution of Nicene Christians in Egypt. Melania fled to Diocaesarea in Palestine with a group of the Nitrian monks, whom she supported.[50] Rufinus reports that he was jailed during the Arian outburst,[51] but whether he spent six years in Egypt (as he later claimed) is uncertain.[52] Jerome's assumption that Rufinus was already in Palestine by 374 (he writes asking to have a commentary copied)[53] may have been mistaken.

By the late 370s, Rufinus had joined Melania in Palestine and they built monasteries for men and women on the Mount of Olives. In the years following, they entertained a steady stream of visitors at their monastic establishment.[54] Melania's extraordinary generosity was well-noted by Palladius: he writes that from her own wealth, she made donations to churches, monasteries, and private individuals, and that upon her death, she endowed her monastery.[55] (Rufinus' wealth, to which Jerome often alludes,[56] can be better assigned to Melania.) An heiress of the *gens Antonia* who married into the *gens Valeria* (A. H. M. Jones, 1971:I.592), she was enormously wealthy. We do not know, however, how many of the mansions and estates owned by her granddaughter Melania the Younger in Rome and its suburbs, Campania, Sicily, Spain, Africa, Mauretania, Britain, Numidia, Aquitania, and Gaul[57] came through Melania the Elder's side of the family.

There can be no doubt that Melania the Elder and Rufinus were a very well-connected monastic pair. They were on the best of terms with John of Jerusalem,[58] who assumed the bishopric of the city in 386. They were linked to Constantinople society in several ways. Melania served as religious mentor to the wealthy heiress Olympias of Constantinople,[59] who renounced "the world" around A.D. 390 and gave her fortune to the Church;[60] according to her *Vita*, she virtually supported the operations of the Church of Constantinople under John Chrysostom's bishopric.[61] Another connection between the Olivet monasteries and Constantinople was through Evagrius Ponticus. Evagrius fled a threatening love affair in the Eastern capital and journeyed to Melania and Rufinus' monastery, where Melania converted him to the ascetic life.[62] In all likelihood, Evagrius' *Rule for Nuns* was written for Melania's use.[63] After a stay on the Mount of Olives, Evagrius went to live among the monks of Egypt[64] and was instrumental in embuing them with Origenist sentiments.[65] Another sojourner at the Jerusalem monastery who subsequently traveled to Egypt was Palladius,[66] who lavished praise on Melania in his *Lausiac History*.[67]

Highly placed visitors came as well. Around 394 arrived Silvia, sister-in-law of the praetorian prefect of the East, Flavius Rufinus. In Melania's monastery she met Palladius, with whom she traveled to Egypt.[68] Perhaps it was through her influence that in late 394 a decree for banishment was issued against Jerome's monks in Bethlehem;[69] nothing came of the decree, however, perhaps because of Count Rufinus' assassination shortly thereafter.[70] Rufinus of Aquileia promised to translate the Pseudo-Clementine *Recognitions* for Silvia, but she died before he accomplished his task.[71] Another highly-placed friend of Rufinus and Melania, who may have influenced the Constantinople regime against Jerome, was Bacurius, *dux Palestinae* sometime between 378–394; a former king of the Iberians, he fought against Eugenius at the battle of the Frigidus.[72] Last, according to the historian Gennadius, Rufinus also corresponded with the women of arguably the wealthiest family of the Western Empire, the Anicii.[73]

Melania and Rufinus journeyed westward at the end of the fourth century and re-established contacts with family and friends there. Melania's arrival in Italy dates to probably A.D. 399–400.[74] According to Palladius, her return was motivated in part by her desire to rescue her granddaughter, Melania the Younger, from falling prey to "heresy."[75] (Given the predilections of both the author and the subjects of the account, this can mean only one thing: the Elder Melania wished to prevent her granddaughter from falling into the hands of Jerome's anti-Origenist faction in Rome.) Upon her disembarkment, Melania the Elder was greeted and entertained by Paulinus of Nola, with whom her entire family enjoyed a close relationship.[76] To Paulinus, Melania brought a coveted present, a piece of the True Cross which John of Jerusalem had given her.[77]

The Elder Melania also met in the West several new family members, including her cousin's husband, Turcius Apronianus, whom we are told she converted.[78] Apronianus was to play an important role as "go-between" for Rufinus. It was from Apronianus that Rufinus received a copy of Jerome's letter to Pammachius and Oceanus attacking Rufinus' views;[79] Apronianus was the rare owner of a corrected copy of Rufinus' translation of the *Peri Archōn*;[80] to Apronianus, Rufinus dedicated his *Apology against Jerome*;[81] and it was Apronianus whom Rufinus beseeched to intercede with Jerome through Pammachius that the controversy be laid to rest.[82] Later, Rufinus dedicated his translation of nine sermons by Gregory Nazianzen[83] and of Origen's *Explanatio super Psalmos XXXVI-XXXVIII*[84] to Apronianus.

In Italy, the Elder Melania also met her granddaughter's wealthy and aristocratic husband Pinianus for the first time (A. H. M. Jones, 1971:I.702). Rufinus became enamored of the young man, calling him "amantissimus filius noster." He also was planning to dedicate to him a translation of Origen's *Homilies on Deuteronomy*, a project he contrived while on Melania's estates in Sicily shortly before his death.[85] The younger generation also learned to revere the friends of the elder: when Palladius fled to Rome in 404–405 to plead on behalf of John Chrysostom, he was given hospitality by the younger Melania and Pinian.[86]

This brief description of Rufinus' circle suggests how tightly the group was linked by kinship, marriage, patronage, religious mentorship, ascetic devotion, gift-giving, and hospitality. Jerome's circle, although not commanding the favor of as many highly-placed individuals,[87] similarly consisted of persons with longstanding, multifaceted relationships with each other. Paula played the role in Jerome's circle that Melania the Elder did in Rufinus'. There can be no doubt that Paula was the soul-mate of Jerome's life:[88] he dedicated many of his commentaries and translations to her,[89] and confessed his inability to estimate the number of letters he sent her, since he wrote daily.[90]

Jerome's Circle

When Jerome first met Paula in Rome in 382, she was an aristocratic widow with five children.[91] Although of senatorial rank, she may not have been as wealthy as Melania the Elder;[92] however, she probably provided much of the money for the Bethlehem monasteries. In Palestine,

Paula and Jerome searched three years for funding to erect their establishments,[93] yet Jerome later was forced to sell some family property to help with costs.[94]

The year 382 saw another important arrival in Rome: Epiphanius attended a bishops' council in Rome that year and stayed at Paula's mansion for the duration.[95] Her hospitality was reciprocated when, in 385, she and Jerome stopped to see him on their way East. On Cyprus, Paula visited "all" the monasteries and left funds for them, such as she could afford.[96] Paula and Jerome stayed in touch with Epiphanius after they reached Palestine. Once when Paula was ill, Jerome secretly appealed to Epiphanius, asking him to convince her to take some wine. According to Jerome, Paula saw through the ruse and almost (but not quite) persuaded Epiphanius never to take a drop again.[97]

Although Paula did not star in the Origenist controversy in Palestine to the degree Marcella did in Rome, she nonetheless had her bouts with Origenists. Jerome reports that an unnamed man tried to trick her with questions about the bodily resurrection, the status of infants' souls before birth, and other disputed topics. Paula turned the matter over to Jerome, who by his own account speedily bested the opposition. But Jerome reveals that Paula "publicly" proclaimed the man and his supporters to be enemies of God.[98]

Paula had another strong relationship in Jerome's circle: with the Roman senator Pammachius, who had married her second daughter, Paulina.[99] When Paulina died in 395, Pammachius adopted an ascetic life while still performing his senatorial duties.[100] Perhaps a schoolmate of Jerome, Pammachius was by all accounts a friend of long standing.[101] Jerome reports that Pammachius had served as a proconsul and was a member of the *gens Furia*, thus a distant relative of Paula.[102] He was also a cousin of Marcella,[103] the principal Hieronyman actress in the Origenist drama. Pammachius may not have been of the highest senatorial aristocracy; nonetheless, he used his abundant income for such charitable projects as a *xenodochium* at Portus and church buildings in Rome.[104]

Pammachius was a key supporter of Jerome in the controversy. It was he who informed Jerome in Bethlehem of the disturbances that had erupted in the Western capital as a result of Rufinus' translation of the *Peri Archōn* and who requested a literal rendition of the work from Jerome.[105] To Pammachius (and Marcella), Jerome sent his *Apology against Rufinus* and his translation of Theophilus of Alexandria's Paschal Letter of 402 condemning Origenism.[106] Most important, Pammachius was responsible for suppressing the friendly letter of reconciliation Jerome wrote to Rufinus in mid-controversy and for circulating instead the hostile one Jerome had intended only for the eyes of his intimate supporters.[107] Thus Rufinus did not know until much later that Jerome was, in 399, ready for reconciliation. (Here it is helpful to recall that Pammachius had earlier suppressed material from Jerome with which he disagreed: shocked by Jerome's *Against Jovinian*, he had hastened about Rome in 394 to remove all the copies from circulation.)[108] To Pammachius, Jerome addressed his tirade *Against John of Jerusalem* and dedicated many of his commentaries on the minor prophets.[109]

Three other Roman friends of Jerome played significant roles in the controversy: Oceanus, Fabiola, and Marcella. Fabiola, perhaps Oceanus' housemate, had been visiting Jerome in Bethlehem when the first phase of the controversy erupted in Palestine.[110] We are told that she enriched many monasteries through her generosity; no doubt the Bethlehem foundations stood high on her gift list. Fabiola shared with Pammachius the expense of building the *xenodochium* at Portus mentioned above.[111] Jerome reports that an important document in the Origenist controversy mysteriously appeared in her and Oceanus' dwelling, but does not identify it.[112]

Of Oceanus' involvement in the controversy we know more. Jerome was informed by another correspondent how ardently Oceanus was battling Origenism in Rome.[113] Along with Pammachius, he wrote to Jerome in Bethlehem asking for a literal translation of the *Peri Archōn*, his request prompted by Rufinus' removal or correction of the offending passages in his translation.[114] Jerome replied, attempting to dissociate himself from Origen as much as possible—but he presumably sent Pammachius and Oceanus his own more literal translation.[115] Jerome also furnished Oceanus with a copy of his *Apology against Rufinus*.[116]

Another important Roman partisan of Jerome was Marcella, whom he had first met on his arrival in the capital in 382.[117] A wealthy widow with a palace on the Aventine, Marcella was a cousin of Pammachius, and is credited by Jerome with being the religious mentor of Paula's daughter Eustochium.[118] Probably the most scholarly of Jerome's women friends, Marcella plied him with questions about Scripture, both before and after his departure from Rome.[119] Never successful in luring Marcella to Palestine, Jerome nonetheless composed Biblical commentaries for her.[120]

Most important for our purposes, Jerome credits Marcella with initiating the condemnation of Origenists at Rome. Although she had at first been reticent to assume a public role, her indignation grew at the number of innocents (including Pope Siricius) who had been duped by Origenist "heretics." She moved to public action: she found witnesses who had been led astray by Origenism, especially by Rufinus' "emended" translation of the *Peri Archōn*, and wrote "countless" letters asking the Origenists to defend themselves publicly—but, according to Jerome, they never would.[121]

Rufinus' report of her activity is understandably different. He writes that "that woman Jezebel" (meaning Marcella) exceeded even Eusebius of Cremona in wickedness: it was she who supplied the allegedly falsified copy of the *Peri Archōn* to Eusebius, which he then broadcast throughout Italy, to Rufinus' dismay. (In his account, Rufinus reveals that he did not know Marcella personally: after he mentions her, he adds, "whoever she may be."[122] Rufinus and Marcella thus constitute two of the few unconnected partisans in the controversy.) To Marcella as well as Pammachius, Jerome sent his translation of Theophilus' Easter Letter, a tirade against Origenism.[123]

Two bishops of Rome were also involved in the controversy: Siricius, who approved Rufinus' statement of faith and gave him a letter of commendation,[124] and Anastasius, his successor in 399, of the opposite persuasion. Although Anastasius claimed (astonishingly enough) that he did not know who Origen was nor did he wish to know, he apparently rejected Rufinus' appeal.[125] He condemned Origen's writings and furnished Eusebius of Cremona with a letter of the Church at Milan so testifying.[126] He also corresponded with others involved in the controversy: Jerome, Theophilus of Alexandria,[127] and John of Jerusalem.[128]

Other partisans and emissaries of Jerome included his monastic companions. His brother Paulinianus accompanied Jerome out of Rome in August 385[129] and re-emerges in the Bethlehem monastery. In Palestine, Paulinianus was ordained by Epiphanius, an ordination that may have given rise to the original hostilities between Epiphanius and John of Jerusalem.[130] Later we find Paulinianus living in Cyprus, presumably near Epiphanius, but frequently visiting Jerome in Bethlehem.[131] Jerome sent him as his emissary to Italy in 397 or 398;[132] while in Rome, he memorized parts of Rufinus' *Apology against Jerome* which he recited to his brother upon his return to Bethlehem.[133] Jerome also honored Paulinianus with his translation of Didymus the Blind's treatise on the Holy Spirit.[134]

Another long-standing friend and monastic companion of Jerome who played an important role in the controversy was the presbyter Vincentius. Apparently at the Council of Constantinople with Jerome in 381–382,[135] Vincentius journeyed to Rome with Jerome and left with him (and thus with Paula and Paulinianus) in 385. Traveling to Cyprus with them, he enjoyed Epiphanius' hospitality.[136] In 394, while at Jerome's monastery,[137] Vincentius served as a significant intermediary: letters from Isidore, a pro-Origenist emissary from Alexandria to John of Jerusalem, were misdelivered to Vincentius, who showed them to Jerome. Although Isidore supposedly had been sent to Palestine as a peacemaker, his letters were decidedly partisan: they encouraged John of Jerusalem not to fear Jerome's "lamentations" and promised that Isidore would come to

Jerusalem and crush John's adversaries.[138] Needless to say, the letters discouraged friendly relations between the Bethlehem and the Jerusalem religious establishments. A few years later, probably in 396 or 397, Jerome sent Vincentius to Rome on a mission.[139] Thus he was in the Western capital when the controversy erupted and reported to Jerome upon his return to Palestine.[140] Jerome dedicated his translations of Eusebius of Caesarea's *Chronicle* and of Origen's *Homily on Ezekiel* to Vincentius.[141]

A third monastic friend and advocate of Jerome was Eusebius of Cremona. Eusebius first surfaces in Jerome's monastery in 394, where he extolled the high character and ascetic devotion of Paulinus of Nola to Jerome.[142] At Eusebius' behest, Jerome translated into Latin Epiphanius' letter criticizing John of Jerusalem. The letter was supposed to remain private, but a "pretended monk" either bribed or stole the letter from Eusebius and gave it to John,[143] thus exacerbating the friction between the Bethlehem and the Jerusalem monasteries. Jerome did not hesitate to claim that Rufinus stood behind the theft of the document.[144]

Eusebius also starred in the Roman act of the controversy. Although Jerome later claimed that he had sent Eusebius to Rome a year after Rufinus' arrival, and on a mission unrelated to Origenism,[145] yet, according to Rufinus, it was Eusebius who changed his translation of the *Peri Archōn* and circulated the faulty copy.[146] We also know that Eusebius journeyed to Milan and in Rufinus' presence read out the allegedly falsified copy, which he claimed he had received from Marcella; Rufinus hotly contended that the version from which Eusebius read was not the version *he* had produced.[147] And Eusebius took more to Milan with him than the *Peri Archōn*: he carried to bishop Simplicianus of Milan the letter from Anastasius of Rome condemning the works of Origen, in which Anastasius divulges that it was Eusebius who pointed out to him the "blasphemous" passages in the *Peri Archōn*.[148] Jerome dedicated his *Commentary on Matthew* to Eusebius and gave him an extra copy for Marcella's monastic housemate in Rome, Principia.[149] In addition, Jerome dedicated his *Commentary on Jewish Questions* to Eusebius.[150]

Two members primarily associated with Rufinus' circle also retained cordial relations with Jerome. One was bishop Chromatius of Aquileia, who baptized Rufinus and presumably knew Jerome at Aquileia during the same period of time.[151] When Rufinus returned West in 397, he spent some years in Aquileia and vicinity (cf. Hammond: 372–427). Chromatius had the distinction of serving as literary patron to both Rufinus and Jerome. He asked Rufinus to translate Eusebius of Caesarea's *Church History* into Latin, perhaps assuming that this massive project would remove Rufinus from controversy for a few years.[152] Yet Chromatius also commissioned Jerome to write commentaries on Chronicles, Jonah,[153] and

Habakkuk, and to translate Proverbs, Ecclesiastes, Song of Songs, Tobit, and Judith.[154] In the preface to his translations of the first three books, Jerome reveals that Chromatius (and Heliodorus) had sent him the necessary supplies for the task and had supported his secretaries and copyists.[155] Here we have documentation of genuine literary patronage. During the heat of the Origenist controversy, however, Chromatius wrote to Jerome, begging him to lay aside his enmity and make peace with Rufinus.[156]

A second friend of Rufinus who at least briefly enjoyed cordial relations with Jerome was Paulinus of Nola. A latecomer to Italy, Paulinus had apparently received a cool reception from Pope Siricius when he journeyed from Spain to take up residence at Nola.[157] Paulinus deeply admired Melania (possibly his relative),[158] whom he entertained upon her return from Palestine and commemorated in *Epistle* 29.[159] Melania in turn brought Paulinus a sliver of the True Cross which John of Jerusalem had given her; Paulinus generously shared his bit with his friend Sulpicius Severus, whose establishment at Primuliacum was awaiting Silvia's promised gift of relics.[160] Melania's entire family, especially her granddaughter's husband Pinian, receive lavish commendation in Paulinus' *Carmen* 21.[161] Through his relationship with Melania, Paulinus also became close friends with Rufinus.[162] A great admirer of Rufinus' translating talent, he asked him to translate the Pseudo-Clementines (which Rufinus still had not done, despite Silvia's earlier request); Paulinus himself had attempted the task, but found his skills inadequate.[163] He also requested that Rufinus write a commentary on the blessings of the patriarchs in Genesis, a request Rufinus was pleased to honor.[164]

Despite these strong links with Rufinus' circle, Paulinus also was an acquaintance of Jerome's Roman friend Pammachius. He composed a moving letter of condolence to Pammachius upon the death of his wife Paulina, thus beating Jerome by a year in expressing his sympathy.[165] Moreover, Paulinus had corresponded with Jerome during 394–395, using Vigilantius as carrier,[166] and had sent Jerome gifts, for which Jerome thanked him in Epistles 53 and 85.[167]

In *Epistle* 85, 2–3 Jerome responds to Paulinus' query about "the hardening of Pharaoh's heart"—that is, to a question about free will in relation to God's predetermination, based on the classic Biblical text. Surprisingly enough, Jerome here, in the very midst of the Origenist controversy (A.D. 400), advises Paulinus that his question is answered in Origen's *Peri Archōn*; Paulinus can borrow a copy of the work from Pammachius, if he wishes to read a Latin translation, although Jerome is sure that Paulinus can manage the Greek original. Jerome's nonchalance in suggesting that Paulinus read the *Peri Archōn* at the very moment when tempers were aflame and friendships breached raises an unsettling doubt about the centrality of theology in Jerome's attack on Origenism.

Last, two people who played "turncoat" roles in the controversy must be briefly considered, Theophilus of Alexandria and Vigilantius. Vigilantius first comes to our attention as a letter carrier between Paulinus of Nola and Sulpicius Severus, and Paulinus and Jerome.[168] In about 395, Jerome calls his messenger Vigilantius a "reverend presbyter."[169] About a year later, Jerome changed his mind: Vigilantius had returned West and spread the report that Jerome held Origenist views, and had indicted Oceanus, Vincentius, Paulinianus and Eusebius of Cremona as well.[170] Jerome lashed out bitterly against this "Judas."[171] He is puzzled how Paulinus of Nola's judgment could have been so mistaken. Jerome had assumed that since Vigilantius was Paulinus' "little client" (*clientulus*), he was trustworthy; Jerome should have trusted his own first impressions instead.[172] Jerome concludes his letter with an apt curse on Vigilantius: may he receive pardon when the Devil obtains it![173]—which to anti-Origenists meant "never."

Most important, Jerome drops a revealing comment about Vigilantius in his *Apology against Rufinus*: it was Rufinus, he claims, who stirred up Vigilantius against Jerome.[174] The reference may pertain only to the Origenist controversy—or it may not. Here recall that Rufinus had taken pains to remind Jerome that his ascetic views were considered "Manichean,"[175] and that within a few years, Vigilantius' critique of Jerome's asceticism[176] would lead Jerome to assert that Jovinian had been reborn in Vigilantius.[177] It is not unlikely that Vigilantius' retreat from Jerome on the Origenist issue may have been coupled with his growing discomfort about Jerome's fanatic asceticism. Rufinus, despite his own monastic vocation, disagreed with Jerome on both issues as well. Thus Vigilantius, at first consideration an unimportant character in the controversy, may have been more central to it than has heretofore been imagined.

Last we come to Theophilus of Alexandria. In the first phase of the Origenist controversy in Palestine, Theophilus had shown decidedly Origenist tendencies. He had expressed his contempt for the narrow theological viewpoints Epiphanius had championed in a letter to Pope Siricius.[178] Theophilus sent an emissary, Isidore, to calm the dispute, but Isidore's neutrality was rightly called into question when letters Isidore had written to John of Jerusalem counseling resistance to Jerome fell into the hands of Jerome's friend Vincentius.[179] Moreover, Isidore refused to deliver letters Theophilus had written to Jerome, and did so allegedly at John of Jerusalem's request.[180] Although Theophilus' immediate response to Jerome after these events was cool, Jerome nonetheless kept up a decidedly one-sided correspondence.[181] In a letter dating from probably 397, Jerome told Theophilus that "many people" considered his stand on Egyptian Origenism too lax, and urged him to greater activity.[182] A year or two later, Theophilus wrote to Jerome, adopting a peacemaker's role.[183] Jerome responded that he also desired peace, but only if it were based on genuine agreement. In passing, Jerome mentions the loving concord that prevailed between Theophilus and the monks of the Egyptian desert.[184] (Indeed, Theophilus had so admired the Tall Brothers that he had coerced them into ecclesiastical service.)[185]

Jerome did not wait long for Theophilus to change his mind. In his Easter Letter of 399, Theophilus had discussed God's incorporeality, a point which angered the simple monks given to Anthropomorphism. They flocked to Alexandria and riots erupted; Theophilus was in serious danger for both his post and his life. So he made a *volte-face:* he agreed with the monks that God had ears, eyes, and other parts (after all, Scripture said so!), and blamed his former friends the Tall Brothers and other Origenists for their disagreement. A time of persecution followed. The Tall Brothers and about eighty other monks fled to Palestine and then to Constantinople, where their cause became tied to that of John Chrysostom.[186]

Meanwhile, Theophilus aligned himself with the anti-Origenists, even enlisting Epiphanius, whose views he had earlier censured.[187] He wrote to Jerome, reporting his rout of the Nitrian monks;[188] he wrote a synodical letter to bishops in Palestine and Cyprus;[189] he wrote to Anastasius.[190] In the next years, Jerome translated Theophilus' Paschal Letters, heavy with criticism of Origenism.[191] There is, however, very little evidence that Theophilus' anti-Origenism had any basis but political expediency. As soon as he had regained his power at home and abroad had engineered the opposition that would lead to Chrysostom's downfall, he quickly reconciled himself to the Origenist monks he had hounded out of Egypt[192]— and resumed his study of Origen's writings. When asked why he now read the books he had so recently condemned, Theophilus allegedly replied that Origen's works could be compared to a meadow: one could pluck the beautiful flowers and step over the thorny ones,[193] a view identical with that held by both Jerome[194] and Rufinus[195] in their more rational moments.

Conclusion: Theological Debate and Mobilized Loyalties

This last point again brings home the extent to which the antagonists agreed in their approach to Origen. So again we ask, why did the controversy develop as it did? We now can bring the network concepts of density, multiplexity, brokerage, and "the strength of weak ties" to bear upon the historical data. The results of this analysis are presented in the tables at the end of the article.

Tables 1 and 2 below summarize a conservative (i.e., based on documentable relationships) calculation of density. For Jerome's cluster, the density is 83.3%; for Rufinus', 78.0%. If all the probable but non-documentable relationships were charted, the figures would be higher, and if second-order relationships were calculated (A and C's indirect relationship through their individual associations with B), the density would be higher still, approximating 100%. Network analysts would claim that the sheer density of these clusters largely explains the complexity and the heat of the controversy: almost everybody knew everybody else directly or through a third party.

The multiplexity of ties in the network is a second factor to note. Seven possible ties have been charted (marriage/kinship; religious mentorship; hospitality; traveling companionship; financial patronage, money, and gifts; literature written to, for, or against members of the network; and carriers of literature and information) and are illustrated in Tables 3–9 below. (The lines of hostility after the controversy's outbreak are schematized in Table 10.) The strong connections *within* clusters are obvious at a glance, the links *between* clusters, less dense. When the individual ties portrayed in Tables 3–9 are reduced to a single chart indicating multiplex relationships (Table 11), the degrees of connectedness are graphically conveyed. To take just two examples: Paulinianus is linked to Jerome by six of the seven categories: as kin, religious mentee, recipient of hospitality, traveling companion, receiver of literature, and carrier of information. Likewise, turning to Rufinus' cluster, we can see that Melania the Elder is linked to Apronianus by kinship and by religious mentorship; insofar as she undoubtedly stayed with family members when she returned to Rome in A.D. 400, we are probably safe in adding the link of hospitality. Rufinus' cluster appears to contain fewer multiplex relations than Jerome's, but the difference can be accounted for by the relative lack of epistolary evidence for Rufinus' circle and the abundance of it for Jerome's.

The role of "brokers" was also of decisive importance. Separated at first by small distances (Jerusalem and Bethlehem) and then by more extensive ones (Italy and Bethlehem), Rufinus and Jerome were in need of speedy and faithful liaisons. Both the development and the rancor of the controversy were influenced by the questionable behavior of their intermediaries. The deliberate nature of the liaisons' misguided actions undoubtedly resulted from the passionate loyalty they gave their respective patrons, and hence their patron's opinions: as Stark observed in his studies, religious commitments tend to follow the lines of personal loyalties to friends and relatives. That seemingly unimportant persons, unknown to the pages of theology textbooks, so strongly influenced the controversy's development is a fact that network analysis has brought to light—a fact totally obscured by a concentration on the theological dimensions of the debate. The following examples illustrate the point.

First, the controversy might not have smouldered on in Palestine had Isidore of Alexandria served as peacemaker, the role in which he had been sent by bishop Theophilus. By allowing his own pro-Origenist letter opposing Jerome to fall (accidentally?) into the hands of Jerome's friend Vincentius, Isidore is at least partially responsible for the deteriorating relations of the Jerusalem and Bethlehem factions. His failure to play his "liaison" role is further indicated by his refusal to deliver letters from Theophilus to Jerome, as he had been directed.

A second case concerns Pammachius, Jerome's supporter in Rome. Instead of delivering Jerome's friendly letter of reconciliation to Rufinus, as he had been instructed by his mentor, he suppressed it and circulated in its place Jerome's hot letter against Rufinus, meant only for the eyes of Pammachius and a few of Jerome's Roman intimates. Thus Rufinus composed his *Apology against Jerome;* Jerome responded with his rancorous *Apology against Rufinus,* and tempers flared.

A third case: Jerome was poorly served by the actions of his emissary Eusebius of Cremona, whom he sent on an allegedly private mission to Rome. According to Rufinus, Eusebius while in Rome pirated an uncorrected copy of Rufinus' translation of the *Peri Archōn,* "emended" it to accentuate its theological unorthodoxy, and trumpeted citations from this falsified version before bishops and aristocrats in Italy. With intermediaries behaving so irresponsibly, it is understandable how difficult it was for Jerome and Rufinus to resolve their feud. The infrastructure of the network depended upon the smooth functioning of these "weak-tied" associations, and when the ties unraveled, the controversy was prolonged and escalated.

A fourth example illustrates how the sheer fact of a person's place in the network's structure, quite aside from his or her relative importance in the larger history, may have influenced the course of events in important ways. Take the case of Silvia, a virtual non-entity except for her kinship with Count Rufinus, praetorian prefect of the East, and briefly the central Eastern wielder of power during Theodosius' Western trip in 394. The few pieces we know of Silvia's story (her journey from Constantinople to Jerusalem, her meeting of Palladius and subsequent travel with him to Egypt, and her role as intended recipient of Rufinus of Aquileia's translation of the Pseudo-Clementine *Recognitions*) suggest that she may have been a (indeed, *the*) missing link in a seemingly mysterious affair: the issuing of an edict of banishment against Jerome. Her "structural" position as intermediary between the Jerusalem religious establishment and the Eastern court perhaps provides a key to an otherwise puzzling aspect of the controversy.

Thus the theological dimensions of the Origenist debate must be set in their proper social context: the networks of kinship, friendship, mentorship, patronage, gifts, travel, and literary dedications that served as the substructure supporting the airy debate on the pre-existence of souls and the bodily resurrection. Indeed, the diminished weight of theology in the controversy prompts a final (and unanswerable) question: if, as Jerome wished, the ship in Macarius' dream had sunk before reaching its Roman destination, would some issue other than Origenism have engaged these clusters of friends and given them outlets for their social, economic and intellectual rivalry?

TABLE 1: DENSITY

JEROME'S CLUSTER

	Jerome	Paula	Pammachius	Fabiola	Marcella	Eusebius of Cremona	Epiphanius of Salamis	Theophilus of Alexandria	Paulinianus	Vincentius	Pope Anastasius	Oceanus
Jerome		X	X	X	X	X	X	X	X	X	X	X
Paula	X		X	?	X	?	X		X	?		?
Pammachius	X	X		X	X	?	?				?	X
Fabiola	X	X	X		?	?						X
Marcella	X	X	X	?		X	?				X	?
Eusebius of Cremona	X	?	?	?	X				?	?	X	?
Epiphanius of Salamis	X	X			?				X		?	
Theophilus of Alexandria	X						X				X	
Paulinianus	X	X	?	?	?	?	X			X		?
Vincentius	X	X	?	?	?		X		X			?
Pope Anastasius	X				X	X	X	X				
Oceanus	X	?	X	X	?		?		?	?		

Density Calculation:

$$\frac{200 \times \text{actual number of links}}{\text{number in cluster} \times \text{number in cluster} - 1}$$

$$\frac{200 \times 55}{12 \times 11} = \frac{11000}{132}$$

83.3% density

TABLE 2: DENSITY
RUFINUS' CLUSTER

	Rufinus of Aquileia	Melania the Elder	Apronianus	Palladius	Paulinus of Nola	Melania the Younger and Pinianus	John of Jerusalem	Isidore of Alexandria	Vigilantius	Evagrius Ponticus	Tall Brothers	Macarius	Pope Siricius	Sylvia
Rufinus of Aquileia		X	X	X	X	X	X	X	X	X	X	X	X	X
Melania the Elder	X		X	X	X	X	X	?		X	X			X
Apronianus	X	X		X	X	X								
Palladius	X	X	X		?	X	?			X	X			X
Paulinus of Nola	X	X	X	?		X			X			?	X	?
Melania the Younger and Pinianus	X	X	X	X	X								?	
John of Jerusalem	X	X		?				X		X	X			?
Isidore of Alexandria	X	?					X			?	X			?
Vigilantius	X				X									
Evagrius Ponticus	X	X		X			X	?			X			?
Tall Brothers	X	X		X			X			X				?
Macarius	X				?									
Pope Siricius	X				X	?								
Sylvia	X	X		X	?		?	?		?	?			

Density Calculation:

$$\frac{200 \times \text{actual number of links}}{\text{number in cluster} \times \text{number in cluster} - 1}$$

$$\frac{200 \times 71}{14 \times 13} = \frac{14200}{182}$$

78.0% density

TABLE 3
MARRIAGE/KINSHIP

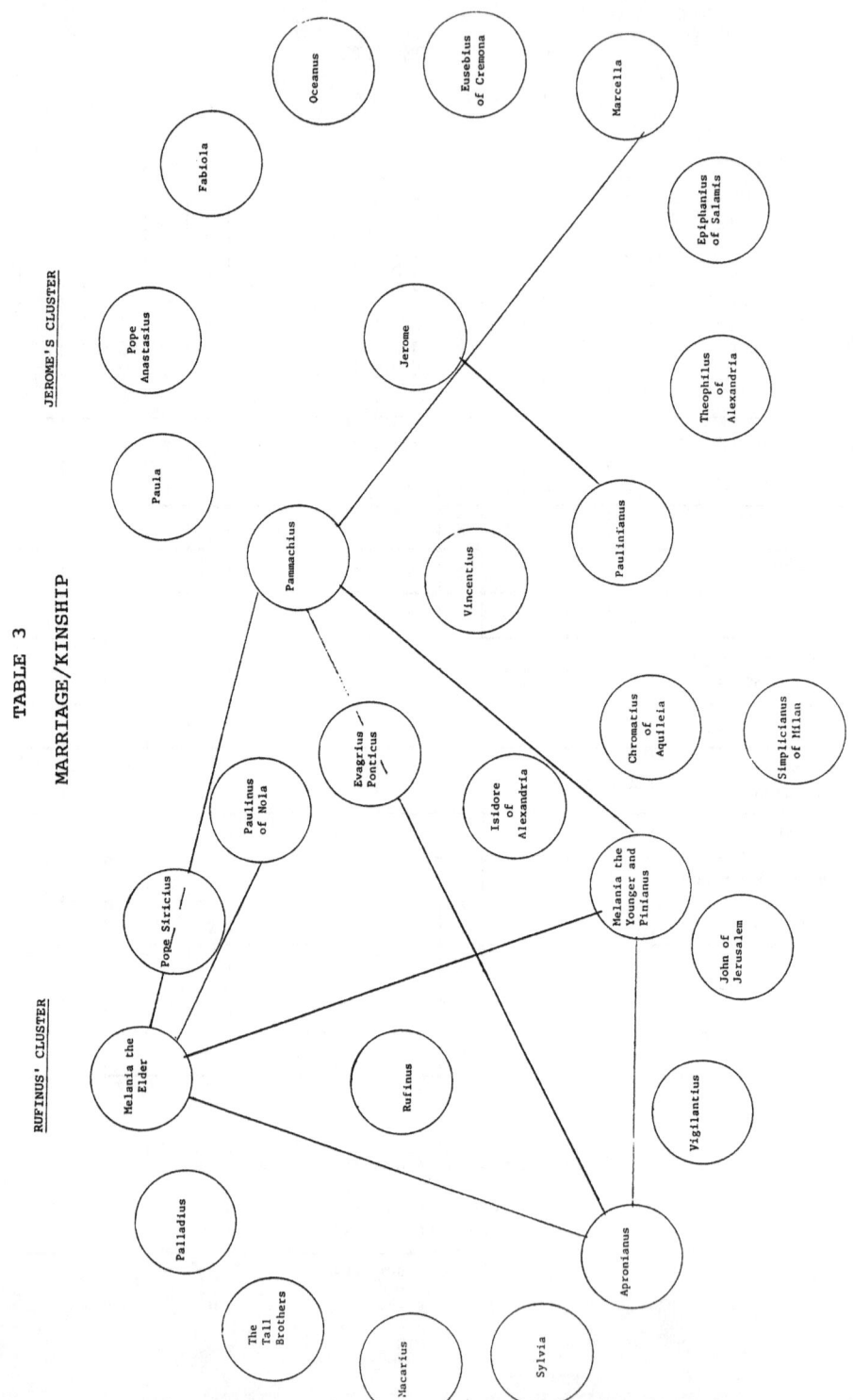

TABLE 4
RELIGIOUS MENTORSHIP

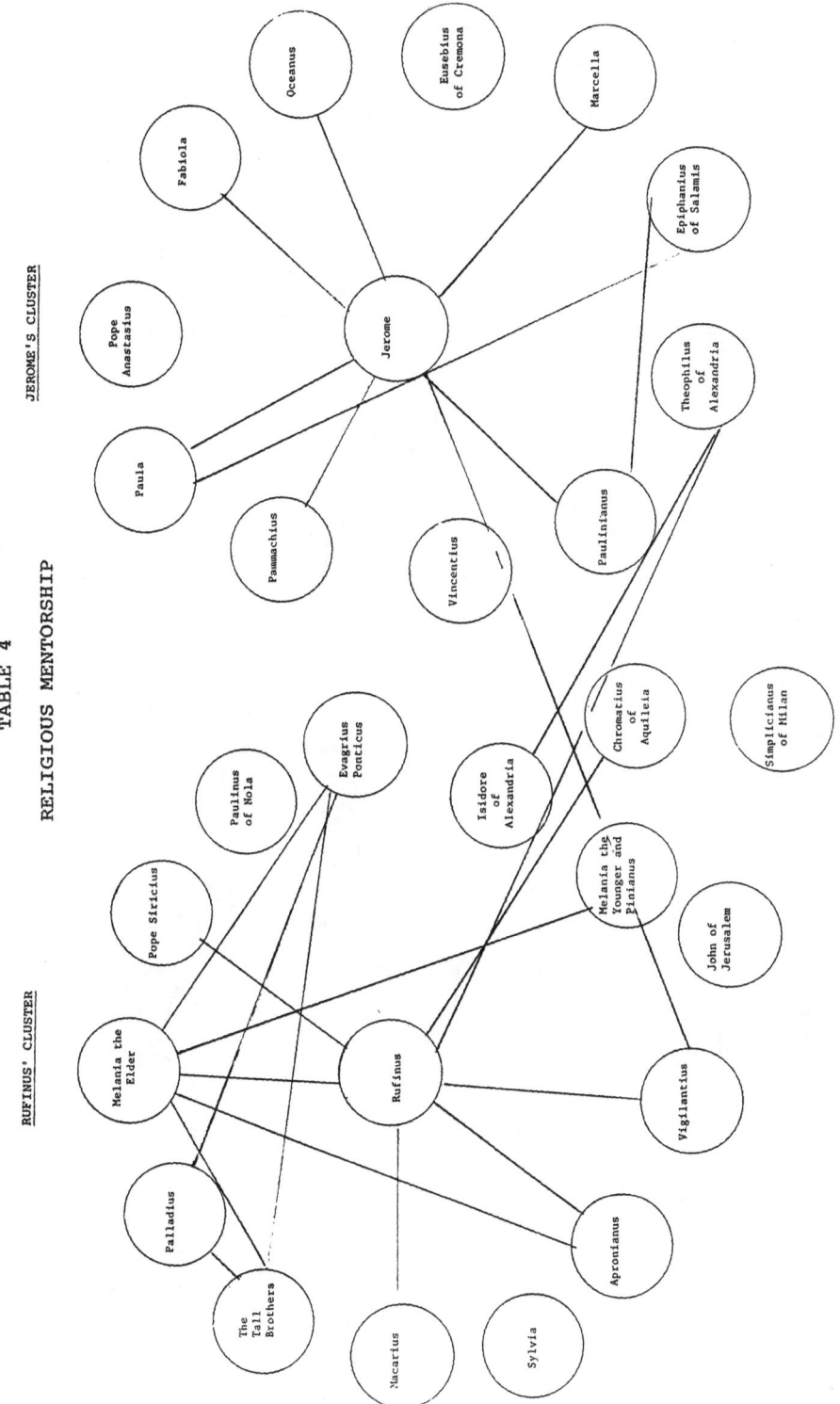

JEROME'S CLUSTER

RUFINUS' CLUSTER

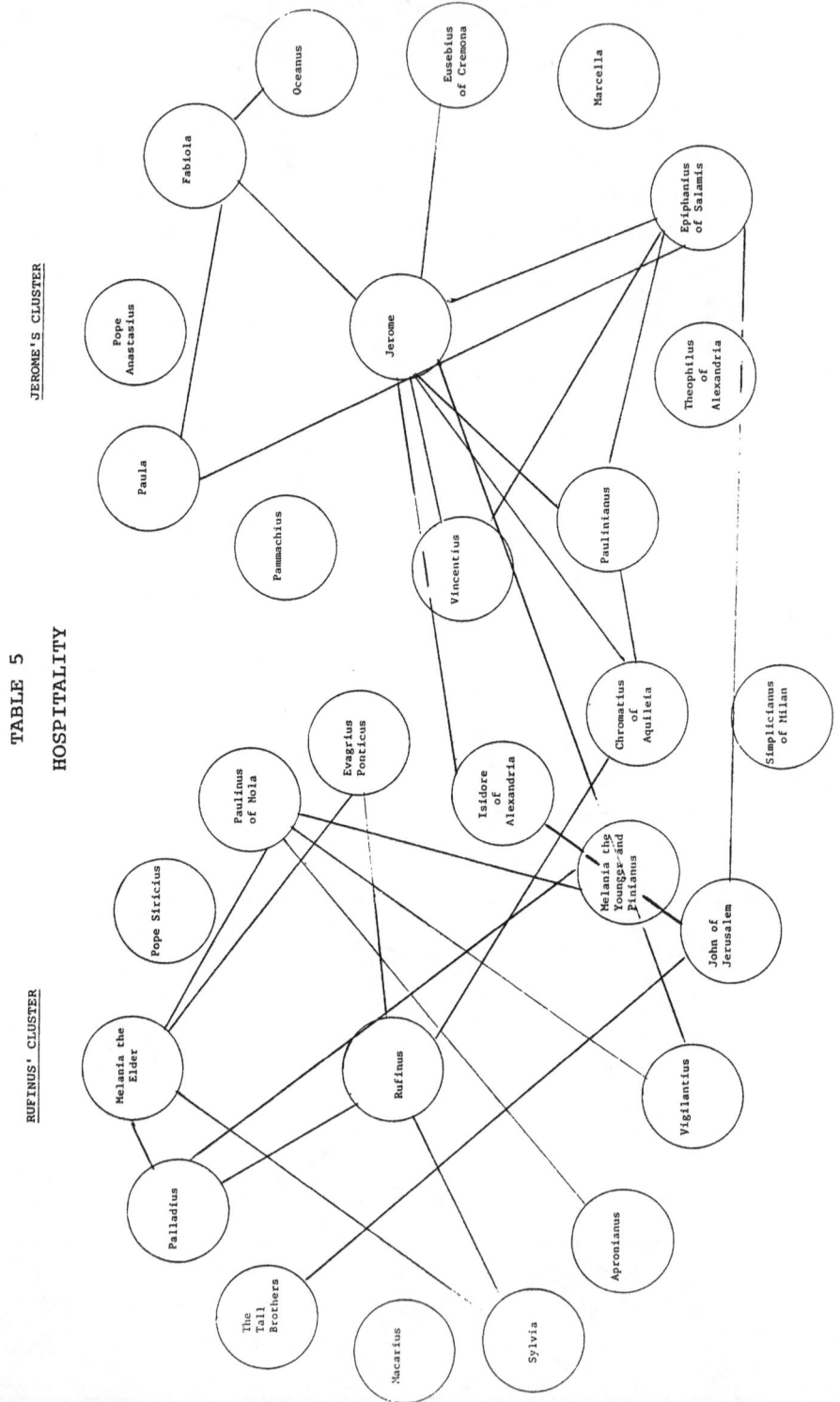

TABLE 5
HOSPITALITY

Clark: Elite Networks and Heresy Accusations

TABLE 6
TRAVELING COMPANIONSHIP

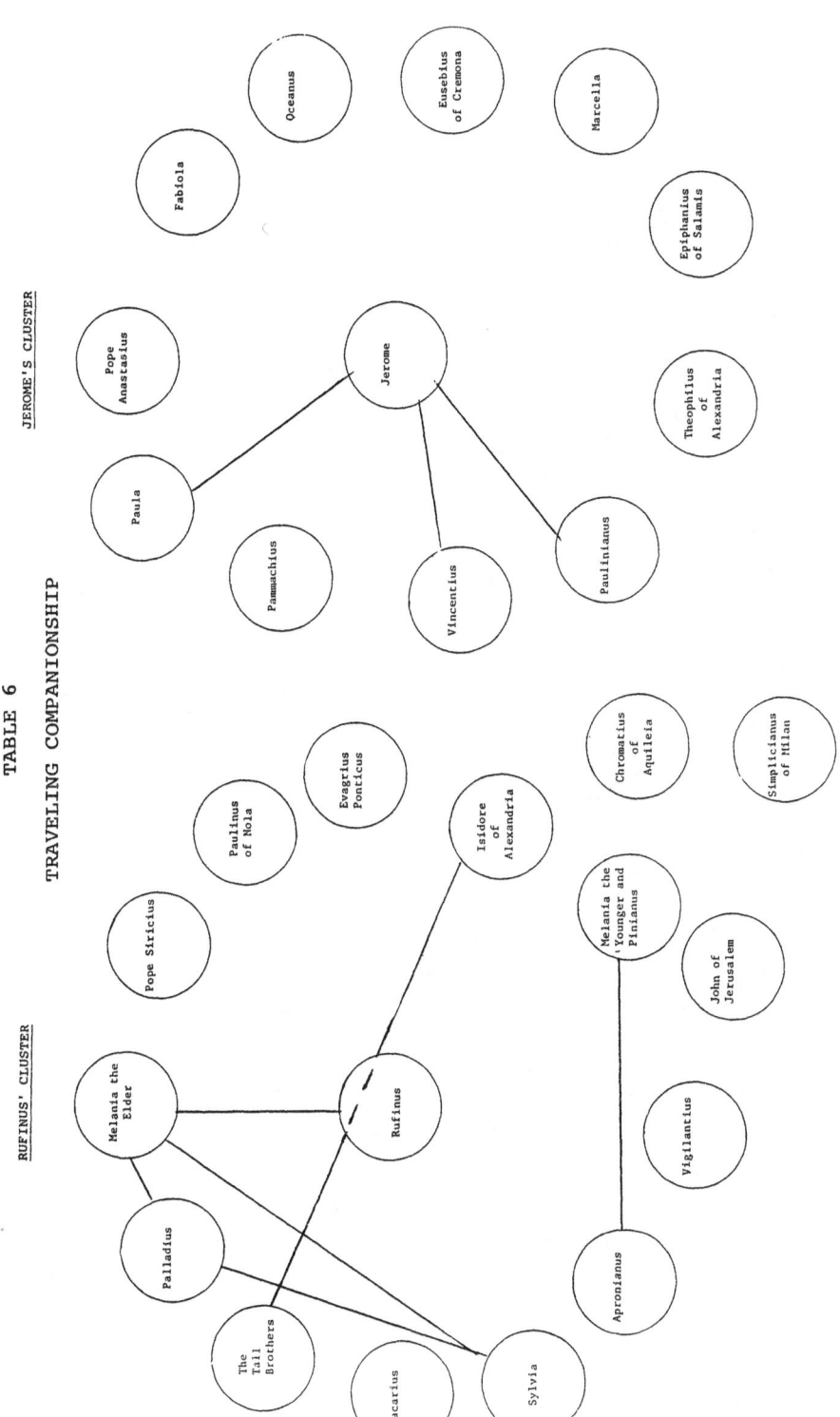

104 Semeia

TABLE 7
FINANCIAL PATRONAGE, MONEY, GIFTS

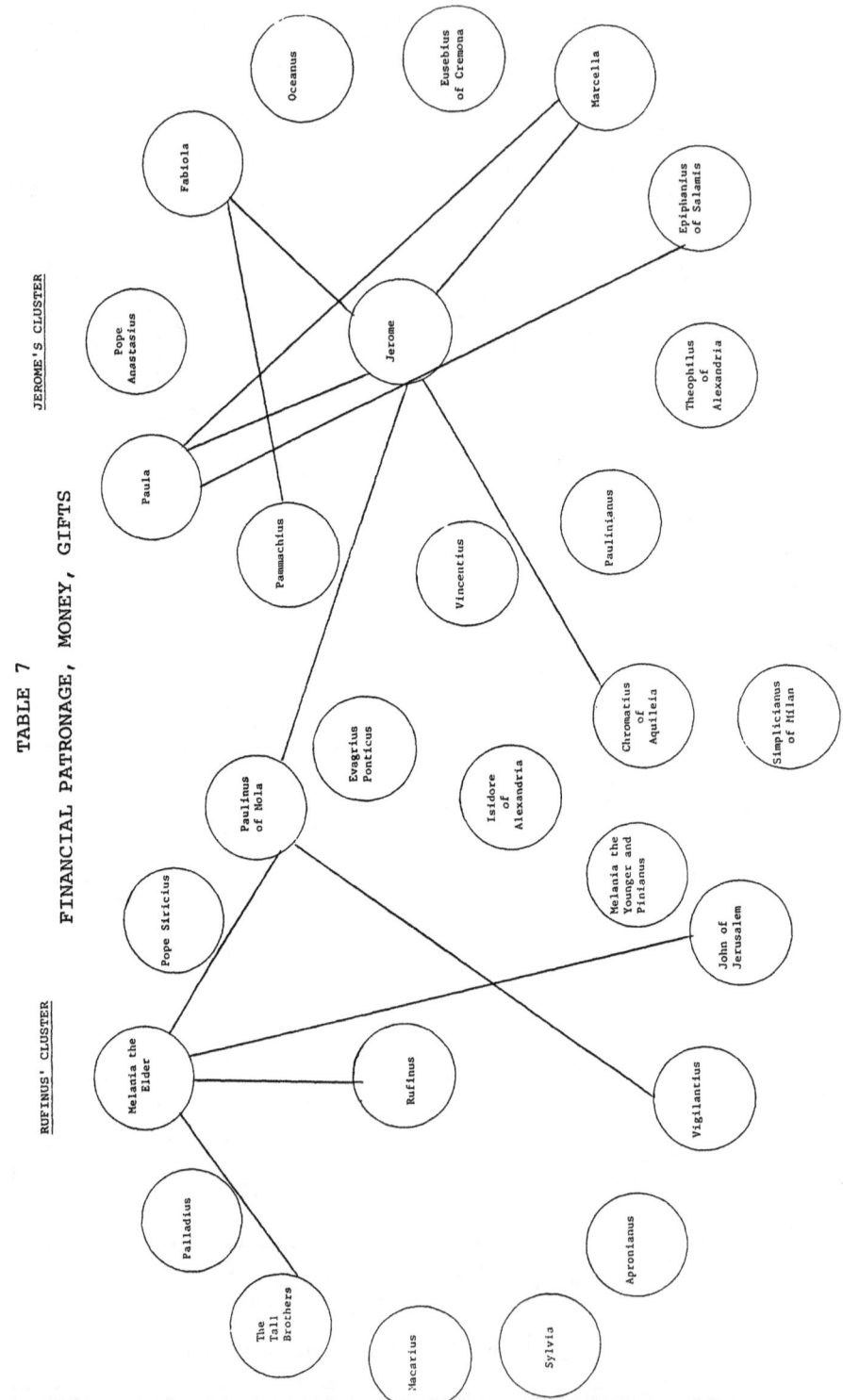

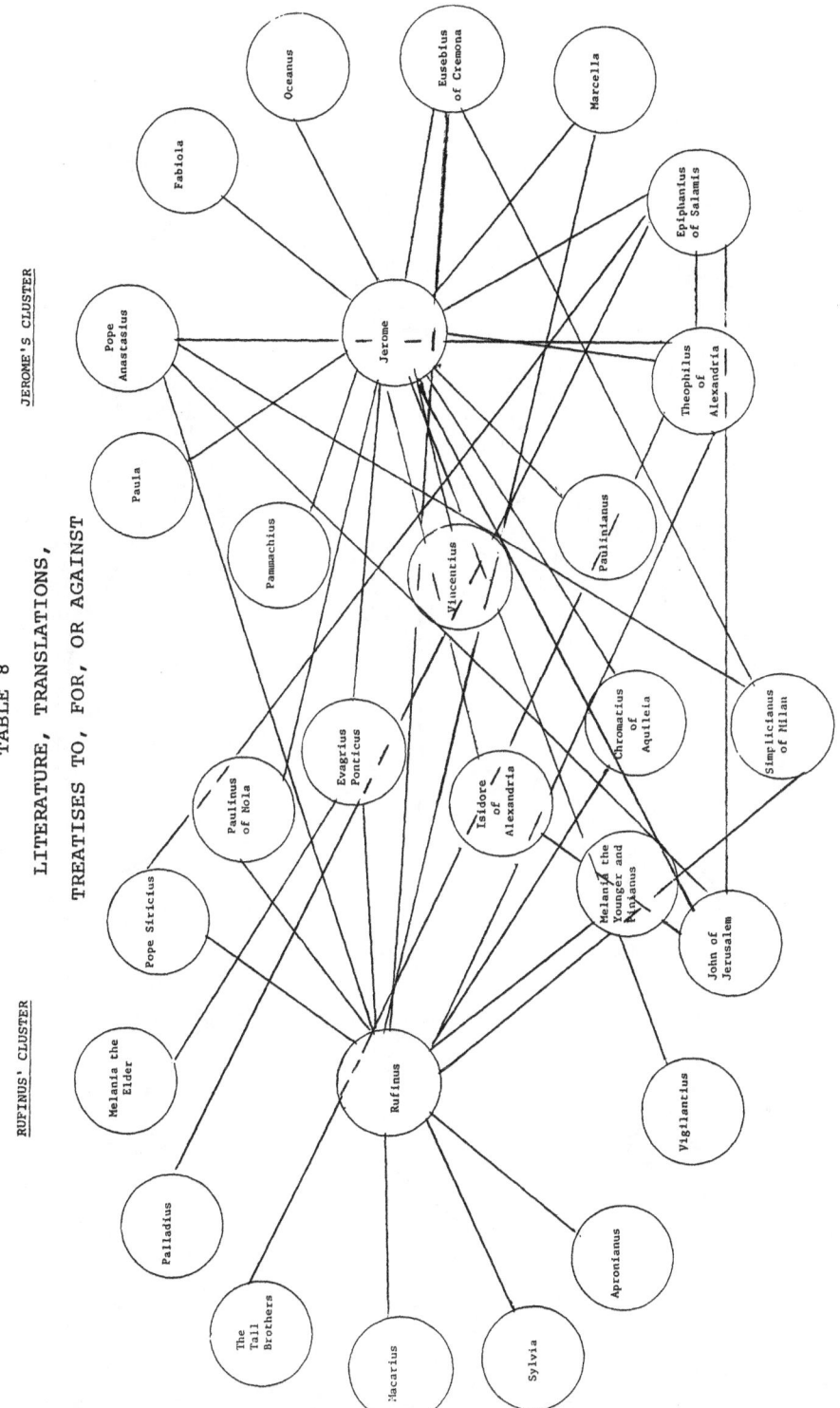

TABLE 8

LITERATURE, TRANSLATIONS, TREATISES TO, FOR, OR AGAINST

106 Semeia

TABLE 9
CARRIERS OF LETTERS, TREATISES, INFORMATION

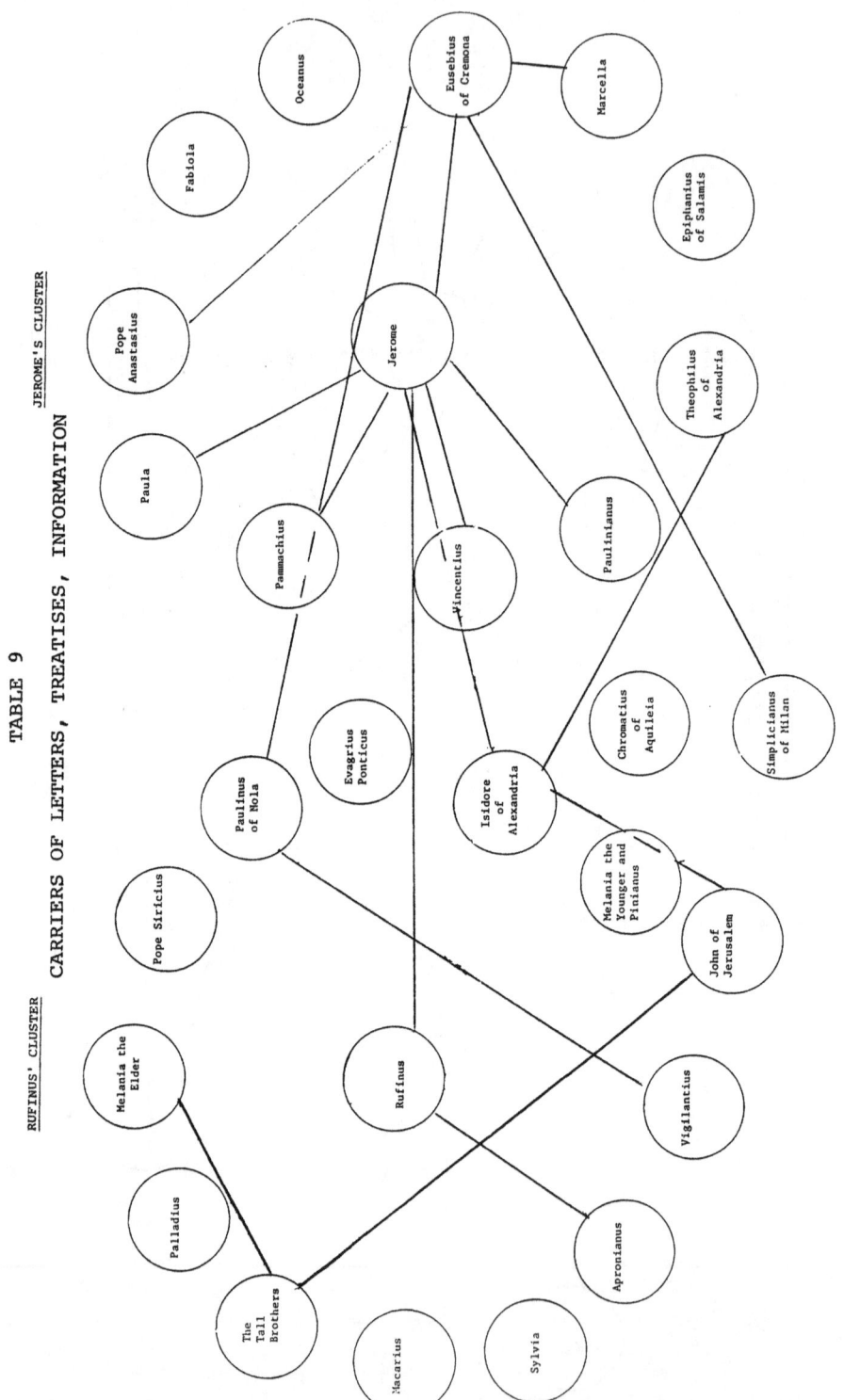

Clark: Elite Networks and Heresy Accusations

TABLE 10

HOSTILITIES

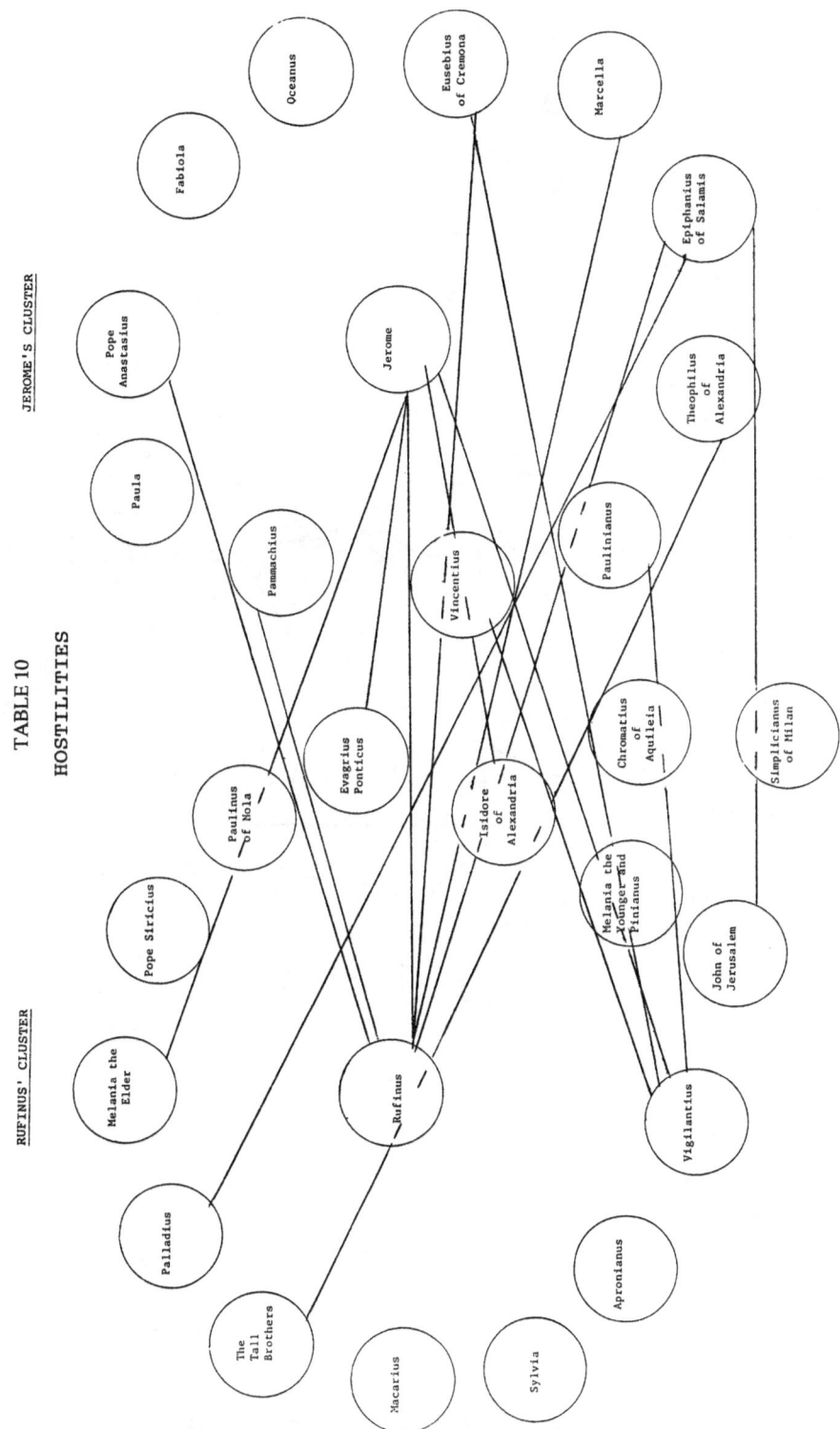

108 Semeia

RUFINUS' CLUSTER

TABLE 10

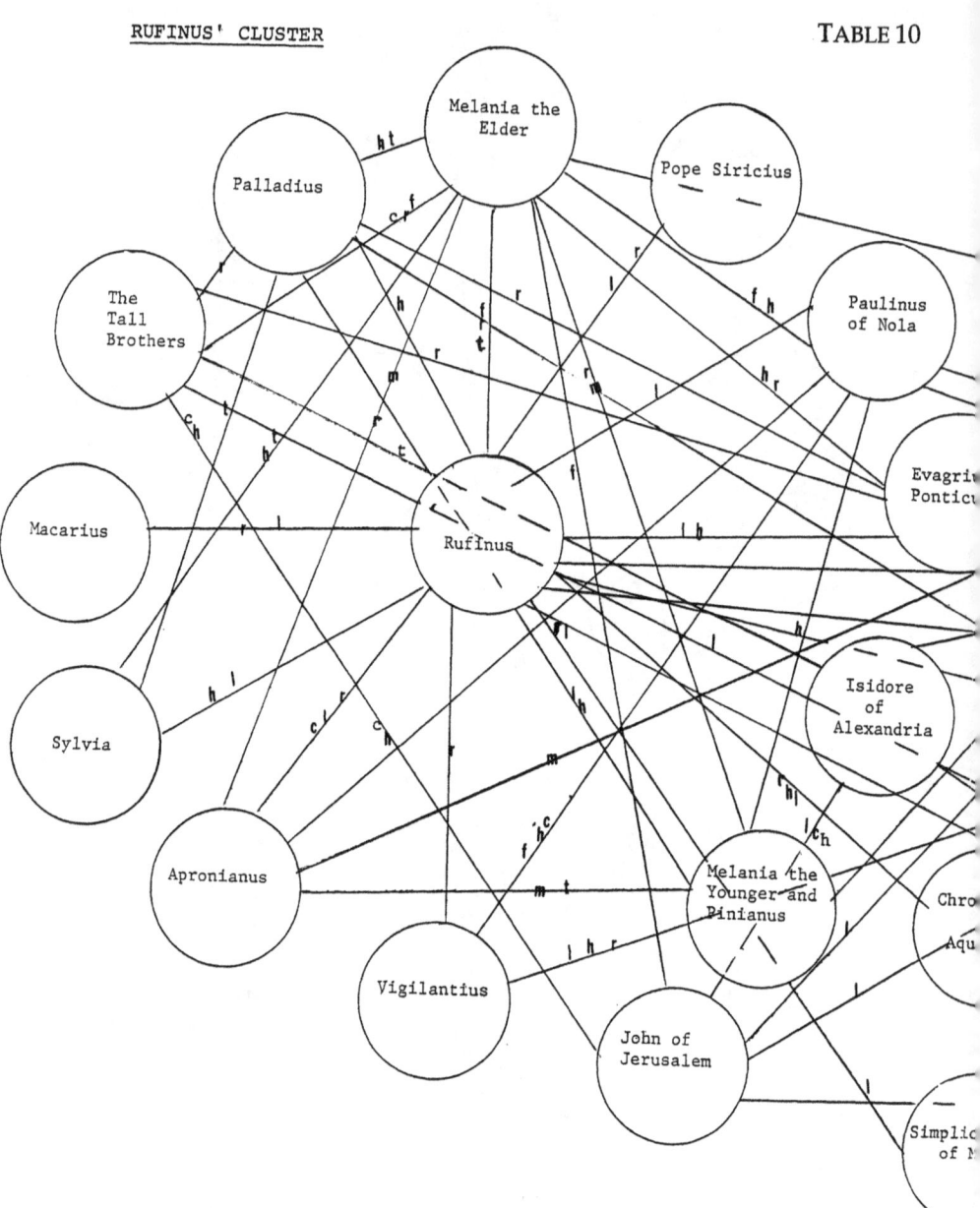

Clark: Elite Networks and Heresy Accusations

MULTIPLEXITY

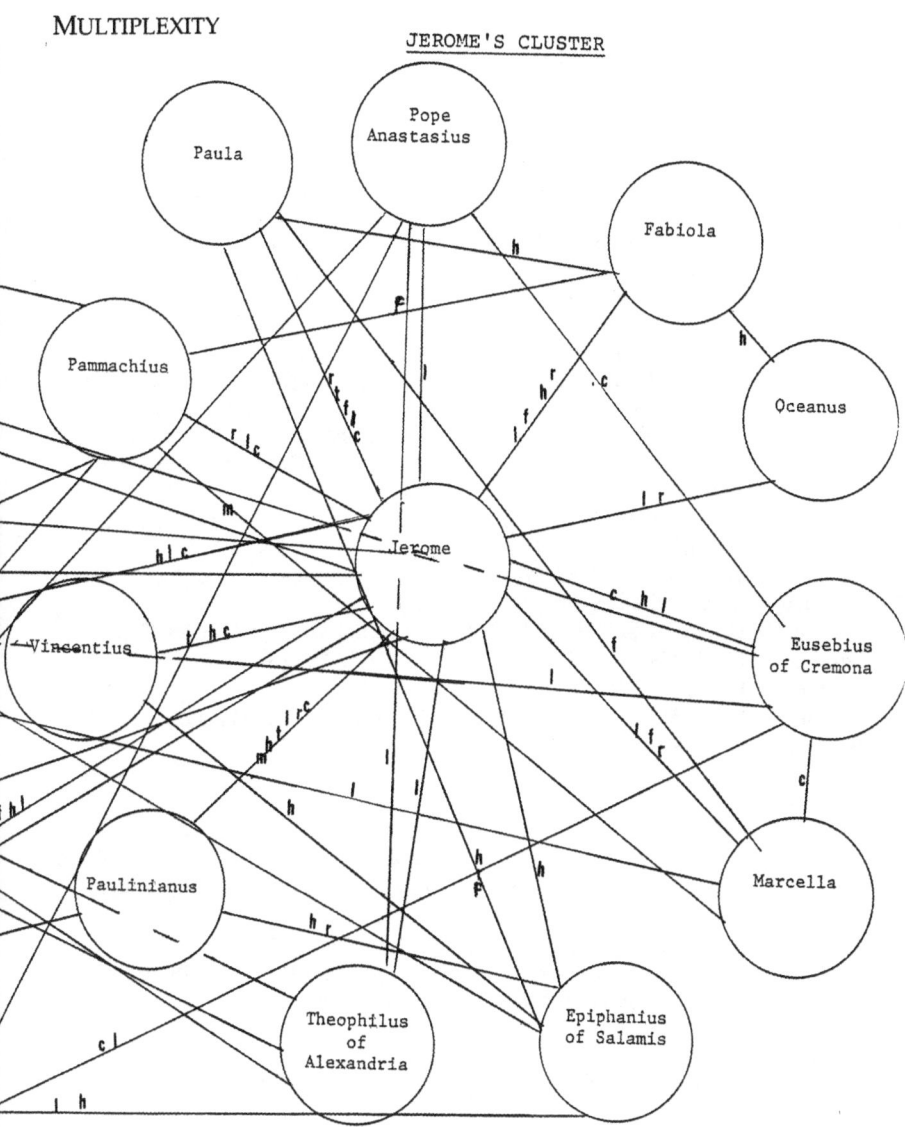

KEY

- m marriage/kinship
- r religious mentorship
- h hospitality
- t traveling companionship
- f financial patronage, money and gifts
- l literature written to, for, or against
- c carriers of literature and information

NOTES

* This paper is a prelude to a larger work on the Origenist controversy forthcoming from Princeton University Press.
I would especially like to thank Professor Angela O'Rand of the Duke University Sociology Department for her help with the network materials.
The numbering of the Latin texts has been followed throughout.

[1] Rufinus, *Apologia contra Hieronymum* I, 11 (CCL 20, 44–45). Macarius is identified as a Roman in Jerome, *Apologia contra Rufinum* III, 32 (CCL 79, 102), and as noble (*vir nobilis*) in III, 24 (CCL 79,96). (Book III of Jerome's *Contra Rufinum* is identified as *Epistula adversus Rufinum* in the CCL edition.) Is Macarius to be identified with a man of the same name who is described by Palladius as an "ex-vicar"? (*Historia Lausiaca* 62 [Butler, II, 157]). Jerome's and Rufinus' *Apologies* against each other will hereafter be cited simply as *Apologia*.

[2] Jerome, *Apologia* III, 29 (CCL 79, 101).

[3] Jerome, *Apologia* III, 32 (CCL 79, 102).

[4] Jerome, *Ep.* 124, 2; 13 (CSEL 56, 97–98, 115–116); *Contra Joannem Hierosolymitanum* 7 (PL 23, 376) (hereafter cited as *Contra Joannem*).

[5] Jerome, *Ep.* 124, 3; 9 (CSEL 56, 98–99, 108–109); *Contra Joannem* 7 (PL 23,376).

[6] Jerome, *Ep.* 124, 3 (CSEL 56, 98); *Contra Joannem* 7 (PL 23, 376).

[7] Jerome, *Ep.* 124, 3; 10 (CSEL 56, 99, 111–112).

[8] Jerome, *Ep.* 124, 4; 5; 9; 10 (CSEL 56, 99–100, 101–102, 109–110, 111–112).

[9] Jerome, *Ep.* 124, 5; 9 (CSEL 56, 101–103, 107–108).

[10] Jerome, *Ep.*124, 7 (CSEL 56, 104–105).

[11] Jerome, *Ep.* 124, 12 (CSEL 56, 114–115).

[12] Jerome, *Contra Joannem* 7 (PL 23, 376).

[13] Jerome, *Apologia* III, 5 (CCL 79, 77): the whole of the *Peri Archōn* needs "emending" to be orthodox, for "everything" hinges on the notion of a universe of rational creatures who fell and who will return to unity.

[14] Epiphanius, *Ep. ad Johannem Episcopum* (= Jerome, *Ep.* 51, 5 [CSEL 54, 404]), commenting on the story of Eden, Genesis 2. Jerome in *Apologia* III, 23 (CCL 79, 94) reveals that Rufinus had called Epiphanius a *delirex senex*. Epiphanius' other objections to Origenism can be found in sections 4–5 of his letter to John.

[15] Rufinus, *Apologia ad Anastasium* 2 (CCL 20, 25); *Apologia* I, 4 (CCL 20,39). The same charge is raised against John of Jerusalem by Jerome in *Contra Joannem* 8 (PL 23, 377).

[16] Jerome, *Apologia* II, 4 (CCL 79, 36): Rufinus may cite his faith in the Trinity all he likes, but the issue is Origen, not Arius. Although Rufinus had changed what Origen had written on the Trinity to make it more orthodox, this was hardly the only point that needed "emendation" (Jerome, *Apologia* I, 6 [CCL 79, 6]).

[17] Rufinus, *Prologus in Apologeticum Pamphili Martyris pro Origene* (CCL 20, 234); *Apologia ad Anastasium* 3;4 (CCL 20, 26); *Apologia* I, 4–9 (CCL 26, 39–43): albeit a spiritual and incorporeal body, following I Corinthians 15:35–54. Rufinus holds Jerome guilty of dispensing with the resurrection body in his *Commentary on Ephesians*: *Apologia* I, 24–25; 41 (CCL 20, 58–60, 75–77).

[18] Rufinus, *Apologia ad Anastasium* 6 (CCL 20, 27). Jerome tried to make it sound as if the Church had ruled in favor of creationism: *Contra Joannem* 22 (PL 23, 389); *Apologia* III, 28; 30 (CCL 79, 99–100, 101–102). Jerome is more cautious after the heat of the controversy died; see *Ep.* 126, 1 (CSEL 56, 143), dated to 412 A.D.

19 Rufinus, *De Adulteratione Librorum Origenis* 1-2, 6-9, 14-16 (CCL 20, 7-8, 10-14, 16-17); Praefatio, *Peri Archōn* 3 (CCL 20, 246); *Apologia ad Anastasium* 7 (CCL 20, 27-28); *Apologia* I, 12 (CCL 20, 45). Rufinus testifies that he sometimes supplanted these interpolated views with orthodox ones Origen expressed elsewhere.

20 Rufinus, Praefatio, *Peri Archōn* 1-2 (CCL 20, 245-246); *Apologia* I, 24-25; 28; 36; 39; 41-43; II, 16-21, 23-25, 49-50 (CCL 20, 58-59, 62-63, 70, 73-74, 75-79, 95-98, 99-102, 121-122). Jerome tries to reduce the extent of his association with Origen. Although he admits he has translated "many tomes," he insists he was interested in the Biblical commentary, not the dogma: *Apologia* I, 22; 24 (CCL 79, 21-22, 24). In *Apologia* II, 16 (CCL 79, 50), he says he possesses all ("omnia") of Origen's works and has read a great many of them. Jerome speaks of his work on Origen in *Epp.* 33, 4-5 (CSEL 54, 255-259); 43, 1-2 (CSEL 54, 318); 61, 1-2 (CSEL 54, 575-578); 82, 7 (CSEL 55, 113-114); 84, 2-3; 7;8;11 (CSEL 55, 121-125, 128-131, 133-134); 85, 3 (CSEL 55, 136-137); 124 (CSEL 56, 96-117);130, 16 (CSEL 56, 196-197), and in many of his Biblical commentaries.

21 Rufinus, *Apologia* I, 22; 25 (CCL 20, 56-57, 58-60).

22 Epiphanius, *Ep. ad Johannem Episcopum* (= Jerome, *Ep.* 51, 1-2 [CSEL 54, 396-399]): Epiphanius claims that Paulinianus was not ordained in a place within John's jurisdiction. Also see Jerome, *Contra Joannem* 10; 40; 41 (PL 23, 379, 410-411); *Ep.* 82, 4; 8 (CSEL 55, 111, 114-115).

23 Rufinus, *Prologus in Apologeticum Pamphili Martyris pro Origene* (CCL 20, 233); Jerome, *Ep.* 84, 11 (CSEL 55, 133-134); *Apologia* I, 8-11; 13; II, 15; 23; III, 12 (CCL 79, 7-11, 12, 48-49, 59-60, 83-85).

24 Jerome, Apologia I, 19; II, 18 (CCL 79, 19, 52-54); *Ep.* 57, 5-6; 12 (CSEL 54, 508-512, 524-526); Rufinus, *Apologia* II, 31 (CCL 20, 106-107); Praefatio, *Peri Archōn* I, 1 (CCL 20, 245). Recall how ardently Jerome desired a Ciceronian style: *Ep.* 22, 30 (CSEL 54, 189-191).

25 Jerome, *Apologia* I, 6; II, 11 (2); III, 14 (CCL 79, 5-6, 45-46, 86-87). In his preface to *Peri Archōn* I, 2, Rufinus says that Jerome emended Origen's language in translating so that nothing would be at variance with the faith (CCL 20, 245-246).

26 Jerome, *Apologia* I, 17; III, 6 (CCL 79, 16, 78-80). In II, 10 (CCL 79,41), Jerome wittily pictures the souls being struck by Rufinus' barbarisms: they didn't encounter as much difficulty in their fall from heaven and assumption of material bodies (in Origen's theory) as they now do, knocked about by the ineloquent sentences of Rufinus.

27 Rufinus, *Apologia* II, 8; 31 (CCL 20, 89, 106-107,).

28 Rufinus, *Apologia* II, 36-41 (CCL 20, 111-116). Jerome defended himself long before the controversy (in 388) in his Preface to *Hebraicae Quaestiones* (CCL 72, 2) as well as later, during the controversy, *Apologia* II, 24-33 (CCL 79, 60-70).

29 Rufinus, *Apologia* II, 6; 7; 9; 11 (CCL 20, 87-89, 90-91, 91-92); cf. Tertullian, *De Praescriptione haereticorum* 7, 9 (CCL 1, 193): "Quid ergo Athenis et Hierosolymis? quid academiae et ecclesiae?"

30 Jerome, *Apologia* I, 30 (CCL 79, 30-31); *Ep.* 70 (CSEL 54, 700-708), Jerome defends his practice.

31 Rufinus, *Apologia* II, 5; 42-43 (CCL 20, 86-87, 116-117).

32 Rufinus, *Apologia* II, 13 (CCL 20, 93).

33 Jerome, *Ep.* 57 ,4;12 (CSEL 54, 507, 526); Apologia I, 17; III, 4 (CCL 79, 16, 76); *In Nahum* III (CCL 76A, 564).

34 Jerome, *Epp.* 57, 12 (CSEL 54, 526); 125,18 (CSEL 56, 138). Is the distinction to be correlated with a possible difference of *Rules* used in the monasteries? Recall that Jerome translated the *Rule of Pachomius* for Eustochium to use with her nuns: Praefatio, *S. Pachomii Regula* 1 (Boon, pp. 3-5), while Rufinus translated the milder *Rule of St. Basil*. See Murphy: 61-62.

35 Mitchell, 1969c: 9; 1974: 281; Boissevain, 1974: 4–19; Eisenstandt and Roniger: 47. Boissevain accuses the structuralist/functionalist approach of serving conservative ends, of supporting a colonialist mentality (1980: 13, 19).

36 E.g., Eisenstadt and Roniger: 48–51, 56, 72–73; Boissevain 1974: chps. 3, 6, 7; Thoden van Velzen: 210–250; Wolf: 1–22; Wellman: 157, 172; Weingood: 41–51, and other essays in Gellner and Waterbury. For the application of these issues to cases in contemporary religious life, see especially Boissevain, 1977: 81–96; and Stark and Bainbridge, 1980: 1376–1395. For a helpful analysis of ancient material by a classicist familiar with network theory, see Saller.

37 For an overview of the controversy, see Brochet: pt. 2; Villain: 5–37, 165–195; Murphy, 1945: 59–157; or Kelly: chs 18, 20–22.

38 Jerome, *Ep.* 57, 2–4 (CSEL 54, 504–508).

39 Jerome's *Contra Joannem Hierosolymitanum* breaks off unfinished. Jerome says that he and Rufinus joined hands in peace at the Church of the Resurrection (*Apologia* III, 33 [CCL 79, 103]).

40 Jerome, Praefatio, *Commentariorum in Esaiam* XII (CCL 73A, 465). Jerome refers to Rufinus as "Grunnius" also in *Ep.* 125, 18 (CSEL 56, 137) and in Prologus 4, *In Hieremiam Prophetam* (CCL 74, 2).

41 Jerome reports this detail later in *Ep.* 5, 2 (CSEL 54, 21–22).

42 Rufinus, *Apologia* I, 4 (CCL 20, 39).

43 The circumstances of Jerome's departure are obscure and hint at unpleasant developments of an unknown sort: see Kelly: 33–35; Cavallera: Note C, II, 75–77.

44 Jerome, *Ep.* 3, 1 (CSEL 54, 13).

45 Jerome, *Ep.* 3, 6 (CSEL 54, 18).

46 Jerome, *Ep.* 3, 3 (CSEL 54, 15).

47 Rufinus, *Apologia* II, 29 (CCL 20, 105); Jerome, *Chronicon* for 374 (GCS 24, 247). Jerome also had praised Melania in *Epp.* 39, 5 and 45, 4–5 (CSEL 54, 305, 325–327).

48 Jerome, *Chronicon* for 377 (GCS 24, 248).

49 Palladius, *Historia Lausiaca* 46, 2–3 (Butler II, 134); for Melania's relation with Pambo, teacher of the Tall Brothers, see 10 (Butler, II, 29–31); on Ammonius, see 11 (Butler, II, 32–34). Rufinus is at Nitria in Jerome, *Ep.* 3, 2 (CSEL 54,14).

50 Palladius, *Historia Lausiaca* 46 (Butler, II, 134–135); Paulinus of Nola, *Ep.* 29, 11 (CSEL 29, 257–258).

51 Rufinus, *Apologia ad Anastasium* 2 (CCL 20, 25).

52 Rufinus, *Apologia* II, 15 (CCL 20, 94).

53 Jerome, *Ep.* 5, 2 (CSEL 54, 21–22).

54 Palladius, *Historia Lausiaca* 46 (Butler, II, 135–136). Exactly when Rufinus arrived in Palestine is a matter of speculation; see Murphy, 1945: 44.

55 Palladius, *Historia Lausiaca* 54 (Butler, II, 146–148).

56 E.g., Jerome, *Epp.* 57, 4; 12 (CSEL 54, 507, 526); 125, 18 (CSEL 56, 137–138); *Apologia* III, 4 (CCL 79, 76), among other references.

57 *Vita Melaniae Junioris* 7; 11; 14; 19 (Gorce, 140, 146, 154, 166, 168); Palladius, *Historia Lausiaca* 61(Butler, II, 156).

58 Jerome charged that John associated daily with "Romans" (*Ep.* 82, 7[CSEL 55, 113–114]); Epiphanius linked John and Rufinus through their mutual esteem for Origen (*Ep. ad Johannem Episcopum* = Jerome, *Ep.* 51, 6 [CSEL 54, 406–407]).

59 Palladius, *Historia Lausiaca* 56 (Butler, II, 149–150).

60 See the *Vita Olympiadis* 5–7 (Malingrey, 416–420).

61 *Vita Olympiadis* 7; 8; 14 (Malingrey, 420, 422, 436).

62 Palladius, *Historia Lausiaca* 38 (Butler, II, 117, 118–120).

63 Muyldermanns: 30. Rufinus may have translated the work into Latin; see the hints in Jerome, *Ep.* 133,3 (CSEL 56, 246–247); Gennadius, *De Scriptoribus Ecclesiasticis* 17 (PG 58, 1070); cf. Wilmart 1911:143–144, 148–151.

64 Palladius, *Historia Lausiaca* 38; 11 (Butler, II, 120,34).

65 Including John Cassian, who emerges later in the Origenist controversy as a partisan of John Chrysostom. For Evagrius and the Nitrian monks, see Guillaumont: 57, 77ff. Guillaumont argues (81–123) that Jerome's complaints against John of Jerusalem's views concern Evagrian theology.

66 Palladius, *Historia Lausiaca* 55 (Butler, II, 148–149) (Palladius is with Melania and Silvia on their way out of Jerusalem); 7 (Butler, II, 24–25). In Egypt, Palladius met Evagrius Ponticus and the Tall Brothers (Palladius, *Historia Lausiaca* 11; 23; 35 [Butler, II, 34, 75, 101]).

67 Palladius, *Historia Lausiaca* 46; 54; part of 55 is also now judged to be about Melania (Butler, II, 134–136, 146–148, 148–149).

68 Palladius, *Historia Lausiaca* 55 (Butler, II, 148–149); see Hunt: 353–4, 357.

69 Jerome, *Contra Joannem* 43 (PL 23, 411); *Ep.* 82, 10 (CSEL 55, 116–117); see Hunt: 358. Jerome blames the decree on John of Jerusalem in *Ep.* 82, 10 (CSEL 55, 116–117).

70 Zosimus, V, 7, 5–6 (Mendelssohn, 225).

71 Rufinus, *Prologus in Clementis Recognitiones* (CCL 20, 281).

72 Rufinus, *Historia Ecclesiae* X, 11; XI, 33 (GCS 9^2, 976, 1038–1039; Socrates, *Historia Ecclesiastica* I, 20 (PG 67, 133); Zosimus, IV, 57,3 (Mendelssohn, 213); A. H. M. Jones, 1971: (*PLRE*) I. 144.

73 So Gennadius, *De Scriptoribus Ecclesiasticis* 17 (PL 58, 1070).

74 The highly complex dating of Melania's history rests ultimately on that of correspondence between Paulinus and others. See Moine: 25–27; and Clark, 1985: 195 n. 9, 196 n. 18.

75 Palladius, *Historia Lausiaca* 54 (Butler, II, 146).

76 Paulinus of Nola, *Epp.* 29, 6; 12–13 (CSEL 29, 251–252, 258–261); 45, 2–3 (CSEL 29, 380–381); *Carmen* 21, 60–83, 210–325 (CSEL 30, 160–161, 165–168).

77 Paulinus of Nola, *Ep.* 31, 1 (CSEL 29, 267–268).

78 Palladius, *Historia Lausiaca* 54 (Butler, II, 146–147).

79 Rufinus, *Apologia* I, 1 (CCL 20, 37).

80 Rufinus, *Apologia* I, 19 (CCL 20, 54).

81 Rufinus, *Apologia* I, 1 (CCL 20, 37).

82 Rufinus, *Apologia* II, 48 (CCL 20, 120).

83 Rufinus, *Praefatio in Gregorii Nazianzeni Orationes* (CCL 20, 255); also a translation of Basil's *Homilies* (*Praefatio in Omelias Sancti Basilii* [CCL 20, 237]).

84 Rufinus, *Prologus in Explanationem Origeniis super Psalmos XXVI-XXVIII* (CCL 20, 251).

85 Rufinus, *Prologus in Omelias Origenis super Numeros* (CCL 20, 285). This was the next project Rufinus planned to undertake. The date of 410 is fixed by the reference to the barbarians' burning of Rhegium across the strait from Sicily.

86 Palladius, *Historia Lausiaca* 61 (Butler, II, 157). Melania the Younger retained contact with Palladius' mentor Lausus, to whom the *Lausiac History* is dedicated: he sent funds for the construction of a bath in her Jerusalem monastery and entertained her when she visited Constantinople in 436: *Vita Melaniae Junioris* (Latin 41 [Rampolla, 24],Greek 53 [Gorce, 230]; Latin 53 [Rampolla, 30]).

87 Jerome's only entrée to the Constantinople aristocracy and court had been Nebridius (briefly the husband of Olympias); in *Ep.* 79 he writes to Salvina, the elder Nebridius' daughter-in-law. Nebridius was long dead when the Origenist controversy flared, and Olympias, by virtue of her relationship with John Chrysostom, would in any case have been on the opposite side of the controversy from Jerome.

88 See Jerome's revealing comments in *Ep.* 45,3 (CSEL 54, 325): Paula was the only Roman woman who had the power to "subdue" him, yet with this one woman to whom he was so attracted, he never even ate dinner.

⁸⁹ To Paula are dedicated Jerome's translations of Job (PL 29, 63);Psalms (PL 29, 122); the books of Solomon (PL 29, 426); Samuel and Kings (PL 28, 604); Esther (PL 28, 1504); Isaiah (PL 28, 828); Jeremiah (PL 28, 904); Daniel (PL 28, 1360); the twelve Minor Prophets (PL 28, 1072); of Origen's *Commentary on Luke* (PL 26, 229); and Jerome's *Commentaries* on Ephesians (PL 26, 467); Philemon (PL 26, 639); Titus (PL 26, 590); Galatians (PL 26, 331); Micah (CCL 76, 473); Nahum (CCL 76A, 526); Zephaniah (CCL 76A, 655); and Haggai (CCL 76A, 713).

⁹⁰ Jerome, *De Viris Illustribus* 135 (PL 23, 759).

⁹¹ Jerome, *Ep.* 108, 4;5 (CSEL 55, 309–310).

⁹² Jerome's attempt to link Paula's family with the Scipios, Gracchi, and Agamemnon (*Ep.* 108, 3 [CSEL 55, 308]), probably a bogus genealogy, may indicate Paula's family was of the *nouveaux riches*. See Hickey: 51–56.

⁹³ Jerome, *Ep.* 108, 14 (CSEL 55, 325).

⁹⁴ Jerome, *Ep.* 66, 14 (CSEL 54, 665).

⁹⁵ Jerome, *Ep.* 108, 6 (CSEL 55, 310–311); for Jerome's arrival along with Epiphanius, see Jerome, *Ep.* 127, 7 (CSEL 56, 150).

⁹⁶ Jerome, *Ep.* 108, 7 (CSEL 55, 312).

⁹⁷ Jerome, *Ep.* 108, 21 (CSEL 55, 337).

⁹⁸ Jerome, *Ep.* 108, 23; 25 (CSEL 55, 339–341, 344).

⁹⁹ Jerome, *Epp.* 108, 4 (CSEL 55, 309–310); 66 on the occasion of Paulina's death.

¹⁰⁰ Jerome, *Ep.* 66, 6 (CSEL 54, 654).

¹⁰¹ Jerome calls Pammachius his "former fellow-learner" in *Ep.* 49 (48 Vall.), 1 (CSEL 54, 351).

¹⁰² Jerome, *Ep.* 66, 6–7 (CSEL 54, 654–655). Paula was related to Furia, according to Jerome in *Ep.* 54, 2 (CSEL 54, 467).

¹⁰³ Jerome, *Ep.* 48 (49 Vall.), 4 (CSEL 54, 349): "consobrina tua."

¹⁰⁴ Jerome said some senators ranked above him: *Ep.* 66,7 (CSEL 54, 655), 11 (CSEL 54, 661); 77,10 (CSEL 55, 47). See A. H. M. Jones, 1971: (*PLRE*) I.663.

¹⁰⁵ Pammachius and Oceanus, *Ep. ad Hieronymum* (= Jerome, *Ep.* 83 [CSEL 55, 119–120]).

¹⁰⁶ Jerome, *Apologia* (CCL 79, 1); *Ep.* 97 (CSEL 55, 182–184).

¹⁰⁷ Jerome, *Ep.* 81 to Rufinus (CSEL 55, 106–107); Pammachius circulated *Ep.*84 (CSEL 55, 121–134), which criticized Origen and Rufinus.

¹⁰⁸ Jerome, *Ep.* 48 (49 Vall.),2 (CSEL 54, 347).

¹⁰⁹ Jerome, *Contra Joannem* 1 (PL 23, 371). Jerome's dedications to Pammachius: the *Commentaries* on Hosea (CCL 76,1), Joel (CCL 76, 159), Amos (CCL 76, 256), Obadiah (CCL 76, 350) Jonah (CCL 76, 300), and Daniel (CCL 75A, 772).

¹¹⁰ Jerome, *Ep.* 77,8 (CSEL 55, 46). In Apologia III, 4 (CCL 79, 76), Jerome speaks of how a document mysteriously appeared in the "chambers of Fabiola and Oceanus," and in *Ep.* 77,8 (CSEL 55, 46), he writes that when Fabiola returned to her native land from Palestine, she "lodged in another's house." Conceivably, she lived in the hospice she and Pammachius had built at Portus? See Jerome, *Ep.* 77, 10 (CSEL 55, 47); also see *Ep.* 66, 11 (CSEL 54, 661). For Fabiola, Jerome wrote on the garments of the high priest (*Ep.* 64) and on the forty-two stopping places of the Exodus (*Ep.* 79).

¹¹¹ Jerome, *Ep.*77,6 (CSEL 55, 44): there was not a monastery not sustained by her riches. Fabiola was of the Fabian family: *Ep.* 77, 2 (CSEL 55, 38).

¹¹² Jerome, *Apologia* III, 4 (CCL 79, 76).

¹¹³ Tranquillinus had so informed Jerome: Jerome, *Ep.* 62, 2 (CSEL 54, 583). Earlier, Jerome had counseled Oceanus against taking too harsh a line against remarriage (*Ep.* 69)—an interesting document to find in the dossier, given Fabiola's checkered marital history (*Ep.*77, 3 [CSEL 55, 39–40]).

¹¹⁴ Pammachius and Oceanus, *Ep. ad Hieronymum* (= Jerome, *Ep.* 83 [CSEL 55,119–120])

115 Jerome, *Ep.* 84 (CSEL 55, 121–134), 12 (CSEL 55, 134).

116 Jerome, *Ep.*126, 1 (CSEL 56, 143).

117 Jerome, *Ep.* 127, 7 (CSEL 56, 150–151).

118 Jerome, *Epp.* 47, 3 (CSEL 54, 346); 48 (Vall. 49), 4 (CSEL 54, 349): Marcella is *consobrina tua*; 127, 5 (CSEL 56, 149).

119 Jerome, *Ep.* 127, 7 (CSEL 56, 151); see also Jerome's prefaces to his *Commentaries* on Galatians and to Books 2 and 3 of Ephesians (PL 26, 331, 507, 546–547), for praise of Marcella. Jerome's letters to Marcella on Scriptural questions she had raised are numbered 32, 34, 59 (and letters 37, 38, 40–44, on other topics).

120 Despite the invitation from Jerome, Paula, and Eustochium in *Ep.* 46. In addition to the mini-commentaries found in his exegetical letters, Jerome dedicated the *Commentary on Daniel* to Marcella and Pammachius (CCL 75A, 772).

121 Jerome, *Ep.* 127, 9–10 (CSEL 56, 152–153).

122 Rufinus, Apologia I, 19 (CCL 20, 54): "de qua ego, quaecumque illa est, nihil dico"—a puzzling admission, since Marcella was one of the first women ascetics in Rome. Even if Jerome overestimates the years of her ascetic devotion (from the 340s: *Ep.* 127, 5–6 [CSEL 56, 149–150]), the 360s probably are not too early. See Grützmacher: I. 227n.3.

123 Jerome, *Ep*. 97; in *Ep.* 98.

124 Jerome, *Apologia* III, 21; 24 (CCL 79, 92, 96); derived from a lost letter of Rufinus to Jerome.

125 Anastasius, *Ep. ad Joannem Episcopum* 3 (PL 20, 69–70). His disclaimer is especially surprising since Jerome in the 380s reports that Origenism had been condemned at Rome (*Ep* . 33,5 [CSEL 54, 259]). That the appeal was rejected is gathered from the fact that Anastasius condemned Origen's writings; see note 126. Rufinus appealed to Anastasius in 400 A.D. (*Apologia ad Anastasium*).

126 Anastasius, *Ep. ad Simplicanus* (= Jerome, *Ep.* 95, 2–3 [CSEL 55, 158]).

127 Seen in Jerome, *Ep.* 88 (CSEL 55, 141).

128 Anastasius, *Ep. ad Joannem Episcopum* (PL 20, 68–73); referred to in Jerome, *Apologia* III, 21 (CCL 79, 92–93).

129 Jerome, *Apologia* III, 22 (CCL 79, 93).

130 Jerome, *Ep.* 82, 4; 8 (CSEL 55, 111, 114–15); *Contra Joannem* 10, 40 (PL 23, 379, 410).

131 Jerome, *Contra Joannem* 41 (PL 23, 410).

132 Jerome, *Apologia* III, 24 (CCL 79, 96); perhaps this was the journey to sell family property mentioned in *Ep.* 66, 14 (CSEL 54, 665).

133 Jerome, *Apologia* I, 21; 23; 28 (CCL 79, 20, 22–23, 27). In *Ep.* 66, 14 (CSEL 54, 665) Paulinianus has already gone, in 397, although in *Apologia* III, 24 (CCL 79, 96) Jerome claims that he did not send Paulinianus until a year after Rufinus left Palestine. Paulinianus had not yet returned in 399, the date of Jerome's friendly (and suppressed) letter to Rufinus: he thinks Rufinus will see Paulinianus at Chromatius' house in Aquileia (*Ep.* 81, 2 [CSEL 55, 107]).

134 Rufinus, *Apologia* II, 26–27 (CCL 20, 102); Jerome, praefatio, *Translatio Libri Didymi de Spiritu Sancto* (PL 23, 107).

135 Jerome, *Contra Joannem* 41 (PL 23, 410) .

136 Jerome, *Apologia* III, 22 (CCL 79, 93).

137 Revealed by Epiphanius in his letter to John of Jerusalem (= Jerome, *Ep.* 51,1 [CSEL 54, 396]).

138 Jerome, *Contra Joannem* 37 (PL 23, 407).

139 Jerome, *Apologia* II, 24 (CCL 79, 96).

140 Jerome, *Ep.* 88 (CSEL 55, 142).

141 Jerome, *Chronicon* (GCS 24, 1); Prologus, *Translatio Homiliarum Origenis in Jeremiam et Ezechielem* (PL 25, 583).

142 Jerome, *Ep.* 53, 11 (CSEL 54, 464).
143 Jerome, *Ep.* 57, 2 (CSEL 54, 504–505); *Apologia* III, 4 (CCL 79, 76).
144 Jerome, *Ep.* 57, 3; 4 (CSEL 54, 506–508).
145 Jerome, *Apologia* III, 24 (CCL 79, 96).
146 Rufinus, *Apologia* I, 19; 21 (CCL 20, 53–54, 55).
147 Rufinus, *Apologia* I, 19–20 (CCL 20, 54–55).
148 Anastasius, *Ep. ad Simplicianum* (= Jerome, *Ep.* 95, 2–3[CSEL 55, 158]).
149 Jerome, *Commentarius in Evangelium secundum Mattheum* (CCL 77, 4, 6); for Principia's relationship with Marcella, see Jerome, *Ep.*127, 1; 8; 13 (CSEL 56, 145, 151, 155).
150 Jerome, Prologus 1, *In Hieremiam* (CCL 74, 1).
151 Rufinus, *Apologia* I, 4 (CCL 20, 39), also inferred from Jerome's letters of the period.
152 Rufinus, Prologus, *In Libros Historiarum Eusebii* (CCL 20, 267), and the suggestion by Hammond: 392.
153 In the Preface to Book III of his *Commentary* on Amos, however, Jerome states that the Jonah *Commentary* was written at the request of Pammachius (CCL 76, 300).
154 Jerome, dedications to Chromatius of the translations of Proverbs, Ecclesiastes, and Song of Songs (PL 28, 1305), Tobit (PL 29, 23), Judith (PL 29,42); and *Commentaries* on Jonah (CCL 76, 379) and Habakkuk (CCL 76A, 579).
155 Jerome, Praefatio, *In Libros Salomonis* (PL 28, 1307).
156 Jerome, *Apologia* III, 2 (CCL 79, 75).
157 Paulinus of Nola, *Ep.* 5, 14 (CSEL 29, 33).
158 Paulinus of Nola, *Ep.* 29, 5 (CSEL 29, 251).
159 Paulinus of Nola, *Ep.* 29, 6; 8–14 (CSEL 29, 251–252, 253–262).
160 Paulinus of Nola, *Epp.* 31, 1; 32, 11 (CSEL 29, 268, 287).
161 Paulinus of Nola, Carmen 21, especially 11. 60–83, 210–325 (CSEL 30, 160–161, 165–168).
162 Paulinus of Nola, *Ep.* 28, 5; *Epp.* 46 and 47 are addressed to Rufinus (CSEL 29, 245–246, 387–389).
163 Paulinus of Nola, *Ep.* 46, 2 (CSEL 29, 387–388).
164 Paulinus of Nola, *Ep.* 47, 2 (CSEL 29, 389); Rufinus, Praefatio, *De Benedictionibus Patriarchum* I; II (CCL 20, 189, 203).
165 Paulinus of Nola, *Ep.* 13 (CSEL 29, 84–107). Paulinus' epistle is dated early 396, while Jerome let two years pass before he wrote to Pammachius (*Ep.* 166, 1 [CSEL 54, 648]). It is interesting to note Paulinus' extended discussions on how souls do not survive without bodies and on the real flesh of Jesus. Although Paulinus makes out that he is describing positions of the philosophical schools, surely there is resonance of the Origenist debate, given the choice of topics (*Ep.* 13, 25–26 [CSEL 29, 105–106]).
166 Jerome, *Ep.* 61, 3 (CSEL 54, 580).
167 Jerome, *Epp.* 53, 1 (CSEL 54, 442); 85, 6 (CSEL 55, 138).
168 Paulinus of Nola, *Ep.* 5, 11 (CSEL 29, 32); Jerome, *Ep.* 61, 3 (CSEL 54, 580).
169 Jerome, *Ep.* 58, 11 (CSEL 54, 541): "sanctum presbyterum."
170 Jerome, *Ep.* 61, 3 (CSEL 54, 579).
171 Jerome, *Ep.* 61, 1 (CSEL 54, 575–576).
172 Jerome, *Ep.* 61, 3 (CSEL 54, 580). Saller (9) offers the interesting observation that "cliens" was usually reserved for the "humble members of the lower classes." Since the term implied "social inferiority and degradation," a writer like Pliny would never use it to refer to his protégés. Jerome not only uses the term of Vigilantius, but puts it in the diminutive, thus doubling the insult.
173 Jerome, *Ep.* 61, 4 (CSEL 54, 582).
174 Jerome, *Apologia* III, 19 (CCL 79, 91).

175 Rufinus, *Apologia* II, 43 (CCL 20, 117). Rufinus criticizes Jerome's ascetic views also in *Apologia* II, 5; 42; 48 (CCL 20, 86–87, 116–117, 120–121).

176 Jerome, *Contra Vigilantium* 2; 17 (PL 23, 355–356, 368).

177 Jerome, *Contra Vigilantium* 1 (PL 23, 355). Jerome's repeating the story (designed to humiliate Vigilantius) of Vigilantius' terrified prayer in the nude during an earthquake in Palestine suggests that Jerome was enraged at his opponent. *Contra Vigilantium* 11 (PL 23, 364). We learn from Jerome's report of Rufinus' nonextant letter that Jerome had apparently claimed Vigilantius was defiled by his communion with "heretics" (no doubt Origenists) at Alexandria: Jerome, *Apologia* III, 19 (CCL 79, 91).

178 Palladius, *Dialogus* 16 (Coleman-Norton, 99); Socrates, *Historia Ecclesiastica* VI, 10 (PG 67, 693–696); Sozomen, *Historia Ecclesiastica* VIII, 14 (Bidez, 367).

179 Jerome, *Contra Joannem* 37 (PL 23, 407).

180 Jerome, *Contra Joannem* 39 (PL 23, 408–409).

181 Jerome, *Ep.* 63, 1 (CSEL 54, 585).

182 Jerome, *Ep.* 63, 3 (CSEL 54, 586).

183 Jerome, *Ep.* 82, 1 (CSEL 55, 107–108).

184 Jerome, *Ep.* 82, 2 (CSEL 55, 108–110).

185 Socrates, *Historia Ecclesiastica* VI, 7 (PG 67, 684–685); Sozomen, *Historia Ecclesiastica* VIII, 12 (Bidez, 364–365).

186 Socrates, *Historia Ecclesiastica* VI, 7 (PG 67, 684–685, 688); Sozomen, *Historia Ecclesiastica* VIII, 11–13 (Bidez, 363–367); Theophilus to Epiphanius (= Jerome, *Ep.* 90). Ammonius and Dioscorus, two of the Tall Brothers, died at Constantinople and were buried in the Church at Chalcedon called "Rufinianae," that is, the church dedicated by Flavius Rufinus, Silvia's brother-in-law: Palladius, *Historia Lausiaca* 11 (Butler, II, 34); Socrates, *Historia Ecclesiastica* VI, 17 (PG 67, 716); and Sozomen, *Historia Ecclesiastica* VIII, 17 (Bidez, 371–372).

187 Theophilus, *Ep. ad Epiphanium* (= Jerome, *Ep.* 90 [CSEL 55, 143–145]); also see Socrates, *Historia Ecclesiastica* VI, 10;12 (PG 67, 693, 696, 700–701); Sozomen, *Historia Ecclesiastica* VIII, 14 (Bidez, 367); Palladius, *Dialogus* 16 (Coleman-Norton, 99).

188 Theophilus, *Ep. ad Hieronymum* (= Jerome, *Ep.*87 [CSEL 55, 140]). According to Theophilus in a letter to Jerome (= Jerome, *Ep.* 89 [CSEL 55, 143]), the Nitrian monks were subdued.

189 Theophilus, *Ep. ad Palaestinos et ad Cyprios Episcopos* (= Jerome, *Ep.* 92 [CSEL 55, 147–155]).

190 Mentioned in Jerome, *Ep.* 88 to Theophilus (CSEL 55, 141): Jerome's information was relayed by Vincentius, returning from Rome to Bethlehem. See also Anastasius' letter to Simplicianus of Milan (= Jerome, *Ep.* 95, 2 [CSEL 55, 158]).

191 Theophilus' Paschal Letters are translated in Jerome as *Epp.* 96, 98, and 100 (CSEL 55, 159–181, 185–211, 213–232).

192 Sozomen, *Historia Ecclesiastica* VIII, 17 (Bidez, 372); Socrates, *Historia Ecclesiastica* VI, 16 (PG 67, 712).

193 Socrates, *Historia Ecclesiastica* VI, 17 (PG 67, 715).

194 Jerome, *Ep.* 61, 1 (CSEL 54, 576): Jerome reads many authors, including Origen, and culls their flowers, holding fast to what is good in them; 61, 2 (CSEL 54, 577): we should accept what is good in Origen's writings and cut away what is evil; *Apologia* II, 23; III, 9; 27 (CCL 79, 59–60, 82, 98); *Epp.* 62, 2 (CSEL 54, 583–584); 84, 2 (CSEL 55, 121–122).

195 Rufinus' attitude toward Origen is shown in *De Adulteratione* (CCL 20, 7–17); Praefatio, *Peri Archōn* 2 (CCL 20, 245–246); *Apologia ad Anastasium* 7 (CCL 20, 27–28).

196 The other possible link of the Jerusalem group to the Eastern court is through their friend Bacurius, *dux Palestinae*. Quite possibly, the Jerusalem group mobilized both of these allies against Jerome.

PART III

NETWORK MODELS AND DYNAMICS IN HISTORICAL CONTEXTS

"BY THE GODS, IT'S MY ONE DESIRE TO SEE AN ACTUAL STOIC": EPICTETUS' RELATIONS WITH STUDENTS AND VISITORS IN HIS PERSONAL NETWORK*

Ronald F. Hock
University of Southern California

ABSTRACT

Studies of Arrian's *Discourses of Epictetus* no longer focus solely on the ideas of this Stoic philosopher, but are now concentrating on the various individuals who appear in the *Discourses* either as Epictetus' students or as visitors to the school. Thus far these studies have investigated the identities and social status of the individuals. This study, however, looks at the relations Epictetus had with them and does so using the anthropological approach of network analysis. Specifically, this study considers the problems and prospects of using this literary source for anthropological analysis. Then it attempts as full a description of Epictetus' network as the *Discourses* allow. Lastly, it tries to account, by means of network analysis, for this problem: why Epictetus—in spite of his sizeable network, strategic location, considerable notoriety, and rhetorical power—was largely unable to convince others of his practical brand of Stoicism and so despaired of ever seeing an actual Stoic.

Introduction

Among the philosophers Domitian banished from Rome in the last months of 93 was the Stoic philosopher Epictetus (c. 50–120) who then crossed over to western Greece and set up a school in Nicopolis of Epirus.[1] Some years later, during the reign of Trajan and, as we will see, most likely between 105 and 113, L. Flavius Arrianus, a young aristocrat from Bithynian Nicomedia, studied with Epictetus and wrote down many of the lectures and conversations with students and visitors that had occurred while he was at the school (cf. Stadter: 19–31; Syme 1982).

These classroom notes, now known as Arrian's *Discourses of Epictetus*,[2] provide the modern reader with a rare firsthand, detailed, and lengthy account of the goings-on in a school of philosophy during the early Roman Empire. Modern scholars have usually read the *Discourses* with history–of–ideas interests and so have paid special attention to the content of Epictetus' brand of Stoicism and especially his dependence on his teacher C. Musonius Rufus and on the older Stoics Zeno and Chrysippus.[3] Recently, however, scholars have also begun to read the *Discourses* as documents of political and social history. Accordingly, interest has shifted from the ideas in the *Discourses* to the various individuals who appear in them.

In particular, scholars have become interested in the identities of these individuals as well as their overall rank and status.[4] But thus far the relations between Epictetus and these persons have not been analyzed. It is the purpose of this article, therefore, to attempt such an analysis, investigating these relations with the help of the anthropological approach known as network analysis.

The analysis will require three steps. In Part I, I will discuss the *Discourses* as a literary source and focus on the problems and prospects this source raises for people doing such an anthropological analysis. In Part II, I will begin the network analysis itself and describe as fully as the *Discourses* allow the social network anchored in Epictetus. Finally in Part III, I will analyze certain morphological and interactional characteristics of Epictetus' network in order to help account for a single, but significant, phenomenon which recurs throughout the *Discourses*: Epictetus' emphasis on a practical understanding of what it means to be Stoic and yet his profound frustation at being unable to get his students and visitors to adopt this understanding.

A final introductory note: This article makes no reference to earliest Christianity. Still, its place in this volume is justified, I think, because of all people contemporary with earliest Christianity Epictetus is surely one of the best known among New Testament scholars, and because a study of a source contemporaneous with the New Testament will help to address methodological problems encountered in early Christian sources and will also provide New Testament scholars with an actual social network with which to compare and contrast Christian networks.

The Problem of Social Description in the Discourses

"Whatever I heard him (*sc.* Epictetus) say I wrote down in his own words as best I could . . . " (*Ep. ad Gell.* 2)—this is what Arrian says about the *Discourses* when writing to a friend in Corinth, L. Gellius Menander,[5] in a letter which at the time served to announce the official, if belated, publication of the *Discourses* and which now serves as their literary preface.[6]

The *Discourses*, however, are not as straightforward as Arrian's statement suggests, even if one agrees more with K. Hartmann's (252–57; cf. von Arnim: 126–28; Brunt: 19) view of the *Discourses* as virtual stenographic records of Epictetus' classroom lectures and conversations than with T. Wirth (207–16) who allows for more literary posturing in Arrian's letter and for considerable invention in the *Discourses* themselves. For

Arrian had a definite purpose in writing down Epictetus' words: " . . . to preserve for myself for later a record of that man's way of thinking (διάνοια) and frankness in speech (παρρησία)" (*Ep. ad Gell.* 2).

Read with this purpose in mind, the *Discourses* emerge as a narrowly focused and therefore limited record of Arrian's stay in Nicopolis. Everything is subordinated to preserving Epictetus' διάνοια and his παρρησία. Consequently, the *Discourses* are a thorough, even repetitious, account of both Epictetus' emphasis on a practical Stoicism and his consistent frankness when speaking to others. In this respect the *Discourses* are of stenographic quality: vivid, detailed, and accurate.

But in other respects—including several of importance to a network analysis—the stenographic quality fades. Accordingly, in matters in which Arrian had little interest or which he simply took for granted, the *Discourses* are vague, incomplete, and haphazard. For example, Arrian tells us surprisingly little about Epictetus himself (aside from his διάνοια and παρρησία) and the little there is appears brief and sporadic: his being an old man (1.9.10; 10.13; 16.20; etc.), lame (1.8.14; 12.24; 16.20), and bearded (1.2.29; 3.1.24); whose class preparation got him up early (1.10.8); whose lamp was once stolen (1.18.15); and whose memories often recalled experiences in Rome, especially those of his teacher "Rufus" (1.1.26–27; 7.32; 9.29; 3.6.10; etc.). More allusive than descriptive, more incidental than important, these items (and many others) only hint at what Epictetus looked like or what he usually did (cf. von Arnim: 126–28; and esp. Millar: 141–43).

Similarly, Arrian says little about the physical description and location of Epictetus' school, except that, in contrast to his practice at Rome (2.12.17–25), he taught in some building, as is known, however, only from words for "entering" which are used of visitors to the school (e.g., εἰσέρχεσθαι in 2.14.1; 3.7.1; 19.1). And the building is never identified— except in the functional sense as a "school" (σχολή: 1.30.2; 2.18.15; 16.20; 34; 17.29; 21.10; etc.)—nor is it described, and only some admittedly ambiguous remarks hint at a location near a gymnasium (2.21.19; 3.16.14; 4.1.113).[7] Just how vague Arrian is in this respect is easily apparent from a comparison with Philostratus' brief but detailed account of his teacher's school, complete with location, fee schedule, library resources, seating arrangements, and classroom schedule.[8]

Nor are the *Discourses* explicit about the time when Arrian studied with Epictetus. Chance references to coins of Nero and Trajan (4.5.17) and especially to the Dacian wars, though not to the Parthian (2.22.22), point to the reign of Trajan and, in fact, to the years 105–113 (Stadter: 5). But the more exact date of 108, which F. Millar (142) has proposed, depends on the questionable identification of a certain *corrector* of the free cities of

Greece who visits Epictetus (3.7.1) with the Maximus named later in the same *Discourse* (3. 10). Millar points out that the younger Pliny wrote (*Ep*. 8.24) in 108 to a Maximus who was assuming this very office (see also Syme, 1982: 184–85; 1985: 329–30), but against this attractive suggestion is the clear sense of the *Discourse* itself in which Maximus is presumably someone other than the visiting *corrector*.[9] Another reason against this identification is Arrian's reluctance to name visitors to the school, a reluctance I will note below.

Finally, the terms used above—vague, incomplete, and haphazard—are especially apt when describing Arrian's treatment of the many persons who appear in the *Discourses*: fellow-students, visitors, and those whom Epictetus merely refers to. These individuals will be the focus of the network analysis below, and so it is unfortunate that, as a group, these people prove to be an elusive lot.

This elusiveness is immediately apparent in Arrian's reluctance, for whatever reason, to give the names of these people. The exceptions—Heraclitus (2.2.17), Maximus (3.7.3, 10), and Lesbius (3.20.19)[10]—only underscore the anonymity of all the others. To be sure, scholars have tried to identify some of these persons, and with some success. For example, they have plausibly identified the *procurator* of Epirus who visits the school (3.4.1) as Cn. Cornelius Pulcher, an aristocrat from Epidaurus who is known from Plutarch and several inscriptions.[11] But to identify the *corrector* of *Discourse* 3.7 with Sextus Quinctilius Maximus is, as we have seen, unwarranted. Other identifications are only possibilities, such as identifying the man who visited Epictetus on his way back to Rome from exile and who later became *praefectus annonae* (1.10.2) as Ser. Sulpicius Similis.[12]

Names, of course, are not always essential for network analysis, especially when other information, as we shall see, is provided. But the lack of names makes tracing network links very difficult, and it will be one problem which we will have to face.

In addition, Arrian's treatment is problematic in other ways. His focus on Epictetus and his words has resulted in a corresponding neglect of others and their words. Arrian's fellow-students, for example, suffer the most, as they become in Arrian's presentation little more than faceless "someones" who ask Epictetus questions (1.2.26; 13.1; 14.1; 3.6.1, 8). As a result, these students will have to be analyzed in terms of a composite portrait.

Visitors fare better but their halves of the conversations show considerable editing, as Arrian usually offers his own brief summary of the circumstances of the visits (1.11.1; 2.14.1; 3.1.1; 4.1; 7.1) and otherwise makes their comments conform to the short and perfunctory agreements or objections of the diatribe's imaginary interlocutor (so, e.g., 2.22.4–9). Indeed, the scholar who visits Epictetus (2.4.1) is not allowed a word until the end of the conversation (10)! This severe editing makes for many gaps, since we are seldom informed about motivations for, or consequences of, the visits to the school, and it makes for ambiguity, since it is difficult to decide sometimes whether Epictetus is engaging an imaginary interlocutor or a real visitor or student in conversation (so, e.g., *Discourse* 2.2).[13]

To sum up: If Arrian had supplied more names of students and visitors, if he had written down their words as faithfully as he did Epictetus', if he had included some more on motivations and outcomes—if he had done all this, then an analysis of Epictetus' personal network would be much easier. But Arrian did not do so because of his literary purpose: to preserve Epictetus' διάνοια and παρρησία. And yet, for all the vagueness, incompleteness, and randomness regarding Epictetus' life, school, and the people he comes in contact with, the *Discourses* still contain large amounts of information that can be used for network analysis. Hence the task in the next two parts will be to pursue that analysis as far as the information allows and so expect some incompleteness and tentativeness. In particular, I cannot expect to trace the network as exactly as I would like, to describe students as individually as I would like, and to analyze many specific incidents as fully as I would like. But the network, at least in its main outlines, is recoverable, and some thematic features of the *Discourses* are subject to network analysis. Such, then, are the problems and prospects of using even a firsthand ancient literary source to answer questions raised by modern social historians.

Network Analysis of the Discourses

Introducing Network Analysis

Only in the last thirty years or so has the common term "network" been made to serve analytical duty among social scientists, especially social anthropologists. The studies of J. Barnes (1954) and E. Bott (1957) are usually credited with initiating this new, technical usage, and the popularity of the concept ever since has been seen as yet another instance of a historical trend among social scientists, which, beginning in the 1940s, has shifted interest away from group structure and inert individuals and toward "active individuals generating patterns [of behavior] by their own decisions in all contexts of interaction" (Whitten and Wolfe: 719).

In any case, periodic reviews of the literature, especially those by J. Mitchell (1969; 1974) and by N. Whitten, Jr. and A. Wolfe (717–22) have brought order and clarity to this area of research and have made it accessible to the rest of us (cf. esp. Boissevain, 1974:1–23). Mitchell, for example, has provided a general definition of a network: " . . . a specific set of linkages among a defined set of persons, with the additional property that the characteristics of these linkages as a whole may be used to interpret the social behavior of the persons involved" (Mitchell, 1969a: 2). A key term in this definition is "characteristics" because implicit in it are the analytical possibilities of the notion of social networks. Mitchell himself, after reviewing various network studies, identifies four morphological characteristics of networks and five interactional ones. The morphological characteristics, which analyze the shape of a network, include: anchorage, reachability, density, and range. The interactional characteristics, which analyze the relations between links in a network, include: content, directedness, durability, intensity, and frequency (Mitchell, 1969a: 11–29).

This list of characteristics is neither authoritative nor exhaustive. J. Boissevain (1974:28–45), for example, offers a similar, though not identical, list, and he adds a number of environmental factors which can also influence networks (1974:67–89). Mitchell (1969a: 26 n. 1) makes a further helpful distinction between actual and proximate networks. Enough has been said, by way of introduction, however, to indicate that a person's social network can be analyzed with a precise, coherent, and incisive set of terms. Accordingly, we turn now, with these terms in mind, to the links and relations which Epictetus had with those persons who appear in Arrian's *Discourses*.

Describing Epictetus' Personal Network

When describing Epictetus' personal network, the concept of "anchorage" (Mitchell, 1969a: 12–15) is an appropriate term with which to begin. Epictetus becomes the anchor or point of orientation of a specific social network. But it is also helpful to think in terms of the "stars" and "zones" (*Ibid.* 13–14) of the network anchored in Epictetus. The primary star consists of those persons who are directly linked to Epictetus, and the primary zone includes the interconnections of those in the star. Similarly, the secondary star is made up of those persons who can be connected with the anchor in two steps, that is, through someone in the primary star, whereas the secondary zone consists of the interconnections of those in this star. Higher level stars and zones are possible, but Mitchell (*Ibid.* 14) doubts that it would ever be necessary to go beyond the secondary star to explain an anchor's behavior. Hence, the description of Epictetus' network will limit itself to primary and secondary stars.

Arrian's *Discourses* contain numerous recollections of Epictetus' experiences in Rome, thereby allowing at least a glimpse of his network there before his exile. To this period, therefore, belong several people with whom he was in direct contact: his (former) master, the imperial freedman Epaphroditus (1.9.29); his teacher Rufus (1.7.32); a rather "wimpish" philosopher named Italicus (3.8.7); an unnamed but wealthy *consul* whom Epictetus had accosted while recruiting in public (2.12.17–25); and, perhaps, the man who was later to visit Epictetus in Nicopolis on his way back to Rome (1.10.2). It is also tempting to link Epictetus with the Cynic Demetrius (1.25.22) and with the unnamed woman who had sent supplies to the exiled Gratilla (2.7.8).[14]

Beyond these persons, however, we can only presume further links—for example, with the other slaves of Epaphroditus, such as Felicio (1.19.19–21), and with other students of Musonius, such as Euphrates of Tyre (3.15.8; 4.8.17–20) and Dio of Prusa (3.23.17). But overall the *Discourses* prove too incomplete regarding Epictetus' links in Rome to pursue network analysis any further.

Consequently, we turn our attention to the far better documented network which Epictetus had in Nicopolis and in particular to those of the primary star. Scholars have already begun to study many of these individuals, with P. Brunt listing sixteen.[15] But the number is actually about forty, divided, for purposes of presentation, into students, visitors, and others who are merely mentioned by Epictetus in one context or another.

First, Epictetus' students: Epictetus' links with students were no doubt the most intense and frequent he had, but they are the most elusive of all, identified usually by no more than the indefinite pronoun "someone" ($\tau\iota\varsigma$). Nevertheless, there are eight identified in this way (1.2.26, 30; 13.1; 14.1; 26.1; 2.25.1; 3.6.1, 8), and scattered and generalized remarks in the *Discourses* about students permit us to add some typical features to these shadowy figures.

These students are mostly young men ($\nu\acute{\epsilon}o\iota$) (1.9.18; 29.34; 30.5; 2.8.15; 17.29; 3.21.8; 23.32; 4.11.25), though not so young as not to have a wife and children (1.18.11; 2.22.4; cf. 1.1.14; 12.20; 2.21.18; 3.17. 7), and they usually have traveled some distance to sit with Epictetus (1.4.21; 3.5.1; 21.8; 23.32; 24.22, 78). In addition, they are, as Brunt puts it, "surely drawn from the better classes" (22), as is clear from their aristocratic experiences and expectations. They have been raised by nurses and *paedagogi* (2.16.39; 3.19.4–5; 24.53) and served by various other slaves (1.1.14; 13.3; 18.19; 2.21.11; 3.19.5; 26.21–22). They have also received a thorough education, including rhetorical training (1.1.2; 2.2.7; 23.36–47; 3.23.6–14, 25; 4.6.12). When they reach Nicopolis they lead a leisurely life: reading books and writing their own compositions (1.4.22; 17.11–19; 2.1.33–34; 17.34–36; 21.10–14); frequenting gymnasia, baths, and symposia (2.16.29; 2.21.14; 1.19.8–10); and going perhaps to a gladiatorial show (3.16.14) or even traveling to Olympia (1.6.23; 4.4.24). And they expect, after leaving school, to return to family and friends (3.21.8), to manage their properties

(4.10.19), to engage in the affairs of their city (2.10.10; 3.24.36), and perhaps to go to Rome and seek out the emperor as a patron of still higher offices and honors (1.25.26; 2.6.20; 4.10.18–21).

But while these eight students need a generalized portrait to give them some identity, other students, even though characterized to some degree, are difficult to distinguish from imaginary interlocutors of Epictetus' diatribal style. Thus two students on Brunt's list—one (Brunt #8) who is going up to Rome (2.6.20–23) and another (#13) who has fallen sick and wants to return home (3.5.1)—may be only imaginary interlocutors. Likewise imaginary may be the student (not listed by Brunt) whose recitations to the public brought at first enthusiastic and then cool responses from his audience (3.23.10–14).

Less likely to be imaginary are three students (not listed by Brunt) who engage Epictetus in conversation. The first interrupts Epictetus' lecture on the topic that only the wise man is able to love (2.22.3) with an objection that he loved his child and yet was foolish (4). Epictetus uses the resulting conversation (5–10) to clarify the issue and then continues the lecture (10–37). The second student, apparently from Athens (3.24.78), is involved in an especially long conversation (7–94), primarily about his continuing attachments to home, family, and friends (22, 27, 58, 82), which prompts Epictetus' censure (28–30) and advice (60, 84–88). But he also seeks advice on how to court a rich man on behalf of family and homeland (44), and Epictetus responds (45–49). The third student is upbraided by Epictetus for changing from a modest person (4.9.6) into one who now has a penchant for erotic writers, fancy clothes, and perfume (6–7).

Two more students are clearly not just imaginary interlocutors (though not listed by Brunt). The first is the γνώριμος who seeks Epictetus' advice about whether to become a Cynic philosopher (3.22.1). The meaning of γνώριμος is disputed. Brunt says that he is "apparently not a student," but M. Billerbeck disagrees, regarding a γνώριμος as an especially close student, and her many examples of this meaning prove the point.[16] Hence we should include among Epictetus' students this person who is elsewhere described as a young man (62) and who already has adopted some of the traits of the Cynic—wearing the rough cloak and sleeping on the ground (10). Epictetus tries to dissuade the young man (2, 9–12, 107), but nothing is said about the outcome.

The second individual is presumably a student and, if so, surely a former one, as Epictetus only refers to him when Arrian was present. In any case, this is the "friend" (ἑταῖρος) whom Epictetus tries to dissuade from commiting suicide (2.15.4–12), and with the help of others was successful (13).

The remaining students all have names. There is of course Arrian himself (not listed by Brunt). Heracleitus of Rhodes (#6) is presumably a student, too, though before Arrian's sojourn in Nicopolis. At any rate, Epictetus refers to him as "my Heracleitus," and his Stoic leanings are apparent in the way he conducted himself in a suit over his property (2.2.17). And from sources other than the *Discourses* we learn about several other students of Epictetus: Demonax, Favorinus, and a certain Onesimus, a slave of Plutarch.[17]

Roughly twenty students, therefore, belong—along with Epictetus' teaching assistant (1.26.13)—to the primary star of Epictetus' network.

Second, visitors to Epictetus' school: Visitors, as already noted, stand out more clearly than students in Arrian's *Discourses*. Hence details about their identity, status, and relations with Epictetus will be especially important for a network analysis.

Three of the nine visitors are from Nicopolis. The first (#7) is a citizen and a scholar (φιλόλογος) (2.4.1, 9–10). He apparently enters the school while Epictetus was discussing faithfulness as a distinctively human trait (1). Since the visitor had once been caught in adultery (1), he becomes for Epictetus an apt illustration of unfaithfulness and thus an object for a verbal attack (2–11). No motivation for the visit is given. But, in the light of Epictetus' attack, which includes a comparison of the man with a useless vessel that is thrown away on a garbage heap (4), it is doubtful that the scholar returned.

The next two visitors are only presumably from Nicopolis, one because of his frequent visits to the school (2.24.1) and another because of the ready availability of his brother (1.15.5). The former (#10) has been repeatedly ignored by Epictetus and so has to confront the philosopher directly in order to engage him in conversation (2.24.2). The visitor, we learn, is rich, handsome, strong, from a good family, and an orator (24–26). But Epictetus' reluctance to say anything to him stems from his lack of skill in listening (5, 11) and from his ignorance (20). Since Epictetus also criticizes the young man's clothing, posture, and expression (22–29), it is doubtful that he ever returned. Still, at the very end, Epictetus holds out some hope: if he learns how to listen, he will find Epictetus more eager to speak to him (29).

The latter (not listed by Brunt) seeks Epictetus' advice on how to deal with an angry brother (1.15.1). Epictetus has no advice because the problem is really the brother's (2–5). When the man then asks how he himself could live according to nature (6), Epictetus backs off again, this time emphasizing how much time he would need to learn how (7–8). Rebuffed twice, the man presumably did not return.

The remaining six are visitors to Nicopolis as well as to Epictetus' school. The first (#3)—a man from Rome (1.11.32), a holder of some public office (1), and rich (38)—is questioned by Epictetus, with the conversation focusing on the man's family and especially on his sick daughter. The man had not been able to endure staying at her bedside and so had fled (4). News of her recovery, however, had reached him, and we find him on his visit to the school on his way home. He was in Nicopolis, therefore, waiting to cross over to Italy and presumably heard about Epictetus during his stopover (cf. 3.9.14). In any case, he drops by and is soon being instructed on proper affection (1.11.16–33) and is in fact persuaded not to repeat his former behavior (34). Finally, the conversation closes with a subtle call to take up philosophy, and the man leaves expressing an openness to the idea (38–40).

On another occasion a father (#9) and son visit (2.14.1). The presence of the son would suggest that the man was seeking a teacher for his son, but the ensuing conversation makes no mention of the boy and in fact focuses entirely on the father. He is perhaps named Naso, probably a Roman of equestrian rank (17),[18] and clearly powerful, as he has many wealthy friends in Rome and even the emperor knows him (18). Epictetus regards him as an amateur in philosophy (2) and thus tells him of the task of the philosopher (7–8) and of his need to learn some basic terms (14–16). Naso, citing his age and military service, objects to his becoming a schoolboy again (17), and Epictetus' next remarks, comparing the man to an ugly person who gets angry at his mirror or to a sick person who gets mad at his doctor, elicit the exiting statement: "He insulted me!" (19–22). Whatever his reasons for coming, he surely also did not return.

The next visitor, a young orator from Corinth (#11) (3.1.1, 34), engages Epictetus in conversation, and the talk focuses on the youth's concern only for external beauty, which prompts Epictetus' censure (1–9). The conversation appears to end (10), but Epictetus, sensing his own responsibility as a philosopher and noticing the young man's ability to listen (11–24), begins to speak again, this time advising him to adorn his reason, not his hair (25–26), and saying that he should especially not pluck out his hairs (cf. 14), as such a practice is not in keeping with his future roles as an active citizen, husband, and father (34–35). While no outcome is given, Epictetus' deferential manner, which is in striking contrast to that shown others, especially the frequent visitor of *Discourse* 2.24, makes future contact highly possible.

But Epictetus' deferential attitude does not last, for the next visitor (#12), the *procurator* of Epirus, Cn. Cornelius Pulcher, is in for the philosopher's παρρησία. Pulcher had been to the theater in Nicopolis and had behaved badly, having taken a highly partisan stance toward the comic named Sophron and used his clout as an official to ensure the performer's victory (3.4.2–4). The others at the theater reviled the *procurator*, and he has sought solace from Epictetus (1). Epictetus, however, defends the people (2) and censures the *procurator* for conduct unbecoming his office and his role as a standard of correct behavior (5–7). Epictetus' παρρησία is especially evident here, for he reprimands him knowing full well that the *procurator* was a friend of Caesar (2). In a sense, Epictetus tries to teach the official, but without any thought of recruiting him and hence with little likelihood of further contact.

Still another powerful visitor, the corrector of the free cities of Greece (#14) (3.7.1), enters the school. At first, Epictetus is deferential, assuming the posture of an amateur in the presence of this man who was also an Epicurean philosopher (1–2), but Epictetus soon takes charge. Thereupon he criticizes the man's Epicurean doctrines (2–20), and even tries to recruit him to Stoicism: "Leave these (Epicurean) doctrines, man" (21). The *corrector*, however, is not persuaded, and the conversation soon becomes anything but deferential and protreptic. He asserts his wealth and connections with Caesar (29–30) and even threatens Epictetus (32–34), while the latter, for his part, accuses the *corrector* of having received his post from kissing slaves' hands, sleeping at men's doors, and sending presents (31), and then gives him a lesson on how to rule (34–36). With their relations strained, thoughts of recruitment must have been forgotten and further contact was most unlikely.

The final visitor is a man from Cnossus (#15) who is en route to Rome (3.9.1). He was in Nicopolis waiting for passage across to Italy. While waiting to gain passage he heard about Epictetus and decided to visit him and seek his help about a legal matter in Rome (14). It is not clear what sort of help he was seeking, but Epictetus censures him on several counts: that formerly as a boy, as a youth, and as a young man, he had never spent time investigating his basic beliefs (8–10), that now a passing visit to Nicopolis was not sufficient time for such an investigation (11–13), and that in the future his desire for wealth and office—in particular, being *patronus* of the Cnossians (6)—would always keep him from this task (15–22). Epictetus fully expects a visitor like this man to leave, muttering about the philosopher's solecisms and barbarisms (14). Further contact is again unlikely.

Outside the *Discourses* there is a tradition that even the Emperor Hadrian visited Epictetus, but such a visit, while surely possible, has occasioned some doubt.[19] In any case, the identities and high social rank of these visitors are rather clear, and Epictetus' relations with them rather strained, to say the least.

Persons referred to by Epictetus: In the course of his lectures and conversations Epictetus refers to several individuals with whom he is (or was) in direct contact and who are thus also links in his primary star. Two such persons have already been discussed above among Epictetus' students: the friend whom he dissuaded from suicide (2.15.4–13) and the Heracleitus whose courtroom conduct drew Epictetus' comment (2.2.17).

The third person (#1) is a Roman who was once prominent and wealthy but who is now an exile living in Nicopolis and impoverished (1.9.27). This man asks Epictetus to write to Rome on his behalf, but Epictetus' letter is so pathetic in tone that the man rejects it, presumably jerked back to (Stoic) reality where exile is no evil (27–28).

The next person (#2) is also an exile, but this time one returning from his place of exile and passing through Nicopolis, presumably in 96,[20] on his way back to Rome (1.10.2). Years later Epictetus recalls their conversation (apparently at the school) and in particular their jesting banter about the man's future life in Rome. The exile was sure he was going to stay out of public life, but Epictetus doubted that such would happen (3–4). Subsequent events proved Epictetus the better prophet, as he immediately entered imperial service and, by the time Epictetus recalled the conversation, had risen to the important equestrian post of *praefectus annonae* (2, 5–6), the emperor's supervisor of the city's grain supply.[21]

The reference to his being *praefectus annonae* has allowed possible identification of this visitor as Sulpicius Similis,[22] but more important for our purposes is the fact that this man was not simply a visitor to the school but apparently a friend of Epictetus. At any rate, Epictetus says that he knows the man (2), possibly already in Rome, and he has obviously kept in touch with him as he has followed the man's subsequent public career, up to his current post (5).

The remaining three persons lived in Nicopolis. Epictetus talked with one of them (#4) about a priesthood of Augustus (1.19.26) the very day he refers to him in a lecture. Epictetus says that he tried to dissuade the man from from accepting this costly honor (26–29), but whether he was successful or not, we do not know. The next person (not listed by Brunt) is named Lesbius and earns Epictetus' best wishes even though Lesbius convicted him daily of complete ignorance (3.20.19). The reason: Epictetus regards him as exercising his patience, composure, and gentleness (cf. 9). Finally, Epictetus recalls a conversation with a man who was angry because another man, named Philostorgus, was doing well (3.17.4). Epictetus points out that Philostorgus was prospering only because he was willing to give up his modesty, something this man would never do. The man then agrees that he was doing well, too—but in the more important area of virtue (4–5).

These various individuals—students, visitors, and others—make up the primary star of Epictetus' network, at least as far as Arrian's *Discourses* permit us to trace its links.

The secondary star, that is, persons who can be linked to Epictetus by means of one intermediate step, is much larger than the primary star, but the *Discourses* permit only a general and partial description.

The best evidence comes from the conversations with visitors. For example, the Roman official whose daughter had recovered is himself the anchor of a network which includes, besides the daughter, his other children (1.11.4), his wife (21), and several of his slaves—nurse and *paedagogus* (22) and the slave who brought news of the girl's recovery (4, cf. 37). Other visitors likewise have household links: brother (1.15.1–5), wife and children (2.14.18), and slaves (2.14.18; 3.4.4). But they also have explicit links to many others, some of them more fleeting, such as the travel companions of the *patronus* from Cnossus (3.9.14), and others more whimsical, such as the attachment of the *procurator* of Epirus to the comic Sophron (3.4.1, 11). More important, the Roman who visits with his son has powerful friends in Rome and is known to Caesar (2.14.18). In fact, friendship with Caesar is quite common, as we have seen: the *praefectus annonae* (1.10.5), the *procurator* of Epirus (3.4.2, 4), the *corrector* of the free cities of Greece (3.7.29–30), and possibly the *patronus* from Cnossus (cf. 3.9.18) all claim such links.

The links of the students' networks do not extend to the emperor, but they are numerous, especially when Epictetus' generalized remarks about his students are considered. Thus there are the obvious links to their respective households: parents (2.21.12; 3.5.12–13; 21.8), brothers (2.21.12; 3.24.78) and slaves (1.13.2; 2.21.11; 3.19.4–6; 24.78). And of course they have friends at home (2.15.5; 3.23.32; 24.78).

Of particular importance are the students' links at Nicopolis. Here they might belong to a youth organization at the gymnasium (2.21.29) or attend symposia (1.26.9; 2.19.8–10) and so make close friends (3.24.82; 4.2.7), make contacts with a senator (1.26.9), or at least impress all present with their command of Stoic literature (2.19.8–10). They might, of course, meet a rich man who warns them against taking their philosophy too seriously (1.22.18–19), but, overall, the *Discourses* emphasize how often Epictetus' students must have regaled the people of Nicopolis with interpretations of Chrysippus (3.21.6–7; cf. 2.17.35; 21.10), with discourses on good and evil (2.9.15–17), and with readings of their own composition (3.23.6–14, 27–28)—all to audiences of perhaps five hundred or more (3.23.19). As a result, the students might attract a following of their own (1.21.2–4).

To sum up: Arrian's *Discourses* contain too little evidence to allow an analysis of Epictetus' network at Rome, even though a few links are still recoverable. The situation for Nicopolis, however, is more promising, as roughly forty persons—students, visitors, and others—can be assigned to Epictetus' primary star. While few of these can be identified specifically, enough is known to indicate their high social rank and local influence. The lack of specific identities makes it especially difficult to trace the further links in Epictetus' network, his secondary star, but the evidence at least suggests a large number, including many in Nicopolis but extending even to the emperor himself. Consequently, with the network described, it is now time to begin the analysis proper.

Characteristics of Epictetus' Personal Network

It is perhaps best to begin the analysis of Epictetus' network which has just been presented with the obvious, and that is that Arrian's *Discourses* contain only a fraction of the links in Epictetus' actual network at Nicopolis, so that we have at best only a sample of links and an unrepresentative sample at that—in a word, a largely intellectual network. Specifically, we are analyzing a network whose links, in Arrian's mind, brought out Epictetus' διάνοια and παρρησία. Those who did not do so are left out—whether students, visitors, or a host of others in Epictetus' world: athletes (1.4.13), booksellers (1.4.16), thieves (1.18.15), judges (2.2.10), sea-captains (2.5.10), fortune-tellers (2.7.2), Jews (2.9.20), musicians (2.13.2), orators (2.16.5), comics (3.4.1), children (3.15.6), nurses and *paedagogi* (3.17.4), shoemakers and vegetable dealers (3.24.44), and priests of Cybele (4.8.5). These are just a few of the sorts of persons Epictetus seems familiar with and thus seems likely to have had relations with as well, but these more social relations lay outside the narrower intellectual world of the school and so are lost to us. Consequently, the analysis which follows is that of Epictetus' personal intellectual network.

Again, to begin with the obvious, we look first at the morphological characteristic known as range, which is a combination of size and social diversity (Mitchell, 1969a: 19–20). Putting size aside for a moment, we notice that Epictetus' network—especially with regard to his primary star—shows little social diversity. It is, for example, exclusively male, with only the woman who sent supplies to the exiled Gratilla (2.7.8) a possible exception and then only for Epictetus' Roman network. His network is likewise confined almost exclusively to aristocrats. Here, as we have seen, are links not only to provincial aristocracies but also to the equestrian and senatorial orders of Rome and, in the secondary star, to the emperor himself. Socially, Epictetus' network ranged only within a narrow, if powerful and prominent, stratum of imperial society.

The only way that Epictetus' network can be regarded as diverse is in terms of geography. For here the range is broad indeed. Epictetus assumes his students are usually from distant lands (3.5.1–3; 23.32; 24.78), and scattered references—taking into account both students and visitors—give some of the specific locales: Athens (3.24.78), Cnossus (3.9.3), Corinth (3.1.34), Epidaurus (assuming Pulcher is the *procurator* of Epirus [3.4.1]), Rhodes (2.2.17), and, of course, Rome (1.10.2; 1.11.32; 2.14.1). Outside the *Discourses* the geographical diversity is also evident, as Demonax is from Cyprus, Onesimus from Chaeroneia, and Favorinus from Arles in Gaul.[23] Finally, Arrian himself is from Nicomedia.

To return now to size, it is tempting to emphasize how large Epictetus' network must have been. This temptation derives from the *Discourses*, in that Arrian recorded only a fraction of the links in Epictetus' network. But it also derives from a consideration of two of the environmental factors in Epictetus' network: occupation and location.[24] As a philosopher Epictetus' network would tend to be large from the continuing parade of students and visitors to the school. Arrian, unfortunately, gives no indication whatever of the number of students sitting with Epictetus while he was there, but even if the number is small, it swells considerably when multiplied by the twenty or so years he taught in Nicopolis. And as a harbor town on a route connecting the Greek East and Rome, Nicopolis is therefore also a factor in the size of Epictetus' network, especially with regard to the visitors who figure so prominently in the *Discourses*. Indeed, Epictetus was something of a tourist attraction in Nicopolis (3.9.14),[25] which could only increase the number of visitors as the years went by, thereby swelling further the size of Epictetus' network.

And yet, it is probably best to resist the temptation of assuming a large network for Epictetus, even though we have only a fraction of the links preserved in the *Discourses* and even though Epictetus' occupation as a philosopher and his residence in Nicopolis might justify extrapolating the evidence we do have into a network of considerable size and influence. For working against these environmental factors are other characteristics of Epictetus' network which undoubtedly diminished their influence and so the size of the network. In fact, it is precisely these other characteristics which present the most interesting prospects for an analysis of this network. The purpose of such an analysis, we recall, is to use the relations an anchor has to interpret his or others' behavior, and one notable feature of Epictetus' network is how strikingly little influence he had on others' behavior. The evidence will be presented more fully below, but Epictetus' lack of influence is succinctly stated in his own cry of frustration: "By the gods, my one desire is to see an actual Stoic!" (2.19.24; cf. 1.29.54; 2.16.17). Accordingly, the question for the following analysis is: What are these other characteristics of Epictetus' network which help to explain why he exerted so little influence over the behavior of others in his network?

We begin with the most important of interactional characteristics: "content" (Mitchell, 1969a: 20–29; Boissevain, 1974: 33). Mitchell says: "The links between an individual and the people with whom he interacts come into being for some purpose or because of some interest which either or both of the parties consciously recognize" (1969a: 20). In Epictetus' case the purpose or interest is Stoic philosophy. But what Stoic philosophy (and hence being a Stoic philosopher) meant to Epictetus—what Arrian has termed Epictetus' διάνοια—is far different from the corresponding notions which students and visitors brought to the school.

Briefly, for Epictetus being a Stoic required a rigorous academic training which included reading various textbooks on philosophy (2.16.34; 17.40; 21.10) but in particular the works of Chrysippus and other Stoics (1.4.6; 10.10; 17.13–19; 2.16.34; etc.), listening to Epictetus' expositions of them (2.6.23; 14.1; 21.11), mastering Stoic logic (1.8.1–4; 17.4–12; 2.25.1), and writing various compositions (1.1.21–25; 2.6.23; 17.35). This curriculum required of students much time and effort (1.11.40; 20.13; 2.21.14; 3.15.11), and Epictetus took it seriously, too, rising early to prepare for class (1.10.8) and employing an assistant to help with the readings (1.26.13).

Nevertheless, far more important for Epictetus is his conviction that being a Stoic means living out the tenets of this philosophy. For most of his students this would simply mean eating like a man, drinking like a man, exercising self-control, marrying, having children, entering politics, putting up with rebuke, enduring an unreasonable brother, father, son, neighbor, or traveler (3.21.5). For others, however, events might call for greater endurance in response to news about the death of a son, the loss of a ship, or condemnation by Caesar (3.8.1–6). In other words, Epictetus' διάνοια, his way of thinking, the content he imparted to those in his network, is a practical Stoicism whose *dogmata*, *praecepta*, and *exempla* were intended to help others *behave* like Stoics.

In contrast, students and visitors came to Epictetus' school with a different notion of the content which the philosopher would give them. For them there is little or no practical consequence to Stoicism; there is only the academic dimension. Epictetus' students came to him only to read and expound books (1.4.22; 2.21.10–14), only to learn syllogisms (2.21.15; cf. 2.17.34), or only to write stylistically pleasing dialogues (2.1.34; 17.35–36; 3.23.35–38). Consequently, they show little interest in discussing how to respond to life's crises (3.8.1–6), but prefer to discuss syllogisms (2.21.19) or show off their Stoic learning at symposia with quotations from Chrysippus, Cleanthes, Archedemus, and Antipater (2.19.8–10; cf. 1.26.9).

Being more concerned with skill in arguments and citing authorities than in living well, students and visitors therefore fall short of Epictetus' expectations. Thus he portrays one student as knowledgeable about Chrysippus, Antipater, and Archedemus but otherwise unchanged—still miserable, quick-tempered, cowardly, and so on (3.2.13–14). Similarly, a local visitor claims that he understands Archedemus (2.4.11) and yet was once caught in adultery (1). In fact, all too often, Epictetus admits, those who call themselves Stoics (2.19.19) are λωποδύται ("clothes-stealers") who have stolen the cloak of philosophy and parade about in it (28). Or, to change the metaphor, they are lions in school, but foxes outside it (4.5.37).

This clash over the purpose of becoming a Stoic is clearly thematic in the *Discourses* (see also 1.4.5–27; 2.17.29–30; 3.10.6–20; 24.78–80; 26.13) and hence not only makes it important but also allows us to refine our question: What are the characteristics of Epictetus' network which kept students and visitors from adopting the Stoic behavior that was so central to the content they received at the school—especially so in light of its repetition and Epictetus' obvious rhetorical skill in expressing it? As we will see, three characteristics of Epictetus' network, when taken together, can account for his inability to change the behavior of those in his network.

The first characteristic is a morphological feature in the primary zone, and that is the presence of dense "clusters," which Boissevain (1974:43–45) describes as segments of networks in which persons are often in contact with one another independently of the anchor. Students make up the clusters in Epictetus' network. They spend much time, to be sure, at his side, but it is also clear that they spend much time with each other as well—reading their compositions to each other (2.17.35–36), strolling together and discussing syllogisms (2.21.19), going together to a show (3.16.14), and joining in on the activities and life of the gymnasial or youth organization at Nicopolis (2.16.29). In addition, the students are linked frequently to people in their own personal networks—to those in Nicopolis who attended symposia with them (1.26.9; 2.19.8–10; 4.2.7–8) or who listened to their public readings and presentations (1.21.2–4; 2.19.15–16; 3.2.10; 21.6–7; 23.6–38), as well as to family and friends at home (1.1.3; 2.21.13; 3.24.22, 27, 82).

The relations in these clusters, however, are not only numerous and frequent; they are also multiplex, a term used to denote interactions involving several contents (Mitchell, 1969a: 22; Boissevain, 1974: 28–32). These contents include mutual assistance and moral support (2.17.35–36;

2.21.19), companionship (2.16.29; 4.2.1–10), friendship (3.24.82), esteem from the public (1.21.2–4; 26.9; 3.2.10), as well as familial affection (3.24.22) and economic assistance (2.21.14) from home. The importance of these multiplex relations within the student clusters is their influence on behavior, as they allow the transmission and constant reinforcement of norms. These norms range from what they hold dear—wealth, property, family, friends, office, reputation, rhetorical skill, and so on (2.2.10–11; 14.18; 24.26; 3.1.34; etc.)—to what they expected of philosophy, and in this respect parents expect their sons to return from a philosopher knowing everything (2.21.13), precisely the academic virtuosity the sons themselves aspired to (see esp. 2.19.8–10). Reinforcement of this norm occurs whenever students applaud each other's compositions (2.17.35–36) or hear the approval of their audience (3.23.17). It also occurs whenever they might meet some old wealthy man who reminds them that all they should learn from a philosopher is a few syllogisms (1.22.18–19; cf. 1.30.1–7). To take philosophy more seriously is foolishness and likely to elicit public ridicule (1.11.39; 2.14.29; 3.15.11).

In other words, the student clusters in Epictetus' network represent a significant morphological characteristic of the primary zone where students can maintain, independently of him, numerous, frequent, and multiplex relations with themselves and others. These relations facilitate the transmission and reinforcement of a solely academic norm of philosophic self-understanding. Within these clusters Epictetus' students could not help but feel the pressure to conform to this norm and so resist their teacher's practical norm. Epictetus, therefore, was effectively isolated within his own network and thus had little influence in promoting this practical norm and so affecting his students' behavior.

The second characteristic of Epictetus' network is interactional, and that is the durability (Mitchell, 1969a: 26–27) of his relations with others. And, overall, Epictetus' relations cannot be described as especially durable, and particularly so with visitors. For example, it seems clear that relations with some visitors lasted no longer than the initial visit. We recall from our earlier discussion that the Roman and his son who leave in anger as a result of Epictetus' belittling and insulting remarks (2.14.14–22) presumably never returned. It is likewise probable that Epictetus' similar παρρησία toward the *procurator* Cornelius Pulcher (3.4.2–7), the *corrector* of the free cities of Greece (3.7.31–34), and the *patronus* from Cnossus (3.9.17–22) hardly prompted any continuing relation with the philosopher. But it should not be forgotten that in rebuffing them, Epictetus was expressing contempt (as διάνοια) for those networks of power and public life which had forced him into exile.

To be sure, some of the visitors themselves may have intended no more than a single, brief visit—in particular those travelers to Nicopolis who regarded Epictetus as only a local attraction to see while stopping over in the city (cf. 3.9.14). But Epictetus behaves no differently with local visitors who might be expected to establish relations of some durability. In any case, it is doubtful that the local citizen who had been caught in adultery and then who was held up by Epictetus as an example of faithlessness (2.4.2–11) ever returned. Similarly, Epictetus drives away the frequent visitor—at least until he is capable of listening (2.24.1, 15, 19, 27–29), and he discourages other visitors and students from coming back with warnings about the amount of time it takes to become a philosopher (1.15.7–8; 3.15.1–13). Epictetus also suggests to homesick students that they may as well go home (3.5.1–3).

There are of course some exceptions. The success Epictetus has with the Roman who fled when his daughter fell sick (1.11.4) as well as the deference he shows the young man from Corinth (3.1.1, 34) suggest the possibility of relations of some duration. In fact, as we have seen, we can assume relations of some duration with the Roman who had risen to the office of *praefectus annonae* (1.10.2–5), with Heracleitus of Rhodes (2.2.17), with the Stoic who attempted suicide (2.15.4), and with the student who had exchanged his modest behavior for fancy clothes and perfume (4.9.6–7). Nevertheless, these exceptions only prove the rule. Indeed, when we add the inherent problem of maintaining relations with students who leave after a year or so, we can further appreciate how difficult it was for Epictetus to have durable relations.

One consequence of this lack of durability in Epictetus' network is to underscore how relatively little time he had to articulate and reinforce his norm of the practical Stoic philosopher. Another consequence is to reduce the size of Epictetus' network, as each year's students and visitors did not so much increase the number of links in the network as simply replace former ones. In other words, Epictetus' actual network—the number of people he was in contact with—was considerably smaller than his proximate (Mitchell, 1969a: 26 n. 1) one—the number of people he was likely to be in contact with. And once again, the result is to isolate Epictetus and hence to diminish his influence on others' behavior.

The third characteristic of Epictetus' network which is relevant to our analysis is the interactional one called directedness (Mitchell, 1969a: 24–26; Boissevain, 1974: 33–34). This term describes the extent to which the flow of content(s) between two people is not reciprocal but instead flows largely in one direction. When viewed in this way, Epictetus' network is directed to an unusually high degree. Indeed, now that Epictetus has given up his earlier Roman practice of accosting people in public (2.12.25), his interactions with those in his primary star are almost never initiated by him but rather the reverse. Students and visitors come to him. Their questions initiate the conversations. In fact, one visitor, after several visits, must actually confront Epictetus and demand that he speak to him (2.24.1–2). Likewise, an exile living in Nicopolis asks Epictetus to write a letter for him (1.9.27), another local man seeks Epictetus' advice about assuming a priesthood of Augustus (1.19.26), another man complains to him about the recent good fortune of a certain Philostorgus (3.17.3), and Lesbius gives Epictetus a daily dose of criticism (3.20.19). It is difficult to think of an instance in which Epictetus himself initiates an interaction, and in fact only one comes to mind: Epictetus goes to a former student after hearing that he was in the third day of a suicidal fast (2.15.5–13). In other words, the strongly directed character of Epictetus' network—with the interactions directed *from others* to him—means that Epictetus is unusually withdrawn within his own network and thus makes no effort to apply pressure, either directly or indirectly, on those whom he thought most needed to adopt his practical brand of Stoicism. This interactional characteristic therefore also helps to explain Epictetus' lack of influence on others' behavior.

To sum up: While such environmental factors as Epictetus' occupation of teaching and his residence in a busy harbor town, when combined with the data about his links concentrated among people of prominence and located throughout the Greek East and Rome, might suggest that the philosopher was at the center of a network of considerable size and influence, we have found almost the opposite to be the case. For other characteristics of his network—in particular, the presence of clusters in the primary zone but also a pattern of interactions which led to low durability and high directedness—tended to make the size of the network smaller than expected and Epictetus' influence over the behavior of others virtually nil, especially with respect to persuading them to adopt his practical brand of Stoicism. As we have seen, these latter characteristics effectively isolated him from those in his primary star and even amounted to his withdrawal from active interaction with them. Isolated and withdrawn, Epictetus was unable to reinforce his norm of Stoic self-understanding and so bring pressure to bear on behalf of it. This isolation and withdrawal were particularly inappropriate because Epictetus' students and visitors were themselves parts of social networks which transmitted and reinforced a merely academic norm for those who wanted to call themselves Stoics. No wonder, then, that Epictetus despaired of ever seeing an actual Stoic!

Conclusion

It should now be clear that social historians have more to investigate in Arrian's *Discourses* than simply the *identities* and *rank and status* of those who appear in them; there are also the *relations* which Epictetus had with these people. These relations, as we have seen, are susceptible to the anthropological approach known as network analysis. To be sure, the *Discourses* are often vague, incomplete, and fickle in their treatment of these relations. Still, it is true that at least a significant portion of Epictetus' intellectual network is recoverable. The description of that network has been attempted here. Moreover, enough is said about the relations to allow the morphological and interactional characteristics of this network to emerge. Again, only rarely can specific incidents be analyzed, but at least more thematic features of Epictetus' relations can be. One such feature, namely, Epictetus' despair at seeing an actual Stoic, has been explained by means of network analysis. Other features await analysis, but already Epictetus himself is emerging more clearly as an isolated, withdrawn, and even frustrated figure, and his place in early imperial society is now more precise as well.

NOTES

* An earlier version of this paper was presented at the Social History of Early Christianity Group of the Society of Biblical Literature during its annual meeting in 1984. I wish to thank Professor L. Michael White for suggestions regarding the revision of this paper.

[1] On the banishment of Epictetus, see Aulus Gellius, 15.11.3–5; on the date, see Sherwin-White, 1957:126–27.

[2] The standard critical text is that of Schenkl (1916). For English translation, see esp. the Loeb edition by Oldfather (1925, 1928). Translations in this paper, however, are my own.

[3] See, e.g., von Arnim; Zeller:765–81; Pohlenz, 1959:327–41; 1955:161–67; and Billerbeck: 44, 46, 49, 60–62, etc.

[4] See esp. Millar; Brunt; and Court. I wish to thank Professor Edwin A. Judge for the last reference which has not been available to me except for its conclusions.

[5] On the identity of this person, see Bowersock 1967 and Syme 1982:186. But for a slightly different identification, see Oliver, 1970:335–37.

[6] On this letter, see esp. Wirth:148–61.

[7] On this location, see also Hijmans:2–3.

[8] See Philostratus, *VS* 604.

[9] See also Stadter, 1980:201 n. 10, following Wirth:176.

[10] The Roman who visits the school with his son (2.14.1) is named Naso in the title of the *Discourse* but not in the course of the conversation itself.

[11] See further Millar:147 and Syme, 1982:186. For his connection with Plutarch, see C. P. Jones:45–46.

[12] Millar (145–46) is not sure about this identification, but Court (222) is. On Sulpicius, see Stein:871–72.

[13] Brunt (20) is also aware of this problem.

[14] Millar (141–42) suspects that Epictetus is dependent on the Stoic martyr-tradition. In any case, he identifies Gratilla as Verulana Gratilla, possibly the wife of Arulenus Rusticus.

[15] Brunt:20–21. Court has structured his study on this list of sixteen.

[16] Brunt:23. Note also the translation "one of his acquaintances" by Oldfather, 1928:131. Billerbeck:41–42.

[17] For Demonax, see Lucian, *Demonax* 3; for Favorinus, see Aulus Gellius, 17.19.1. According to Galen (frag. 30 Barigazzi), Favorinus wrote a dialogue in which Epictetus and the slave Onesimus converse, on which see Schmid:2083 and Jones, 1971:36.

[18] For possible identifications, see Millar, 1965:144 n. 55. For Court (222) the identification remains open. On his rank, see Brunt:20 n. 7.

[19] See the *Historia Augusta*, Hadrian 16.10. Brunt 19 n. 1 is doubtful, but see von Arnim:127; Zeller:765 n. 3; and Syme, 1982:186.

[20] On the return of exiles under Nerva, see Millar:145.

[21] On this post, see Rickman:62, 66, 74, 80–88.

[22] For this identification, see the views at n. 12 above.

[23] For references, see above n. 17.

[24] On these and other environmental factors, see Boissevain, 1974:67–89.

[25] See Brunt:22: "Epictetus' school was a striking feature of life at Nicopolis, and ... it made him a man of importance there."

CHRIST AS PATRON IN THE ACTS OF PETER

Robert F. Stoops, Jr.
Western Washington University

ABSTRACT

The *Acts of Peter* shows both the positive functions of patronage networks in the expansion of early Christianity and some of the problems associated with patronage. The author of *APt* uses the relationship between patron and client as a model for understanding faith and uses the promise of divine patronage as a means of promoting faith in Christ. Faith is understood as giving loyalty and honor to Christ in response to the material and spiritual benefits which he provides. *APt* claims that Christ should function as the sole patron of believers. This claim gives the author the means for winning converts and strengthening the faith of believers in the face of competition from other cults. At the same time it requires a reassessment of the role of human patrons. Even the apostle Peter is treated as a broker for Christ's benefits. Peter is not to receive honor himself, because he is only a temporary anchor in a network which has its proper center in God or Christ.

Introduction

The *Acts of Peter* is one of many accounts of a conflict between Simon Magus and the apostle Peter. Written near the middle of the second century, probably in northern Asia Minor (Ficker: 37–40), *APt* presents the conflict between Peter and Simon Magus as a miracle contest. Christ works wonders of many types through Peter. Christ also guides Peter and the other believers by means of visions. Simon's works, however, are exposed as empty deceptions.

The *APt* has usually been studied as part of a group of early apocryphal acts. Discussion of the apocryphal acts has focused on questions of text criticism, genre, theology (Kaestli: 1981; Plümacher), and more recently the social context of these writings (Davies; MacDonald; Burrus). Unfortunately, generalizations based on a group of five or more texts have not fit *APt* well.

As a genre, the aprocryphal acts have been compared to both Hellenistic romances (Von Dobschütz; Kee, 1983: 274–89) and the lives of philosophers (Reitzenstein: 1–34; Junod). While *APt* does show some features of these genres, it does not fit them as closely as some other apocryphal acts. In *APt* travel is a matter of getting from one place to another; it is not beset with dangers. Erotic motifs play a minor role. There are no separations or recognition scenes. *APt* is not primarily intended to enhance the reputation of the apostle as a divine man or teacher. Christ is clearly identified as the source of the wonders, and teaching material is relatively unimportant (Junod: 210, 214–15). *APt* is largely a collection of miracle stories which have been given a novelistic framework. It does share with other Graeco-Roman novelistic literature strong protreptic or propagandistic interests (Söder: 181–87; Koester: 2.324).

The theological *Tendenz* of the apocryphal acts has been treated as a question of their gnostic or orthodox affiliations. *APt* has been assigned to each side. Lipsius, in fact, proposed two levels of redaction—one gnostic, the other orthodox (1883: 1.1–3). This approach wrongly assumes that theology was the author's primary concern and reduces the miracles to devices which lend authority or interest to the teachings of the apostle (Lipsius, 1883: 1.78; Achtemeier: 171–73; Kee, 1983: 294–95). Peter does very little teaching in *APt*. Peter's first sermon in Rome gives as much attention to the miracles of Christ and Satan as to the issue of salvation (*APt* 7). In *APt* 21 Peter recounts the story of Christ's transfiguraton in a manner which interprets the miracles which accompany the sermon. Peter's lengthy instructions on the meaning of the cross (*APt* 37–39) stand as a testament. They are not representative of Peter's normal activity (Schneemelcher: 273). Moreover, Simon is not treated as an heresiarch in this document, in sharp contrast to other uses of the Simon Magus tradition for theological polemic. When *APt* is considered as a whole, Simon represents a composite of all forms of competition rather than a consistent theological position. The accusations against Simon focus on deception and theft. The theological debates that do appear in *APt* are brief and quickly give way to the miracle contest (*APt* 23–28). The contrast to the Pseudo-Clementine literature is striking. Gnostic and orthodox traditions appear side by side in *APt* because the author was not concerned about theological consistency.

Most investigations of the social location and function of the apocryphal acts have interpreted them as vehicles for the promotion of chastity, which is understood as an expression of female autonomy in a male-dominated world (Davies; MacDonald; Burrus; cf. Kaestli, 1986). These concerns are not the primary interests of *APt*. Procreation is nowhere treated as evil; Peter has a daughter. While sex outside of marriage, and concubinage in particular, is condemned, the author's attitudes toward sexuality follow the conventions of the period (Plümacher: 44–48; Kaestli, 1981:59). The theme of persecution arising from vows of chastity appears only in the martyrdom section, where it serves to denigrate the persecutor (cf. Justin Martyr, *Second Apology* 2) rather than extol female autonomy (Stoops, 1983:235, 294–96; Kaestli, 1986:121, 124). In *APt* widows are indeed treated as models of faith, but several of them have children. Virgins are mentioned only in the company of widows. These women are of interest for reasons other than their chastity, which is taken for granted.

Although the specific social function proposed for the apocryphal acts as a group does not fit *APt* well, the propagandistic character of *APt* demands explication. Analysis of the aims of the text and the means by which it pursued its goals will help to locate *APt* in the social history of early Christianity. Approaching *APt* on its own terms means recognizing that the primary message is carried by the stories of miracles and visions which make up the bulk of the text. Peter himself advises, "We must not put faith in words, but in actions and deeds" (*APt* 17; cf. *APt* 7).

The miracle stories and vision reports in *APt* belong to a well-established pattern of religious propaganda, aretalogy. The stories are drawn from a variety of sources, and some have close parallels either inside or outside of the Christian tradition. Form-critical and redaction-critical investigation of the aretalogical materials in *APt* can illuminate the author's situation and purposes. The contest which provides a literary frame for assembling stories probably reflects the author's situation. The Mediterranean world of the second century teemed with lively religious competition (cf. MacMullen, 1981:65, 107, 113). In that setting, miracle stories could be effective propaganda both to win converts and to strengthen the faith of those who were already believers. *APt* has Jesus appear in a vision to reassure Peter that the signs and wonders will accomplish these purposes (*APt* 16).

The use of miracle stories for propaganda requires adjustment to the contemporary "life-world." That life-world is a social construction with a history of its own (Kee, 1983: 293–96). It is to be expected that the use of miracle stories in *APt* will differ from the function of classical aretalogies. Older miracle reports such as the inscriptions honoring Asclepius at Epidauros were meant to engender confidence that additional miracles could be performed should the need arise. The author of *APt* presents miracles as the basis for an ongoing relationship with Christ. The stories treat miracles as demonstrations of Christ's ability to care for his own and show that the proper response to these demonstrations is a continuing and exclusive loyalty to Christ. The miracles in *APt* bring those who are aided and, perhaps more importantly, those who witness the miracles into a lasting relationship with Christ. The collection of stories in *APt* was no doubt intended to have the same effect on those who read or heard them. Similar attitudes toward miracles can be observed in non-Christian texts which are contemporary with *APt* (Kee, 1983: 252–56). Only the demand for an exclusive loyalty to Christ sets *APt* apart (Nock, 1933: 13–16).

Christ as Patron

In *APt* the relationship binding believers to Christ is in many ways analogous to that which attached clients to patrons in Roman society at large. Patronage networks were cemented by the exchange of gifts between persons of unequal status (Saller: 1, 27, 70; see Gellner: 4; Boissevain, 1977: 81).* The patron, who acted as anchor, offered *beneficia* such as material support, influence, and protection. In return the client displayed *gratia* in the form of honor, loyalty, gifts or whatever favors the patron might require (Saller: 8–21, 69–72, 121–24, 126–29; MacMullen: 1974, 113–14, 124–25). In some cases brokers played important roles as mediators. They provided access to or influence with those who controlled first-order benefits (Saller: 74–78). The exchange of tangible and intangible goods affected the social status of each participant (ibid.: 35, 127, 134). Patronage networks were a fundamental structure of Roman society under the empire (ibid.: 69, 193–94, 205–08). Such networks were especially important in the provinces (ibid.: 134, 145, 154–56, 165–66, 169–70, 180–87, 189; Bund: 559–60; Hausmaninger: 1254–55). The protection and support offered by patrons was crucial to associations as well as individuals (MacMullen, 1974:74–76). It should not be surprising that patronage could play important roles in religious propaganda (Boissevain, 1977: 90–94).

In *APt* Christ is never explicitly called a patron, but the term is not a sure guide to the presence of the phenomenon (Saller: 7–11, 22). Christ's ability to take care of the needs of those who are loyal to him is repeatedly emphasized. Christ offers material aid, spiritual guidance and protection at the final judgment. Faith (*fides*) is understood as a matter of continuing personal loyalty and worship given in return to Christ.

Joining oneself to Christ in the second century disrupted many social affiliations. Believers reconstructed or replaced those broken relationships within a new community. As a result early Christian literature is filled with references to brethren, household, etc. In *APt* believers are usually referred to as "servants" of Christ, a designation which emphasizes their dependence and loyalty. *Minister* translates both *diakonos* and *doulos*. Christ stands at the the head of a patronage network offering benefits which are ultimately more real than those offered by competing cults or the secular society. Even the network anchored on the emperor is shown to be inferior (*APt* 8, 11).

Christ is the ideal patron because only he is able to care for his servants on both the material and the spiritual levels. This point is made in the story of the healing of a blind widow in *APt* 20. The story follows the pattern of a typical healing miracle except that most of the expected motifs appear twice. In each section of the story there is a reference to a helping hand as well as a reference to vision. The double motifs produce a story that addresses both the physical and spiritual needs of the widow.

> So Peter went in and saw one of the old people, a widow that was blind, and her daughter giving her a hand and leading her to Marcellus' house. And Peter said to her, "Mother, come here; from this day onward, Jesus gives you his right hand through whom we have light unapproachable which no darkness hides; and he says to you through me, 'Open your eyes and see, and walk on your own.'" And at once the widow saw Peter laying his hand on her (*APt* 20).

The widow is able to walk on her own because Jesus takes the place of the daughter who had guided her. Christ speaks to the woman through Peter. Peter is a broker who distributes Christ's benefits. Peter's status is not changed by the miracle story; rather he includes himself among the recipients of divine aid.

In *APt*, miracles are consistently presented as demonstrations of Christ's ability to care for his own. The redactional framework often stresses the public character of these demonstrations through phrases like "before all these witnesses" (*P. Berol.* 8502 130; *APt* 1, 2, 9, 10, 11, 12, 13, 22, 26, 28, 32) while Simon sometimes prefers private displays of power (*APt* 31). The miracles which Christ performs through the apostles benefit the poor or the infirm directly, but they also convert the crowds who witness them. Even a *Strafwunder*, such as the story of Rufina (*APt* 2), can be retold without describing the promised cure. Attention is shifted away from the fate of the adulteress toward the witnesses' response to the demonstration of Christ's power.

The relationship between miracles and faith is treated at length in the stories of Peter's daughter drawn from *APt* (C. Schmidt, 1903: 23–25) by the compiler of a fourth-century Coptic codex, *P. Berolensis* 8502:

> On the first day of the week, which is the Lord's day, a crowd collected, and they brought a crowd who were sick to Peter for him to heal them. But one of the crowd dared to say to Peter, "Look, Peter, before our eyes you have made many blind to see, and the deaf to hear, and the lame to walk, and you have helped the weak and given them strength. Why have you not helped your virgin daughter, who has grown up beautiful and has believed on the name of God? For she is completely paralyzed on one side, and she lies there stretched out in the corner helpless. We see the people you have healed; but your own daughter you have neglected." But Peter smiled and said to him, "My son, it is evident to God alone why her body is not well. You must know, then, that God is not weak or powerless to grant his gift to my daughter. But to convince your soul and increase the faith of those who are here"—He looked then towards his daughter, and spoke to her: "Rise up from your place and with no man giving a hand but Jesus alone and walk naturally before them all and come to me." And she rose up and went to him; but the crowd rejoiced at what had happened. Then Peter said to them, "Look, your heart is convinced that God is not powerless in all the things

which we ask of him." Then they rejoiced even more and praised God (*P. Berol.* 128–30).

The introductory remarks interpret the cure as a demonstration of the sufficient power of Christ. The demonstration is given for the benefit of the questioner and the crowd of observers.

Having displayed Christ's power to heal, Peter sends his daughter back to her place and paralyzed condition (*P. Berol.* 131). He explains that it is best for her and for him that she remain as she was. Peter's explanation of the reversal of the healing miracle is not completely preserved, but it is clear that the author of *APt* has modified the traditional pattern of a rescue miracle in this section. Earlier forms of the story may have emphasized the importance of sexual purity. The girl was saved from sexual defilement by a sudden paralysis. The paralysis was a divine response to her parents' prayer for help (Augustine, *c. Adimantum* 17). *APt*, however, shifts the emphasis from chastity to the public demonstration of God's ability to care for his own.

Peter's speech goes on to deal with Ptolemy, the villain who had abducted the girl. Initially Ptolemy was blinded by grief over being deprived of the object of his desire. However, he too received a miraculous cure from Christ. He then became a benefactor of the community of believers. "He did good to them and brought them the gift of God." Ptolemy also willed property to Peter's daughter. Peter sold the land and gave the money to the poor. Legacies were a recognized way of repaying an obligation to a benefactor (Saller: 71–74). In this case the legacy is turned over to Christ's clients, because Christ was the source of the original benefit.

The fundamental concern of *APt* is documenting the care given to believers by God/Christ and modeling the response to such care. Miracles are only one means by which that care is provided. Turning the wealth of the converted, like Ptolemy, to the support of the community is equally important. In both areas, Peter's role is limited to that of broker. His reputation may be enhanced through the exchange of benefits, but that is incidental to the primary purpose of the story. The conclusion of Peter's speech interprets both the temporary cure of his daughter and the stories linked to it as unmistakable demonstrations of Christ's ability to care for believers.

Know then, O servant of Jesus Christ, that God takes care of his own and prepares good for each one (*P. Berol.* 139–40).

APt often treats the material benefits conferred in miracle stories as pointers to the more important spiritual benefits which Christ also provides: guidance in this life and a promise of protection at the judgment on the last day (*APt* 6, 7, 17). While spiritual benefits are considered more important than material ones, the reality of material benefits is never denied. In most cases some form of material aid accompanies the granting of spiritual aid and serves as the concrete demonstration of the reality of Christ's benefits. When Ptolemy's blindness was cured, the eyes of his soul were also opened (*P. Berol.* 121). When Eubula recovers the property stolen from her by Simon, she is encouraged to recover her lost soul as well (*APt* 17).

The compound story of the healing of the blind widows in *APt* 21 provides a complete paradigm for the relationship between miracle and belief in *APt*. In the course of a healing miracle, the widows encounter the Lord whom they see with their minds' eyes. Each widow sees a different figure, while the others present in the room see only a blinding light. All encounter Christ as one who is willing and able to care for his own. Christ is shown to be both immediately present and unknowable in his transcendence. The power of the spirit can be manifested physically, but the Lord remains incomprehensible even to those whom he touches (cf. Georgi, 1964:140). Christ's transcendence is such that he meets each believer in a form appropriate to each one. He meets them in order to help them both physically and spiritually. The apparently docetic motifs do not indicate a rejection of the material world but an interest in the inclusiveness of Christ's care (Cartlidge: 63). Christ is available to all at all times (*APt* 17). The universal and unmediated character of Christ's benefactions overcomes one of the major obstacles that plagued the imperial patronage network, namely distance (Saller: 68–9).

Christ's role as patron is not the whole of the author's Christology, but it shapes the stories throughout *APt*. Christ is presented as the one who takes care of and saves those who are faithful to him. That care is the basis for conversion and faith, which is understood as trust and loyalty. Continued loyalty to Christ is rewarded with knowledge, care, and future salvation (*APt* 6, 7, 17). Christ is presented as the ideal patron. Christ also claims the exclusive loyalty of his followers. Therefore, competition with the cults of other divinities offering protection and guidance is a major issue for *APt*. The role of the apostles and of human benefactors must be carefully delineated. Even the structure of the community of believers may have been influenced by the patronage model of faith.

The Context of Competition

The expansion of Christianity in the second century was part of a general upsurge of interest in religion that swept the Roman empire at that time. That era of religious ferment provided opportunities for gaining new adherents but also presented dangers. Believers might be lost to revivals of old traditions or to exotic new concoctions such as the cult of Glykon founded by Alexander of Abonoteichus. *APt* is intended to promote faith in Jesus in the face of this lively competition for religious loyalties. *APt* treats competition with other Graeco-Roman religions as a question of which divinity can provide the best benefits and is therefore deserving of loyalty and worship. The issue is one of patronage.

On the literary level the challenge from other cults is dealt with in the figure of Simon Magus. In *APt* Simon Magus is not so much a gnostic heretic as an embodiment of various competitive challenges facing the Jesus-faith. Simon is a composite figure. He is called a Jew (*APt* 6, 22), but he is also hailed as "god in Italy" and "Savior of the Romans" (*APt* 4, 6, 22). Some think that he may be the Christ (*APt* 4). At other points he presents the arguments of educated Roman sensibility against the Christian faith (*APt* 14, 23). Simon claims his wonders are demonstrations that he is the great power of God (cf. Acts 8:10). Simon threatens the relationship between Christ and believers by offering benefits which appear to be superior. It is for this reason that he is called a persecutor (*APt* 7). No matter what Simon preaches, his works are rejected as empty deceptions, attributable to magic (*APt* 28, 31) or the power of Satan (*APt* 7). By recounting a contest of miracles between the apostle Peter and Simon Magus, the author of *APt* was able to locate in the past the decisive victory of the Lord over all types of competitors.

The Role of the Apostles

APt shows more interest in promoting faith in Christ than in enhancing the reputation of Peter as a divine man or teacher. The career of the apostle shows that the promises made by others are false. Peter also guarantees the link between believers and their God. Peter had known Jesus in human form and had witnessed his miracles (*APt* 7, 10). Even though Peter had not fully understood those miracles at the time, he was later in a position to indicate the source of Christ's miracles with certainty, and to testify to the Lord's transcendence (*APt* 21).

The apostles indicate both the channels through which divine patronage flows and the response with which it should be met. However, the apostles are presented in a way that prevents them from becoming objects of loyalty who could threaten the loyalty owed to Christ. The apostles' role in the stories is that of intermediary between the divine and human realms. They are brokers who provide second-order benefits of access and intercession. Peter and Paul never act as patrons in their own right. Peter and Paul care for the Lord's servants, but they do so at the Lord's direction (*APt* 4). They give Christ credit for being the source of the benefits they distribute (*APt* 20). They are called servants of God, as are other believers, more often (13 times) than they are called apostles (11 times). At most Peter acts as the steward (*procurator*) among the servants of Christ (*APt* 10). Unlike Marcellus (*APt* 8), Peter has no material resources of his own and takes no interest in the wealth that passes through his hands (*P. Berol.* 139). When the crowd worships Peter as a god (*APt* 29), they are mistaken (*APt* 28). Converts may attach themselves to Peter temporarily, but they are directed to join the community of worshipers (*APt* 32).

For the author of *APt*, the connection between spirit and flesh allows movement in one direction only. The spirit is able to benefit the flesh. The miracles which Jesus worked through Peter demonstrate this fact above everything else. The miracles and visions encountered in the flesh reveal the presence of the spirit. In these miracles the invisible Lord can be seen working for the benefit of his believers. Material patrons, however, are not able to provide spiritual goods and should not be honored as spiritual leaders.

The Role of Human Patrons

The image of Christ as divine benefactor would appeal to poor and disenfranchised members of Roman society in obvious ways. Christ offered aid and protection to people who experienced themselves as weak and blind, whether on the physical or spiritual levels. The presentation of Christ as the patron of individual believers and their community did not preclude an interest in human patrons. Wealthy patrons were an important mechanism by which Christ provides for the material needs of his followers. Not everything in *APt* is accomplished through miracles. The community depended on the resources of the wealthy for meeting places (*APt* 8, 13, 28), money (*P. Berol.* 139; *APt* 8, 17, 19, 29), and prestige (*APt* 17, 27). Converted patrons could bring a network of clients along with them (*APt* 8, 14). Conversely, dependents could bring the message about Christ to their patrons (*APt* 28). In either case the ability to incorporate existing household or patronage networks into the community of believers probably contributed to the expansion of the faith (cf. Stark, 1986: 318–19, 322–25).

Because wealthy converts were useful to the community some of the stories in *APt* are designed to appeal to potential patrons (*APt* 11, 17, 22, 27–28; Stoops, 1983:193–94, 205–19; 1986:93–95). However, wealthy converts also caused problems. The author of *APt* found it necessary to redefine the role of human patrons in order to control their influence. In the normal cycle of patronage, gifts and protection evoke a response of loyalty and honor, producing a well-defined hierarchy. The author of *APt* proposed to short circuit the cycle of patronage so that the honor and loyalty human benefactors expected in return for their gifts were directed to Christ instead. No human benefactor, not even an apostle, is allowed to divert loyalty from Christ, who is the source of all good things.

The author of *APt* used a number of devices to indicate the proper role of patrons within the community. Several stories show wealthy converts who give support to the community after receiving aid from Christ and then disappear from the story. The senator who was raised from the dead and his mother both respond with money for the community (*APt* 29). Eubula also acts as a benefactress after her conversion, but she does not become a leader in the community (*APt* 17). This pattern suggests that potential patrons should give freely in recognition of the spiritual benefits they have received from Christ.

The story of Chryse (*APt* 30) suggests that these gifts should not be understood as simple almsgiving. Her story is designed to show definitively that those who are patrons on the material level are not suited to be spiritual leaders and should not receive honor or authority within the community. Because of her luxurious and promiscuous way of life, Chryse cannot become a leader or even a member of the community. Yet Chryse's gift is accepted as coming from Christ, because she was "indebted" to him. Loans and gifts of money were a common element in Roman patronage exchanges (Saller: 55, 64–66, 120–26). Peter and the community of believers can accept the gift without falling under obligation to a person of low reputation, because the giver is discharging an obligation to their common benefactor. Rather than receiving honor or loyalty in return for her material gift, this potential patroness is presented as a recipient of Christ's benefits. Peter, who is called a servant of Christ himself in the story, explains that the whole transaction is Christ's way of caring for his servants, especially those who were afflicted.

The extensive subplot constructed around the figure of Marcellus deals directly with the problems of patrons (Stoops, 1986:96–98). Marcellus' reactions have been appended to several of the stories in the contest between Simon and Peter (Stoops: 1983:195–205). The author portrays Marcellus as one who had held a secure position near the top of the worldly network of Roman society. Marcellus is a senator. Before his seduction by Simon, believers had called him a patron of the poor (*APt* 8; cf. Saller: 10). His patronage of believers was problematic. It conflicted with the normal structures of patronage in Roman society by diverting the flow of goods to and from the emperor (*APt* 8). On the other hand, believers who honored Marcellus as their patron followed him in his apostasy:

... if he (Marcellus) had not been won over, we in turn should not have deserted the holy faith in our Lord God (*APt* 8).

Marcellus is reconverted when the speaking dog accosts Simon (*APt* 9–10). The episode is set in Marcellus' house, and Marcellus' reaction is added to the end of the story. He announces his willingness to abandon those things which had given him the status of patron and admits the instability of his faith. Although restored as a believer, Marcellus never becomes a model of faith. He is always in danger of misstepping precisely because of the wealth and senatorial status which put him in the position to be a patron. Shortly thereafter Peter exorcizes a laughing youth in the house of Marcellus. The departing demon topples a statue (*APt* 11; cf. Philostratus, *Life of Apollonius* 4.20). The anticipated acclamation of the crowd has been replaced by Marcellus' fearful reaction. Because the statue was an image of the emperor, Marcellus fears reprisals. In spite of his earlier willingness to renounce his wealth, his position in society continues to conflict with his loyalty to Christ. Even in dream, Marcellus' social standing prevents him from defending the faithful (*APt* 22). At the end of *APt*, Marcellus fails to understand that his wealth cannot confer honor on the martyred apostle but is to be used to support the poor among the faithful and thereby bring honor to Christ (*APt* 40; cf. the statue raised in Simon's honor, *APt* 10).

One of the most important patron-client relationships in Roman society was that between manumitted slaves and their former masters. In *APt* 28 Peter dramatically intervenes in a manumission and restructures the patronage relationship so that loyalty to Christ is primary. The story is part of a complex in which three dead men are restored to life by Christ at Peter's request. The first man, a protégé of the prefect, was killed by Simon's magic as part of the public contest (*APt* 25–26). The second corpse belongs to the son of a widow who is distraught because her son had been her only source of material support (*APt* 25, 27). Her story, along with others involving the poor and widows has a clear appeal to the disenfranchised. The third man to be resuscitated is a young senator (*APt* 28). This story is constructed as a parallel to that of the widow's son but it is composed in terms which would appeal to another group of potential believers (Stoops, 1986:94). His mother—no father is mentioned—is not worried about financial matters. She asks only for light for her son, without revealing the fact that he has died. This mother is wealthy enough to free her son's slaves in order to swell his funeral procession. Resurrection of the propertied dead, however, creates social stress. What is to be the status of those who were freed to honor the dead man if he is no longer dead? The question is particularly important because some of the slaves seem to be believers in Christ. Before raising the senator, Peter negotiates not only freedom, but also support for the slaves. These freedmen will serve their former master as dependent clients. However, when he is finally revived, the senator makes it plain that he now belongs to Christ. Therefore, the former slaves are integrated into the network anchored in Christ with no conflicts of loyalties. The mother's potential role as benefactress is limited when she is not allowed to provide hospitality to Peter. Both mother and son respond to Christ's aid by making large donations for the care of the widows and thereby conform to the pattern set for benefactors in *APt*.

The author of *APt* thought it necessary to redefine and limit the role of patrons before they could be integrated into the community of believers without destroying its fabric. The author wanted to obligate the wealthy to fulfill their duties as benefactors, without granting them the honor and loyalty which are the normal responses to such patronage. The credit, as manifested by worship and loyalty are owed directly to Jesus who is the ultimate source of all blessings. Those who benefit from the contributions of the wealthy should respond with loyalty to Jesus rather than to figures like Marcellus (*APt* 19). The wealthy should support the community, not as the patrons of the other believers, but as grateful recipients of Christ's patronage (*APt* 17, 29).

The Role of Widows

Some believers receive special attention in *APt* not as leaders but as examples of humility and dependence. *APt* gives one group of women special status as widows. *APt* agrees with pastoral epistles in viewing widows primarily in terms of their lack of male sources of support (Fiorenza, 1983:310; Bassler:37). They are grouped with the poor and the orphans. Maturity and chastity are assumed. Eubula (*APt* 17) is too wealthy to be designated a widow. The mother of the senator appears to be a widow in the ordinary sense (*APt* 29). However, she controls significant wealth and is never called a widow in the text. When these wealthy women are aided by Christ, they become believers and respond by giving gifts for the support of the widows or virgins and the poor (*APt* 17, 29).

The author is interested in widows because their absolute dependence on the material and spiritual support coming from Christ makes them model believers. Their acceptance of gifts derived from Christ confirms their status as true "servants of Christ" (*APt* 19). The widows and virgins may enjoy a kind of autonomy in the sense that they depend on no one but Christ (*APt* 21), but their position is not envied. It is considered better to have your son restored to life than to be free of his control (*APt* 27). The widows are never considered as potential leaders within the community, nor do they have their own houses. There is no polemic aimed at limiting their influence or autonomy. Apparently their direct relationship to Christ was not threatening to the author of *APt* (cf. MacDonald:73–77; Bassler: 31–39).

The Nature of the Community

Because the author was describing events of a past, apostolic, age *APt* gives little certain information about the social structure of the community for which it was written. The relatively large number of women who appear in the stories may reflect the makeup of that community. It seems likely that the community included or anticipated including some members who could be expected to function as patrons. *APt* treats the relationship binding the believers to Christ as the primary dimension of faith. The relationship among believers derives from it, because loyalty to Christ is given concrete expression by joining with other believers for collective instruction and worship (*APt* 13, 32). Christ appears to Ptolemy to explain the link between believers:

> ". . . it is not right for you, a believer in me, to defile my virgin, one whom you ought to know as your sister, as if I were for the two of you a single spirit" (*P. Berol.* 137).

APt applies a common motif based on Genesis 2:24 to solidarity among believers rather than the salvation of the individual. The bond is spiritual and is anchored on Christ.

The relationship among believers is not one that could easily allow for distinctions in status. All believers ought to be on equal footing as fellow-servants of the same master. Even the apostles, Peter and Paul, are most often called servants of God. The absence of strong, institutionalized leadership may have contributed to the community's vulnerability to the influence of human patrons. Peter and Paul offer temporary leadership, but no other figures are able to counter the influence of Simon Magus. The only church officer seen at work, Narcissus, the presbyter, remained loyal to Christ but was ineffective against Simon. Similarly Ariston's prophetic visions could not protect the majority of believers from Simon's charms (*APt* 6). If the issue of competition had been settled by the apostles, the gifts exercised by lesser figures could be construed as the means by which Christ continued to care for believers. Perhaps the author thought that leadership should rotate among believers to be exercised by each as long as Christ chose to act through that person. Such a pattern would have preserved the basic equality among the servants of Christ (Fiorenza, 1983:286).

The Christology and the understanding of faith put forward in *APt* could support the development of different types of theology and church structure. If church officers were given clear and permanent roles as mediators of Christ's benefits, the patron-Christology of *APt* would support an orthodox hierarchy. The ordained clergy would stand between Christ and believers to guarantee the bond of loyalty. Ignatius seems to have had something like this in mind when he advised his fellow bishop Polycarp concerning the care of widows in the church (Ignatius, *Polycarp* 4.1):

> Do not let the widows be neglected. You, after the Lord, be their guardian. Let nothing be done without your consent, and you do nothing without God, as you do nothing. Stand firm.

Peter Brown (1981) has shown how this process unfolded in the Latin church. The prediction that the anonymous, resurrected son of the widow would serve as a deacon and bishop (*APt* 27) may point in this direction. However, *APt* does not present Peter as a model bishop. He is never called a bishop, and an association between apostles and bishops cannot be assumed for Asia Minor in the mid-second century (Stoops, 1987:167–68). In the absence of a permanent mediator standing between Christ and believer, the direct relationship between the two could collapse into spiritual identification, congenial to gnostic forms of Christology and soteriology. Other apocryphal acts may represent developments in this direction, perhaps under the pressure of persecutions (MacDonald: 40–53, 78–85). *APt*, however, has not yet made a choice between the gnostic and orthodox options.

Conclusion

The author of *APt* was interested in the networks which bound patrons and clients together because they provided a means of maintaining and expanding the Jesus-faith. In his contribution to this volume, Holland Hendrix has shown that the introduction of new patrons into a community could lead to significant shifts in religious loyalties. The author of *APt* sought to promote loyalty to Jesus by showing it to be the best way of securing both material and spiritual benefits. The superior benefits offered by Christ were the basis for conversion. His care gave a reason for continued loyalty. Even so, making this model work for the author's view of faith and the community required some reworking of existing notions of patronage.

The problems addressed in *APt* are those that arise from the author's understanding of faith. When faith is understood as loyalty based on the ability of the divine patron to provide for clients, individual believers and the community as a whole are left vulnerable to competing claims made on the same grounds. Simon Magus represents this threat from other cults. Peter's prayer in response to Simon's last miracle (*APt* 32) shows that the author of *APt* recognized that the faith of believers might still be vulnerable.

On the human level patronage can only flow downward. The apostle acts as broker enlarging and maintaining the network anchored on Christ but does not properly become the object of worship himself (*APt* 28, 29, 40). Human patrons give *beneficia* in the form of material support, but the *gratia* due as honor, worship, and loyalty is directed to Christ. The patrons, rather than becoming guides for the community, recognize themselves as grateful recipients of Christ's aid. They too are clients, fellow servants of Christ, along with all other believers. They discharge their obligations to Christ by supporting his clients. The models of faith are the poor, the sick, and the widows, those who are most obviously in need of Christ's aid.

APt shows that at least one early Christian author recognized the importance of the patron-client network as a means of winning converts and strengthening the faith of believers. At the same time the author presented a new understanding of how patronage should work within the community of those bound to each other by their common loyalty to Christ. While it is unlikely that any community of Jesus-believers ever organized themselves as this author suggested they ought, *APt* demonstrates the importance of social conventions in early Christian literature and reminds us that social and religious categories can never be completely separated. Many of the stories in *APt* will be misunderstood unless it is recognized that the author has shaped the literary presentation of aretalogical materials to fit patterns rooted in social experience. *APt* reflects a stage in the development of Christianity when it could present itself as a superior version of established social structures rather than as an apocalyptic antithesis to them. This strategy made Christianity broadly accessible and prepared the way for later accommodations with Roman imperial structures. *APt* gives evidence that the impact of patronage networks on the development of early Christianity was both complex and open to manipulation.

NOTE

* This study was completed before Wallace-Hadrill 1989 became available to the author. In particular it should be noted that the articles by Saller and Wallace-Hadrill in this volume support the approach taken here toward patronage in the imperial period.

EPIDEMICS, NETWORKS, AND THE RISE OF CHRISTIANITY

Rodney Stark
University of Washington

ABSTRACT

The early Christian movement achieved unprecedented growth during the second and third centuries A.D. Numerous historical and sociological explanations have been advanced to account for this phenomenon and its role in the eventual "triumph" of Christianity under Constantine. Long overlooked in this endeavor has been the role of several spectacular disasters that hit the empire in this same period. Most notable are two periods of widespread and devastating epidemic that hit especially hard in the eastern provinces in the 160s and again in the 250s. This article suggests that the fabric of Roman society was substantially disrupted and demoralized by these catastrophes, and that this opened the door for Christian ascendancy, both theologically and numerically. To demonstrate this contention the character of the epidemics will be described. Then, three main theses will be advanced and explored. First, the Christians offered a more satisfactory explanation of the catastrophic events. Second, Christian values of love and charity were translated into practices of social service in the times of crisis, thereby creating a network of medical care. Third, with even minimal medical attention, the survival rate among the Christians (and any of their pagan neighbors whom they treated) was substantially higher than that in the general population. Over time, the proportion of Christians in the total population was thereby dramatically increased. When coupled with the network effect of those pagans now disengaged from traditional ties and attracted by Christian benevolence to new attachments, the result was to alter irreversibly the balance of the Roman empire.

Introduction

In 165 A.D., during the reign of Marcus Aurelius, a devastating epidemic swept through the Roman Empire. Some medical historians suspect that it was the first appearance of smallpox in the West (Zinsser, 1960). But, whatever the actual disease, it was lethal. During the 15 year duration of the epidemic, from a quarter to a third of the population of the empire died from it, including Marcus Aurelius himself, in 180 in Vienna (Boak, 1947; Russell, 1958; Gilliam; McNeill). Then, in 251 a new and equally devastating epidemic again swept the empire, hitting the rural areas as hard as the cities (Boak, 1955a, 1955b; Russell, 1958; McNeill). This time it may have been measles. Both smallpox and measles can produce massive mortality rates when they strike a previously unexposed population (Neel, et al.).

Although, as we shall see, these demographic disasters were reported by contemporary writers, the role they likely played in the decline of Rome was ignored by historians until modern times (Zinsser; Boak, 1947). Now, however, historians recognize that acute depopulation was responsible for policies once attributed to moral degeneration. For example, massive resettlement of "barbarians" as landholders within the empire and their induction into the legions did not reflect Roman decadence, but were rational policies by a state with an abundance of vacant estates and lacking manpower (Boak, 1955b). In his now classic and pioneering work on the impact of epidemics on history, Hans Zinsser (99) pointed out that:

> ... again and again, the forward march of Roman power and world organization was interrupted by the only force against which political genius and military valor were utterly helpless—epidemic disease ... and when it came, as though carried by storm clouds, all other things gave way, and men crouched in terror, abandoning all their quarrels, undertakings and ambitions, until the tempest had blown over.

But, while historians of Rome have been busy making good the oversights of earlier generations, the same cannot be said of historians of the early Christian era. The words "epidemic," "plague," or "disease" do not even appear in the index of the most respected recent works on the rise of Christianity (Frend; MacMullen, 1984). This is no small omission. Indeed, Cyprian, Dionysius, Eusebius, and other church fathers thought the epidemics made major contributions to the Christian cause. I think so, too. In this essay I suggest that had classical society not been disrupted and demoralized by these catastrophes, Christianity might never have become so dominant a faith. To this end, I shall develop three theses.

The first of these can be found in the writings of Cyprian, bishop of Carthage. The epidemics swamped the explanatory and comforting capacities of paganism and of Hellenic philosophies. In contrast, Christianity offered a much more satisfactory account of why these terrible times had fallen upon humanity and it projected a hopeful, even enthusiastic, portrait of the future.

The second is to be found in an Easter letter by Dionysius, bishop of Alexandria. Christian values of love and charity had, from the beginning, been translated into norms of social service and community solidarity. When disasters struck, the Christians were better able to cope and this resulted in *substantially higher rates of survival*. This meant that in the aftermath of each epidemic, Christians made up a larger percentage of the population even without new converts. Moreover, their noticeably better survival rate would have seemed a "miracle" to Christians and pagans alike and this ought to have influenced conversion.

Let me acknowledge that, as I consulted sources on the historical impact of epidemics, I discovered these two points discussed briefly in William H. McNeill's superb *Plagues and Peoples*, 1976. I cannot recall having read them before. I must have done so, but at a time when I was more interested in the fall of Rome than in the rise of Christianity. In any event, both points have a substantial social scientific pedigree as elements in the analysis of "revitalization movements"—the rise of new religions as a response to social crises (Wallace, 1956, 1966; Carroll; Thornton; Champagne; Stark and Bainbridge, 1985, 1987).

My third proposition is an application of control theories of conformity (Hirschi, 1969; Stark and Bainbridge, 1985, 1987). When an epidemic destroys a substantial proportion of a population, it leaves large numbers of people without the interpersonal attachments which had, in the past, bound them to the conventional moral order. As mortality mounted during each of these epidemics, large numbers of people, especially pagans, would have *lost the bonds* that once might have restrained them from becoming Christians. Meanwhile, the superior rates of survival of Christian social networks would have provided pagans with a much greater probability of replacing their lost attachments with new ones to Christians. In this way, very substantial numbers of pagans would have been shifted from mainly pagan to mainly Christian social networks. In any era, such a shifting of social networks will result in religious conversions (Lofland and Stark, 1965; Stark and Bainbridge, 1985, 1987).

In what follows I will expand each of these arguments and offer evidence that it applies. But first, I must sketch the extent of these two epidemics and their demographic impact.

The Epidemics

The great epidemic of the second century, which is sometimes referred to as the "Plague of Galen," first struck the army of Verus, while campaigning in the East in 165 A.D., and from there spread across the Empire. The mortality was so high in many cities that Marcus Aurelius spoke of caravans of carts and wagons hauling the dead from cities. Hans Zinsser (100) noted that

> ... so many people died that cities and villages in Italy and in the provinces were abandoned and fell into ruin. Distress and disorganization was so severe that a campaign against the Marcommani was postponed. When, in 169, the war was finally resumed, Haeser records that many of the Germanic warriors—men and women—were found dead on the field without wounds, having died from the epidemic.

We cannot know the actual mortality rate with any certainty, although there is no doubt that it was high. Seeck's estimate, made in 1910, that over half the population of the Empire perished, now seems too high (in Littman and Littman). Conversely, Gilliam's conclusion that only 1 percent died is incompatible even with his own assertion that "a great and destructive epidemic took place under Marcus Aurelius."

The Littmans propose a rate of seven to ten percent, but do so by selecting smallpox epidemics in Minneapolis during 1924–25 and in West Prussia in 1874 as the relevant comparisons, and ignoring the far higher fatalities for smallpox epidemics in less modern societies with populations lacking substantial prior exposure. I am most persuaded by McNeill's estimate that from a quarter to a third of the population perished during this epidemic. Such high mortality is consistent with modern knowledge of epidemiology. It also is consistent with analyses of subsequent manpower shortages (Boak, 1955b).

Almost a century later a second terrible epidemic struck the Roman world. At its height, 5,000 people a day were reported to have died in the city of Rome alone (McNeill). And for this epidemic we have excellent contemporary reports, especially from Christian sources. Thus Cyprian, bishop of Carthage, wrote in 251 that "many of us are dying" from "this plague and pestilence." Several years later Dionysius, bishop of Alexandria, wrote in an Easter message that "out of the blue came this disease, a thing ... more frightful than any disaster whatever."

These disasters were not limited to the cities. McNeill suggests that the death toll may have been even higher in rural areas. Boak (1955a) has calculated that the small town of Karanis, in Egypt, may have lost more than a third of its population during the first epidemic. Calculations based on Dionysius' account, suggest two-thirds of the population of Alexandria may have perished (Boak, 1947). Such death rates have been documented in many other times and places when a serious infectious disease has struck a population not recently exposed to it. For example, in 1707 smallpox killed more than 30 percent of the population of Iceland (D. R. Hopkins). In any event, my concern here is not epidemiological. It is, rather, with the human experience of such crisis and calamity.

Crisis and Faith

Frequently in human history, crises produced by natural or social disasters have been translated into crises of faith. Typically this occurs because the disaster places demands upon the prevailing religion that it *appears unable to meet*. This inability can occur at two levels. First, the religion may fail to provide a satisfactory explanation of *why* the disaster occurred. Second, the religion may seem to be *unavailing* against the disaster, which becomes truly critical when all non-religious means also prove inadequate—when the supernatural remains the *only plausible source* of help. In response to these "failures" of their traditional faiths, societies frequently have evolved or adopted new faiths. The classic instance is the series of messianic movements that periodically swept through the Indians of North America in response to their failures to withstand encroachments by European settlers (Mooney, 1896). The prevalence of new religious movements in societies undergoing rapid modernization also illustrates the point. Bryan Wilson has surveyed many such episodes from around the world.

In a now famous essay, Anthony F. C. Wallace argued that *all* religions arise in response to crises. That seems a needlessly extreme view, but there is abundant evidence that faith seldom is "blind," in the sense that religions frequently *are discarded* and new ones accepted in troubled times. Elsewhere I have attempted to specify the process by which this occurs and explain why the new faith often will retain many elements of the old (Stark and Bainbridge, 1985, 1987). Here my concern is simply to contrast the ability of Christianity to explain the epidemics with that of its competitors in the Graeco-Roman world.

I also will examine the many ways in which Christianity not only seemed to be, but actually was *efficacious*. This too is typical. Indeed, this is why the term "revitalization movement" is applied to new religions that arise during times of crisis—the name indicates the positive contributions such movements often make by "revitalizing" the capacity of a culture to deal with its problems. How do religions "revitalize?" Primarily by effectively mobilizing people to attempt collective actions. Thus the new religious movements among the North American Indians during the eighteenth and nineteenth centuries initially revitalized these societies by greatly reducing drunkenness and despair and then provided an effective framework for joining fragmented bands into an organized political unit capable of concerted action. That these proved unable to withstand white encroachments in the *long run*, must not obscure the obvious early benefits and how these "proved" the validity of the new faith. In this way new ideas or theologies often generate new social arrangements that are better-suited to the new circumstances.

As a sociologist, I was trained to be suspicious of "theological" or "ideological" explanations—those that attribute behavior to ideas. However, as I shall demonstrate in this essay, ideas often are critical factors in determining not only individual behavior but, indeed, the path of history. Put another way, for people in the Graeco-Roman world, to be a Christian or a pagan was not simply a matter of "denominational preference."

Rather, the *contents* of Christian and pagan beliefs were *different* in ways that greatly determined not only their explanatory capacities, but also their relative capacities to mobilize human resources.

To assess these differences between pagans and Christians, let us imagine ourselves in their places, faced with one of these terrible epidemics.*

Here we are in a city stinking of death. All around us, our family and friends are dropping. We can never be sure if or when we will fall sick too. In the midst of such appalling circumstances, humans are driven to ask: *Why?* Why is this happening? Why them and not me? Will we all die? Why does the world exist, anyway? What's going to happen next? What can we do?

If we are pagans we probably already know that our priests profess ignorance. They don't know why the gods have sent such misery—or if, in fact, the gods are involved or even care (Harnack, 1908). Worse yet, many of our priests have fled the city, as have the highest civil authorities and the wealthiest families, which adds to the disorder and suffering.

Suppose that instead of being pagans we are philosophers. Even if we reject the gods and profess one or another school of Greek philosophy we still have no answers. Natural law is no help in saying *why* suffering abounds, at least not if we seek to find *meaning* in the reasons. To say that survival is a matter of luck makes the life of the individual seem trivial. Cicero expressed the incapacity of classical as well as modern humanism to provide meaning (or perhaps we should say meaningfulness), when he explained that

> ... it depends on fortune or (as we should say) "conditions" whether we are to experience prosperity or adversity. Certain events are, indeed, due to natural causes beyond human control (in Cochrane, 1957:100).

Moreover, for a science that knows nothing of bacteria the phrase "natural causes" in connection with these great epidemics is simply how philosophers say "who knows?" I am not here disputing that survival *was in fact* substantially random or that the epidemics had natural causes. But I do claim that people will prefer explanations that assert that such events reflect underlying historical intentions, that the larger contours of life are coherent and explicable. Not only were the philosophers of the time unable to provide such meanings, but from the point of view of classical science and philosophy these events were indeed beyond human control, for no useful medical courses of action could be suggested. Indeed, the philosophers of the period could think of nothing more insightful than to anthropomorphize society and blame senility. As Cochrane (1957:155) put it, "while a deadly plague was ravaging the empire ... the sophists prattled vaguely about the exhaustion of virtue in a world growing old."

But if we are Christians, our faith does claim to have answers. McNeill summed them up this way:

> Another advantage Christians enjoyed over pagans was that the teachings of their faith made life meaningful even amid sudden and surprising death... even a shattered remnant of survivors who had somehow made it through war or pestilence or both could find warm, immediate and healing consolation in the vision of a heavenly existence for those missing relatives and friends.... Christianity was, therefore, a system of thought and feeling thoroughly adapted to a time of troubles in which hardship, disease, and violent death commonly prevailed (108).

Cyprian, bishop of Carthage, seems almost to have welcomed the great epidemic of his time. Writing in 251 he claimed that only non-Christians had anything to fear from the plague. Moreover, he noted that although:

> ... the just are dying with the unjust, it is not for you to think that the destruction is a common one for both the evil and the good. The just are called to refreshment, the unjust are carried off to torture; protection is more quickly given to the faithful; punishment to the faithless.... How suitable, how necessary it is that this plague and pestilence, which seems horrible and deadly, searches out the justice of each and every one and examines the minds of the human race; whether the well care for the sick, whether relatives dutifully love their kinsmen as they should, whether masters show compassion for their ailing slaves, whether physicians do not desert the afflicted... Although this mortality has contributed nothing else, it has especially accomplished this for Christians and servants of God, that we have begun gladly to seek martyrdom while we are learning not to fear death. These are trying exercises for us, not deaths; they give to the mind the glory of fortitude; by contempt of death they prepare for the crown ... our brethren who have been freed from the world by the summons of the Lord should not be mourned, since we know that they are not lost but sent before; that in departing they lead the way; that as travellers, as voyagers are wont to be, they should be longed for, not lamented ... and that no occasion should be given to pagans to censure us deservedly and justly, on the ground that we grieve for those who we say are living with God.... (Cyprian, *On the Mortality*, 15–20).

His fellow bishop Dionysius addressed his Alexandrian members in similar tones. "Other people would not think this a time for festival," he wrote, but "far from being a time of distress, it is a time of unimaginable joy" (*Festal Letters*, quoted by Eusebius, *Church History* 7,22). Acknowledging the huge death rate, Dionysius noted that though this terrified the pagans, Christians greeted the epidemic as merely "schooling and testing." Thus, at a time when all other faiths were called to question, Christianity offered explanation and comfort. Even more important, Christian doctrine provided a *prescription for action*. That is, the Christian way appeared to work.

Survival Rates and the Golden Rule

At the height of the second great epidemic, around 260, in the Easter letter already quoted above, Dionysius wrote a lengthy tribute to the heroic nursing efforts of local Christians, many of whom lost their lives while caring for others.

> Most of our brother-Christians showed unbounded love and loyalty, never sparing themselves and thinking only of one another. Heedless of danger, they took charge of the sick, attending to their every need and ministering to them in Christ, and with them departed this life serenely happy; for they were infected by others with the disease, drawing on themselves the sickness of their neighbors and cheerfully accepting their pains. Many, in nursing and curing others, transferred their death to themselves and died in their stead.... The best of our brothers lost their lives in this manner, a number of presbyters, deacons, and laymen winning high commendation so that death in this form, the result of great piety and strong faith, seems in every way the equal of martyrdom.

Dionysius noted the heavy mortality of the epidemic by saying how much happier had they merely, like the Egyptians in the time of Moses, lost the firstborn from each house. For "there is not a house in which there is not one dead—how I wish it had been only one." But, while the epidemic had not passed over the Christians, he suggests pagans fared much worse: "its full impact fell on the heathen."

Dionyius also offered an explanation of this mortality differential. Having noted at length how the Christian community nursed the sick and dying and even spared nothing in preparing the dead for proper burial, he wrote:

> The heathen behaved in the very opposite way. At the first onset of the disease, they pushed the sufferers away and fled from their dearest, throwing them into the roads before they were dead and treated unburied corpses as dirt, hoping thereby to avert the spread and contagion of the fatal disease; but do what they might, they found it difficult to escape.

But, should we believe him? To assess Dionysius' claims, it must be demonstrated that the Christians actually did minister to the sick while the pagans mostly did not. It also must be shown that these different patterns of responses would result in substantial differences in mortality.

Christian and Pagan Responses

It seems highly unlikely that a bishop would write a pastoral letter full of false claims *about things that his parishioners would know from direct observation*. So, if he claims that lots of leading members of the diocese have perished while nursing the sick, it must have happened. Moreover, there is compelling evidence *from pagan sources* that this was characteristic Christian behavior. Thus, a century later, the Emperor Julian launched a campaign to institute pagan charities in an effort to match the Christians. Julian complained in a letter to the high priest of Galatia in 362 that the pagans needed to equal the virtues of Christians, for recent Christian growth was caused by their "moral character, even if pretended" and by their "benevolence toward strangers and care for the graves of the dead." In a letter to another priest, Julian wrote, "I think that when the poor happened to be neglected and overlooked by the priests, the impious Galileans observed this and devoted themselves to benevolence." And he also wrote, ". . . the impious Galileans support not only their poor, but ours as well, everyone can see that our people lack aid from us" (Johnson, 1976:75; Ayerst and Fisher:179–181).

Clearly, Julian loathed "the Galileans." He even suspected that their benevolence had ulterior motives. But he recognized that his charities and that of organized paganism paled in comparison with Christian efforts which had created "a miniature welfare state in an empire which for the most part lacked social services" (Johnson, 1976:75). By Julian's day in the fourth century it was too late to overtake this colossal result, the seeds for which had been planted in such teachings as "I am my brother's keeper," "Do unto others as you would have them do onto you," and "It is more blessed to give than to receive" (Grant).

Julian's testimony also supports the claim that pagan communities did not match Christian levels of benevolence during the epidemics, since they did not do so even in normal times when the risks entailed by benevolence were much lower. But there is other evidence.

Some of the most detailed reporting on epidemics in the classical world is to be found in Thucydides' *History of the Peloponnesian War* (Book II, 47–55). Thucydides was himself a survivor of a deadly plague that struck Athens in 431 B.C., having contracted the disease in the first days of the epidemic. Modern medical writers praise Thucydides' careful and detailed account of symptoms (Marks and Beatty). At least as much can be said for his account of public responses.

Thucydides began by noting the ineffectiveness of both science and religion:

> . . . the doctors were quite incapable of treating the disease because of their ignorance of the right methods. . . . Equally useless were prayers made in the temples, consultation of the oracles, and so forth; indeed, in the end people were so overcome by their sufferings that they paid no further attention to such things (49).

Then he reported that once the contagious nature of the disease was recognized people "were afraid to visit one another." As a result:

> ... they died with no one to look after them; indeed there were many houses in which all the inhabitants perished through lack of any attention.... The bodies of the dying were heaped one on top of the other, and half-dead creatures could be seen staggering about in the streets or flocking around the fountains in their desire for water. The temples in which they took up their quarters were full of the dead bodies of people who had died inside them. For the catastrophe was so overwhelming that men, not knowing what would happen next to them, became indifferent to every rule of religion or of law.... No fear of god or law of man had a restraining influence. As for the gods, it seemed to be the same thing whether one worshipped them or not, when one saw the good and the bad dying indiscriminately (51–53).

Although separated by nearly seven centuries, this description of how pagan Athens reacted to a killing epidemic is strikingly similar to Dionysius' account of pagan responses to the epidemic in Alexandria. Thucydides acknowledged that some, who like himself had recovered from the disease and thus were immune, did try to nurse the sick, but their numbers seem to have been few. Moreover, Thucydides accepted that it was only sensible to flee epidemics and to shun contact with the sick.

It also is worth noting that the famous classical physician Galen lived through the first epidemic during the reign of Marcus Aurelius. What did he do? He got out of Rome quickly, retiring to a country estate in Asia Minor until the danger receded. In fact, modern medical historians have noted that Galen's description of the disease "is uncharacteristically incomplete" and suggest this may have been due to his hasty departure (D. Hopkins). Granted that this is but one man's response, albeit a man much admired by later generations as the greatest physician of the age. But, although at least one modern medical historian has felt the need to write an exculpatory essay on Galen's flight, it was not seen as unusual or discreditable at the time (Walsh). It was what any prudent person would have done, had they the means—unless, of course, they were "Galileans."

Here issues of doctrine must be addressed. For something distinctive did come into the world with the development of Christianity—the linking of a highly *social* ethical code with religion. There was nothing new in the idea that the supernatural makes behavioral demands upon humans—the gods have always wanted sacrifices and worship. Nor was there anything new in the notion that the supernatural will respond to offerings—that the gods can be induced to exchange services for sacrifices. What was new was the notion that more than self-interested exchange relations were possible between humans and the supernatural. The Christian teaching that God *loves* those who love Him was alien to pagan beliefs. MacMullen (1981:53) has noted that from the pagan perspective:

> What mattered was ... the service that the deity could provide, since a god (as Aristotle had long taught) could feel no love in response to that offered.

Equally alien to paganism was the notion that because God loves humanity, Christians cannot please God unless they *love one another.* Indeed, as God demonstrates his love through sacrifice, humans must demonstrate their love through sacrifice on behalf of *one another.* Moreover, such responsibilities were to be extended beyond the bonds of family and tribe, indeed to "all those who in every place call on the name of our Lord Jesus Christ" (1 Cor. 1:2). These were revolutionary ideas.

Pagan and Christian writers are unanimous that not only did Christian scripture stress love and charity as the central duties of faith, but that these were sustained in everyday behavior. Lucian wrote of the Christians: "Their original lawgiver taught them that they were all brethren, one of the other." I suggest reading the following passage from Matthew (25:35–40) as if for the very first time, in order to gain insight into the power of this new morality when it was *new*, not centuries later in more cynical and worldly times:

> "For I was hungry and you gave me food, I was thirsty and you gave me drink, I was a stranger and you welcomed me, I was naked and you clothed me, I was sick and you visited me, I was in prison and you came to me.... Truly, I say to you, as you did it to one of the least of these my brethren, you did it to me."

When the New Testament was *new*, these were the norms of the Christian communities. Tertullian claimed (*Apology*, 39):

> It is our care of the helpless, our practice of loving kindness that brands us in the eyes of many of our opponents. "Only look," they say, "look how they love one another!"

Harnack (1908:161) quoted the duties of deacons as outlined in the *Apostolic Constitutions* to show that they were set apart for the support of the sick, infirm, poor and disabled:

> They are to be doers of good works, exercising a general supervision day and night, neither scorning the poor nor respecting the person of the rich; they must ascertain who are in distress and not exclude them from a share in church funds, compelling also the well-to-do to put money aside for good works.

Or, let us read what Pontianus reports in his biography of Cyprian about how the bishop instructed his Carthaginian flock:

> The people being assembled together, he first of all urges on them the benefits of mercy.... Then he proceeds to add that there is nothing remarkable in cherishing merely our own people with the due attentions of love, but that one might become perfect who should *do something more than heathen men or publicans*, one who, overcoming evil with good, and practicing a merciful kindness like that of God, should love his enemies as well.... Thus the good

was done to all men, not merely to the household of faith (in Harnack, 1908:172–173).

And, as we have seen, that is precisely what most concerned Julian as he worked to reverse the rise of Christianity and restore paganism. But, for all that he urged pagan priests to match these Christian practices, there was little or no response because *there were no doctrinal bases or traditional practices* for them to build upon. Pagan gods did not punish ethical violations because they imposed no ethical demands—humans offended the gods only through neglect or by violation of ritual standards (MacMullen, 1981:58). Since pagan gods only required propitiation and beyond that left human affairs in human hands, a pagan priest could not preach that those lacking in the spirit of charity risked their salvation. Indeed, the pagan gods offered no salvation. They might be bribed to perform various services, but the gods did not provide an escape from mortality. We must keep that in sight as we compare the reactions of Christians and pagans to the shadow of sudden death. Galen lacked belief in life beyond death. The Christians were certain that this life was but prelude. For Galen to have remained in Rome to treat the afflicted would have required bravery far beyond that needed by Christians to do likewise.

Differential Mortality

But, how much could it have mattered? Not even the best of Graeco-Roman science knew anything to do to *treat* these epidemics other than to avoid all contact with those who had the disease. So, even if the Christians did obey the injunction to minister to the sick, what could they do to help? At the risk of their own lives they could, in fact, save an immense number of lives. McNeill (108) pointed out:

> When all normal services break down, quite elementary nursing will greatly reduce mortality. Simple provision of food and water, for instance, will allow persons who are temporarily too weak to cope for themselves to recover instead of perishing miserably.

Some hypothetical numbers may help us grasp just how much impact Christian nursing could have had on mortality rates in these epidemics. Let us begin with a city having 100,000 inhabitants in 160, just before the first epidemic. Let us suppose that 15,000 of these inhabitants are Christians, all of the others pagans. That is a ratio of 1 Christian to 5.7 pagans. Now, let us assume an epidemic generating mortality rates of 30 percent over its course in a population left without nursing. Modern medical experts believe that conscientious nursing *without any medications* could cut the mortality rate by two-thirds or even more. So, let us assume a Christian mortality rate of 10 percent. Imposing these mortality rates results in 13,500 Christian and 59,500 pagan survivors after the epidemic. Now the ratio of Christians to pagans is 1 to 4.4. To keep things simple, let us suppose that the population of this city is static over the next 90 years, until hit by the second epidemic. Let us assume the same mortality rates of 10 and 30 percent apply again. After this epidemic was over, there would be 12,150 Christian and 41,650 pagan survivors. And this is a ratio of 1 Christian to 3.4 pagans. In fact, of course, the population would not have been static for this period. In the days before modern medicine, epidemics always were especially hard on the young and on pregnant women and those suffering from birth-related infections (Russell, 1958). Hence, in the aftermath of serious epidemics the birth rate declined. With a much lower mortality rate, the Christian birth rate also would have been much less influenced and this too would have increased the ratio of Christians to pagans.

Thus an immense Christian gain would have occurred without their having made a single convert during the period. But, of course, these same trends ought to have resulted in a lot of converts. For one thing, if, during the crisis, Christians fulfilled their ideal of ministering to *everyone*, there would be a lot of pagan survivors who owed their lives to their Christian neighbors. For another, no one could help but notice that Christians not only found the capacity to risk death, but that they were much less likely to die.

As Kee (1983) has so powerfully reminded us, miracle was intrinsic to religious credibility in the Graeco-Roman world. Modern scholars have too long been content to dismiss reports of miracles in the New Testament and in other similar sources as purely literary, not as things that happened. Yet we remain aware that in tabernacles all over modern America, healings are taking place. One need not propose that God is the active agent in these "cures" to recognize their reality both as events and as perceptions. Why then should we not accept that "miracles" were being done in New Testament times too and that people expected them as proof of religious authenticity? Indeed, MacMullen (1981:126) regards it as self-evident that a great deal of conversion was based on a "visible show of divinity at work." He suggests that martyrdom would have been perceived as a miracle, for example. But, accepting the immense weight of testimony by eyewitness, MacMullen (1981:96) stresses the centrality of healing miracles: "*That* is what produced converts. Nothing else is attested."

Against this background, consider that a much superior Christian survival rate hardly could seem other than miraculous. Moreover, superior survival rates would have produced a much larger proportion of Christians who were *immune*, and who could, therefore, pass among the afflicted with seeming invulnerability. In fact, those Christians most active in nursing the sick were likely to have contracted the disease very early and to have survived it as they, in turn, were cared for. In this way was created a whole force of miracle workers to heal the "dying." And who was to say that it was the soup they so patiently spooned to the helpless that healed them, rather than the *prayers* the Christians offered on their behalf?

Mortality, Flight, and Attachments

It has long been taken for granted that theology plays a primary role in conversion—that people are attracted to a religion because of the way its system of beliefs meets their needs. However, sociologists have found that theology seldom attracts converts, but plays a relatively passive, filtering role in conversion. One of these filters is that people already deeply committed to one set of beliefs do not exchange them for another. A second filtering function is that people who utterly reject the possibility of the supernatural do not embrace a religion. Within these general limits, however, theology often plays the more important role *after* conversion. Part of being socialized into the role of a member of a faith is learning to act in accordance with its doctrines. Moreover, it is typical for people to be taught retrospectively to attribute their conversion to theological appeals, as the culmination of a spiritual search. In fact, however, observation of people *during the process of conversion* has revealed that most were not seeking a new faith at all (Lofland and Stark, 1965; Stark and Bainbridge, 1985, 1987).

People convert because of their social ties to others who already belong. Accepting a new faith is part of conforming to the expectations and examples of one's family and friends. Hence, religious movements can grow in two primary ways. First, they grow as members *form* new relationships with outsiders. Conversion occurs to the extent that these relationships come to outweigh the outsider's ties to other outsiders. A second way movements grow is by spreading through *pre-existing* social networks as members in turn bring in their families and friends. The latter pattern has far greater potential for rapid growth.

The importance of attachments in the conversion process is simply an application of the primary proposition of control theories of conformity and deviance. People tend to conform to the expectations of their friends in order to maintain their respect and affection. That is, our attachments to others give us a stake in conformity. People who lack or lose their attachments are thereby "free" to deviate. If people lose their attachments to one group and gain attachments in another, their basis for conformity also shifts—it will be to the norms of their new group that they will conform.

What this leads to is, of course, a comparative analysis of the impact of epidemics on the social networks of Christians and pagans and how this would have changed their relative patterns of attachments. In general, I will demonstrate that an epidemic would have caused chaos in pagan social relations leaving large numbers with but few attachments to other pagans and meanwhile greatly increasing the relative probabilities of strong bonds between pagans and Christians.

Let us return to our hypothetical city of 100,000 inhabitants, 15,000 of them Christians and the other 85,000 pagans. Let us focus attention on three varieties of interpersonal attachments: 1) Christian-Christian; 2) Christian-pagan; 3) pagan-pagan. If we apply the differential mortality rates used above (10% for Christians, 30% for pagans) we can calculate the *survival odds* for each variety of *attachment*. That is, our interest here is not in the survival of individuals but of an attachment, hence our measure is the odds that both persons survive the epidemic. The survival rate for Christian-Christian bonds is .81 (or 81%). The survival rate for Christian-pagan bonds is .63. The survival rate for pagan-pagan bonds is .49. Thus not only are attachments among pagans almost twice as likely to perish as attachments among Christians, pagan bonds to Christians also are much more likely to survive.

These attachment survival rates take only differential mortality into account. But attachments also are severed if one person leaves. Since we know that substantial numbers of pagans fled epidemics (while Christians stayed), this too must be considered. Let us suppose that 20 percent of the pagan population fled. Now the survival rate of pagan-pagan attachments is .25 and of Christian-pagan attachments .45, while the Christian–Christian rate remains .81.

These rates assume, of course, that Christian victims of an epidemic received nursing care, while pagans did not. In fact, however, our sources testify that *some pagans* were nursed by Christians. Given the relative sizes of the Christian and pagan populations at the onset of the epidemic, Christians would not have had the resources to nurse all or even most sick pagans. Presumably, proximity and attachments would have determined which pagans would be cared for by Christians. That is, pagans who lived near Christians and/or who had close Christian friends (even relatives) would have been most likely to be nursed. Let us assume that Christian nursing was as effective on pagan survival as on their own. That means that pagans nursed by Christians had noticeably higher survival rates than other pagans. But it also means that we should recalculate the Christian-pagan attachment survival rate. If we assume that pagans in these relationships had as good a chance of living as did the Christians, then the survival rate for these attachments is .81—more than three times the survival rate of pagan-pagan attachments.

Another way to look at this is to put oneself in the place of a pagan who, before the epidemic, had three very close attachments, two with pagans and one with a Christian. We could express this as a pagan/Christian attachment ratio of 2 to 1. Let us assume that this pagan remains in the city and survives. Subtracting mortality rates results in a pagan/Christian attachment ratio of 1 to .9. What has happened is that where once there were two pagans to one Christian in this pagan's intimate circle, now there is, in effect, one of each—a dramatic equalization.

Not only would pagan survivors have a much higher proportion of their attachments to Christians simply because of the greater survival rate of those relationships, during and after the epidemic the formation of new relationships would be increasingly biased in favor of Christians. One reason is that the nursing function is itself a major opportunity to form new bonds. Another is that it is easier to attach to a social network that is more rather than less intact. To see this let us once again focus on the pagan who, after the epidemic, has one close Christian and one close pagan attachment. Suppose that he or she wishes to replace the lost attachment—a spouse, perhaps. The Christian friend still has many other attachments to connect this pagan to. The pagan friend, however, is very deficient in attachments. For the Christian, there is a 90 percent probability that any one of his or her Christian friends or relatives survived the epidemic and remained in the city. For the pagan, these odds are only 50 percent.

The consequence of all this is that pagan survivors faced greatly increased odds of conversion because of their increased attachments to Christians.

Conclusion

Several modern writers have warned against analyzing the rise of Christianity as though it were inevitable. That is, since we know that indeed the tiny and obscure Jesus movement managed, over the course of several centuries, to dominate Western civilization, our historical perceptions suffer from overconfidence. As a result, scholars more often recount rather than try to *account for*, the Christianization of the West, and in doing so seem to take "the end of paganism for granted," as Peter Brown (1964:109) has noted.

In fact, of course, the rise of Christianity was long and perilous. There were many crisis points when different outcomes easily could have followed. Moreover, in this essay I have argued that had some crises *not occurred* the Christians would have been deprived of major, possibly crucial, opportunities.

MacMullen (1981:134) has warned us that this "enormous thing called paganism, then, did not one day just topple over dead." But neither did it simply wither away as increasing numbers of people came to recognize the "superiority" of Christian teachings. Paganism, afterall, was an active, vital part of the rise of the Hellenic and Roman empires and therefore *must have had* the capacity to fulfill basic religious impluses. As an antidote to the tendency to underestimate paganism, one might read the unself-conscious and sincere piety expressed repeatedly by the leading figures in Xenophon's *The Persian Expedition*.

True enough, Christianity brought forth some very appealing doctrinal innovations. But, the classical world had gotten along adequately without them for many centuries. Moreover, as noted above, there is substantial research showing that theological attractions are not the primary basis for conversion and therefore "theological" explanations *by themselves* seem woefully inadequate to account for the rise of Christianity.

Viewed on its own terms in the middle of the second century, paganism was not in its last days. To the contrary, it required some truly devastating blows to bring down this "enormous thing,"—blows far beyond any the Christian movement could have dealt it directly during normal times. In this essay I have argued that the terrific crises produced by two disastrous epidemics may well have tipped the scales. If I am right, then in a sense paganism did "topple over dead," a victim of its relative inability to confront these crises socially or spiritually.

*See also the article by Robinson, pp. 71–72 above. Ed.

Works Consulted

WORKS CONSULTED

Achtemeier, Paul
    1976   "Jesus and the Disciples as Miracle Workers in the Apocryphal New Testament." Pp. 146–86 in *Aspects of Religious Propaganda in Judaism and Early Christianity*. Ed. Elizabeth Schüssler Fiorenza. South Bend: Notre Dame University Press.

Akurgal, E.
    1973   *Ancient Civilizations and Ruins of Turkey*. Istanbul.

Alföldy, Géza
    1988   *The Social History of Rome*. Trans. D. Braund and F. Pollock. Rev. ed. London: Routledge.

Arnheim, M. T. W.
    1972   *The Senatorial Aristocracy in the Later Roman Empire*. Oxford: Clarendon.

Arnim, Hans von
    1907   "Epiktetos." *Pauly's Real-encyklopädie der classichen Altertumswissenschaft*. Ed. G. Wissowa. Stuttgart: Metzler. 6: 126–31.

Ayerst, David and A.S.T. Fisher
    1971   *Records of Christianity: Volume I*. Oxford: Basil Blackwell.

Badian, E.
    1958   *Foreign Clientelae (264–70 B.C.)*. Oxford: Clarendon.
    1968   *Roman Imperialism in the Late Republic*. Ithaca: Cornell University Press.

Bainbridge, W. S.
    1978   *Satan's Power*. Berkeley: University of California Press.

Banton, Michael, ed.
    1966   *The Social Anthropology of Complex Societies*. London: Tavistock; New York: Frederick Praeger.

Barnes, John A.
    1954   "Class and Committees in a Norwegian Island Parish." *Human Relations* 7:39–58.

1969   "Networks and Social Process." Pp. 51–76 in *Social Networks in Urban Situations*. Ed. J. Clyde Mitchell. Manchester: Manchester University Press.

1972   *Social Networks*. Addison-Wesley Module in Anthropology, 26. Reading, Mass.: Addison-Welsey Publishing.

Barrow, R. H.
1983   *Prefect and Emperor: The Relationes of Symmachus, A.D. 384*. Oxford: Clarendon.

Bassler, Jouette M.
1984   "The Widow's Tale: A Fresh Look at 1 Tim 5:3–16." *JBL* 203:23–41.

Bates, Frederick L.
1956   "Position, Role, and Status: A Reformulation of Concepts." *Social Forces* 34:313–321.

Bean, G. E.
1966   *Aegean Turkey, An Archaeological Guide*. London: Benn.

Bell, H. I., and V. Martin, H. E. W. Turner, D. van Berchem
1962   *The Abinnaeus Archive: Papers of a Roman Officer in the Reign of Constantius II*. Oxford: Blackwell.

Billerbeck, Margarethe
1978   *Epiktet, Vom Kynismus*. Leiden: E. J. Brill.

Bloch, Herbert
1963   "The Pagan Revival in the West at the End of the Fourth Century." Pp. 193–217 in *The Conflict between Paganism and Christianity in the Fourth Century*. Ed. A. Momigliano. Oxford: Clarendon.

Bloch, Marc
1961   *Feudal Society*. Chicago: University of Chicago Press.

Boak, Arthur E. R.
1947   *A History of Rome to 565 A.D.* 3rd. ed. New York: Macmillan.

1955a   "The Populations of Roman and Byzantine Karanis." *Historia* 4:157–62.

1955b   *Manpower Shortage and the Fall of the Roman Empire in the West*. Ann Arbor: University of Michigan Press.

Boissevain, Jeremy
- 1974 *Friends of Friends: Networks, Manipulators and Coalitions.* New York: St. Martin's; London: Macmillan.
- 1977 "When the Saints Go Marching Out: Reflection on the Decline of Patronage in Malta." Pp. 81–96 in *Patrons and Clients in Mediterranean Societies.* Ed. Ernest Gellner and John Waterbury. London: Duckworth.

Boissevain, J. and J. C. Mitchell, eds.
- 1973 *Network Analysis: Studies in Human Interaction.* The Hague: Mouton.

Boswell, D. M.
- 1969 "Personal Crisis and the Mobilization of the Social Network." Pp. 245–295 in *Social Networks in Urban Situations.* Ed. J. C. Mitchell. Manchester: Manchester University Press.

Bott, Elizabeth
- 1957 *Family and Social Network.* London: Tavistock.
- 1975 *Family and Social Network: Roles, Norms, and External Relationships in Ordinary Urban Families.* 2nd ed. (enlarged). New York: The Free Press.

Bovon, François, ed.
- 1981 *Les actes apocryphes des Apôtres: Christianisme et monde païen.* Publication de la Faculté de théologie de l'Université de Genève 4. Geneva: Labor et Fides.

Bowersock, Glen Warren
- 1964 *Augustus and the Greek World.* Oxford: Oxford University Press.
- 1967 "A New Inscription of Arrian." *GRBS* 8:279–80.

Brochet, J.
- 1905 *Saint Jérôme et ses ennemis.* Part 2. Paris: Albert Fontemoing.

Brooten, Bernadette
- 1982 *Women Leaders in the Ancient Synagogue.* Brown Judaic Studies 36. Chico: Scholars Press.

Brown, Peter R. L.
- 1964 "St. Augustine's Attitude to Religious Coercion." *Journal of Roman Studies* 54:107–116.
- 1971 "Rise and Function of the Holy Man in Late Antiquity." *Journal of Roman Studies* 61:80–101.

1972   *Religion and Society in the Age of St. Augustine.* New York: Harper and Row.

1978   *The Making of Late Antiquity.* Cambridge: Harvard University Press.

1981   *The Cult of the Saints: Its Rise and Function in Latin Christianity.* Chicago: University of Chicago Press.

Brunt, P. A.
1977   "From Epictetus to Arrian." *Athenaeum* 55:19–48.

Bund, E.
1964   "Patronus." *Der kleine Pauly Lexikon der Antike.* Stuttgart: Druckenmüller. IV:559–60.

Buresch, Karl
1889   *Klaros: Untersuchungen zum Orakelwesen des späteren Altertums.* Leipzig: Teubner.

Burrus, Virginia
1986   "Chastity as Autonomy: Women in the Stories of the Apocryphal Acts." *Semeia* 38:101–17.

Carney, T. F.
1975   *The Shape of the Past: Models and Antiquity.* Lawrence, KS: Coronado.

Cavallera, F.
1922   *Saint Jérôme. Sa vie et son oeuvre.* Louvain: Spicilegium Sacrum Lovaniense; Paris: H. and E. Champion.

Carroll, Michael P.
1975   "Revitalization Movements and Social Structure: Some Quantitative Tests." *American Sociological Review.* 40:389–401.

Cartlidge, David R.
1986   "Transfigurations and Metamorphosis Traditions in the Acts of John, Thomas, and Peter." *Semeia* 38:53–66.

Champagne, Duane
1983   "Social Structure, Revitalization Movements and State Building: Social Change in Four Native American Societies." *American Sociological Review* 48:754–763.

Chastagnol, Andre
1960   *La Préfecture urbaine à Rome sous le Bas-Empire.* Paris: Boucard.

Cichorius, C.
    1961   *Römische Studien*. Stuttgart: B. G. Teubner.

Clark, Elizabeth A.
    1979   *Jerome, Chrysostom, and Friends*. New York/Toronto: Edw. Mellen.
    1985   *The Life of Melania the Younger: Introduction, Translation, Commentary*. New York/Toronto: Edw. Mellen.
    1986   *Ascetic Piety and Women's Faith: Essays on Late Ancient Christianity*. Lewiston: Edw. Mellen.

Cochrane, Charles Norris
    1957   *Christianity and Classical Culture: A Study of Thought and Action from Augustus to Augustine*. Oxford: Clarendon, 1940; repr. Oxford University Press.

Coster, C.H.
    1968   *Late Roman Studies*. Cambridge: Harvard University Press.

Countryman, L. William
    1980   *The Rich Christian in the Church of the Early Empire: Contradictions and Accommodations*. TSR 7. New York/Toronto: Edw. Mellen.

Court, John D.
    1986   *Some Aspects of Rank and Status in Epictetus: Development of a Methodology*. Master's Thesis, Macquarie University.

Cyprian
    1958   *Treatises*. New York: Fathers of the Church.

Danker, Frederick
    1982   *Benefactor. Epigraphic Study of a Graeco-Roman and New Testament Semantic Field*. St. Louis: Clayton.

D'Arms, John H.
    1970   *Romans on the Bay of Naples*. Cambridge: Harvard University Press.
    1981   *Commerce and Social Standing in Ancient Rome*. Cambridge: Harvard University Press.

Davies, Stevan L.
    1980   *The Revolt of the Widows: The Social World of the Apocryphal Acts*. New York: Winston/Seabury.

Davis, J.
1977   *People of the Mediterranean: An Essay in Comparative Social Anthropology*. London: Routledge and Kegan Paul.

Dibelius, Martin
1917   "Die Isisweihe bei Apuleius und verwandte Initiations-Riten." Repr. in *Botschaft und Geschicht*, vol. 2. Tübingen: Mohr, 1956. English trans. in *Conflict at Colossae*, ed. F. O. Francis and W. A. Meeks. Missoula, Mont.: SBL, 1973. [Page numbers refer to the Eng. ed.]

Dodds, E. R.
1965   *Pagan and Christian in an Age of Anxiety: Some Aspects of Religious Experience From Marcus Aurelius to Constantine*. Cambridge: Cambridge University Press.

Duncan-Jones, Richard
1974   *The Economy of the Roman Empire: Quantitative Studies*. Cambridge: Cambridge University Press.

Edson, Charles
1972   *Inscriptiones graecae Epiri, Macedoniae, Thraciae, Scythiae, Pars II Inscriptiones Thessalonicae et viviniae*. Berlin: Walter de Gruyter.

Eisenstadt, S. N. and Louis Roniger
1980   "Patron-Client Relations as a Model of Structuring Social Exchange." *Comparative Studies in Society and History* 22:42–77.

Erbse, Hartmut
1941   *Fragmente griechischer Theosophien*. Hamburg: Hansischer Gildenverlag.

Eusebius
1965   *The History of the Church*. London: Penguin.

Evans-Pritchard, E. E.
1964   *Essays in Social Anthropology*. London: Faber.

Fears, J. R.
1981   "The Theology of Victory at Rome." Pp. 736–826, 758–59 in *Aufstieg und Niedergang der Römischen Welt: Geschichte und Kultur Roms im Spiegel der neueren Forschung* 17.2. Berlin: Walter de Gruyter.

Fehr, F.
    1971/2   "Zur Geschichte des Apollon-Heiligtums von Didyma." *Marburger Winckelmann-Programm*. Pp. 14–59.

Ficker, G.
    1903   *Die Petrusakten: Beiträge zu ihren Verständnis*. Leipzig: Barth.

Finn, Thomas M.
    1982   "Social Mobility, Imperial Civil Service and the Spread of Early Christianity." Pp. 31–37 in *Studia Patristica* XVIII. Ed. E. A. Livingstone. Oxford and New York: Pergamon.

Fiorenza, Elizabeth Schüssler
    1976   *Aspects of Religious Propaganda in Judaism and Early Christianity*. South Bend: Notre Dame University Press.
    1983   *In Memory of Her: A Feminist Theological Reconstruction of Christian Origins*. New York: Crossroad.

Fontenrose, Joseph
    1978   *The Delphic Oracle: Its Responses and Operations*. Berkeley: University of California.

Frankel, M.
    1895   *Die Inschriften von Pergamon*. Berlin: Spemann. No. 324.

Franklin, James L.
    1980   *Pompeii: The Electoral Programmata, Campaigns and Politics, A.D. 71–79*. Papers and Monographs of the American Academy in Rome XXVIII. Rome: American Academy in Rome.

Frend, W.H.C.
    1984   *The Rise of Christianity*. Philadelphia: Fortress.

Frischer, Bernard
    1982   *The Sculpted Word: Epicureanism and Philosophical Recruitment in Ancient Greece*. Berkeley: University of California Press.

Fustel de Coulanges, N. D.
    1873   *The Ancient City: A Study on the Religion, Laws, and Institutions of Greece and Rome*. Trans. W. Small from the French edition of 1864. Garden City: Anchor-Doubleday.

Gager, John G.
    1975   *Kingdom and Community: The Social World of Early Christianity*. Englewood Cliffs: Prentice Hall.

Geertz, Clifford
1971   *Islam Observed*. Chicago: University of Chicago Press.

Gellner, Ernest
1977   "Patrons and Clients." Pp. 1–6 in *Patrons and Clients in Mediterranean Societies*. Ed. E. Gellner and J. Waterbury. London: Duckworth.

Gellner, E. and John Waterbury, eds.
1977   *Patrons and Clients in Mediterranean Societies*. London: Duckworth.

Gelzer, Matthias
1969   *The Roman Nobility*. Trans. R. Seader. Oxford: Basil Blackwell; 2nd impression, 1975.

Georgi, Dieter
1964   *Die Gegner des Paulus im 2. Korintherbrief*. Wissenschaftliche Monographien zum Alten und Neuen Testament 11. Neukirchen-Vluyn: Neukirchener.
1976   "Socioeconomic Reasons for the 'Divine Man' as a Propagandistic Pattern." Pp. 27–42 in *Aspects of Religious Propaganda in Judaism and Early Christianity*. Ed. Elizabeth Schüssler Fiorenza. South Bend: Notre Dame University Press.

Gilliam, J.F.
1961   "The Plague Under Marcus Aurelius." *American Journal of Philology*. 82:225–251.

Gilmore, David D.
1982   "Anthropology of the Mediterranean Area," *Annual Review of Anthropology* 11:175–205.

Gow, A. S. F. and D. L. Page, eds.
1968   *The Greek Anthology. The Garland of Philip and Some Contemporary Epigrams*. 2 vols. Cambridge: Cambridge University Press.

Granovetter, Mark S.
1973   "The Strength of Weak Ties." *American Journal of Sociology* 78: 160–76.
1983   "The Strength of Weak Ties: A Network Theory Revisited." Pp. 201–219 in *Sociological Theory 1983*. Ed. Randall Collins. San Francisco: Jossey-Bass.

Grant, Robert M.
1977   *Early Christianity and Society: Seven Studies.* San Francisco: Harper and Row.

Gruen, Erich
1984   *The Hellenistic World and the Coming of Rome.* 2 vols. Berkeley: University of California Press.

Grützmacher, Georg
1969   *Hieronymus: Eine Biographische Studie zur alten Kirchengeschichte.* 1901–1908; Rpt. Aalen: Scientia Verlag.

Guillaumont, Antoine
1962   *Les 'Kephalaia Gnostica' d'Evagre le Pontique et l'histoire de l'Origènisme chez les Syriens.* Patristica Sorbonensia 5. Paris: Seuil. Pp. 57 ff., 77ff.

Günther, W.
1971   *Das Orakel von Didyma in hellenistischer Zeit: eine Interpretation von Steinurkunden.* MDAI(I), Beih. 4. Tübingen: Wasmuth.
1980   "Inschriftenfunde 1978 (nr 1–3) und 1979 (nr. 4 und 5) aus Didyma," *MDAI(I)* 30:170–76, no. 5.

Habicht. C.
1969   *Die Inschriften des Asklepieions: Altertümer von Pergamon 8.3.* Berlin: de Gruyter.
1990   *Cicero the Politician.* Baltimore: The Johns Hopkins University Press.

Hammond, C.P.
1977   "The Last Ten Years of Rufinus' Life and the Date of His Move South from Aquileia." *Journal of Theological Studies,* n.s. 28:372–427.

Harnack, Adolf
1908   *The Mission and Expansion of Christianity in the First Centuries.* Trans. J. Moffatt from the 2nd (1906) German ed. 2 vols. London: Williams and Norgate.

Hartmann, Karl
1905   "Arrian und Epiktet." *Neue Jahrb* 15:248–75.

Haselberger, L.
1983   "Bericht über die Arbeit am Jüungeren Apollontempel von Didyma." *MDAI(I)* 33:90–123.

Hausmaniger, H.
1964 "Clientes." *Der kleine Pauly Lexikon der Antike*. Stuttgart: Druckenmüller. I:1254–55.

Haussoullier, Bernard
1898 "L'oracle d'Apollon à Claros," *RPh* 22:257–73.
1902 *Etudes sur l'histoire de Milet et du Didymeion*. Paris: Boullon.
1920 "Comment avait lieu la consultation de l'oracle?" *RPh* 44:268–77.

Henrichs, Albert
1975 "Democritus and Prodicus on Religion." in *Harvard Studies in Classical Philology* 79:93–123.

Hendrix, Holland
1984 "Thessalonicans Honor Romans." Unpublished Ph.D. dissertation, Harvard Divinity School.

Herman, Gabriel
1980/1 "The 'friends' of the early hellenistic rulers: servants or officials?" *Talanta* 12/13:103–149.
1987 *Ritualized Friendship in the Greek City*. Cambridge: Cambridge University Press.

Hermann, P.
1971 "Athena Polias in Milet," *Chiron* 1: 291–298.

Hickey, Anne Ewing
1983 *Women of the Senatorial Aristocracy of Late Rome as Christian Monastics: A Sociological and Cultural Analysis of Motivation*. Unpublished PhD. dissertation, Vanderbilt University.

Hijmans, B. L.
1959 *ΑΣΚΗΣΙΣ. Notes on Epictetus' Educational System*. Assen: Van Gorcum.

Hirschi, Travis
1969 *Causes of Delinquency*. Berkeley: University of California Press.

Hommel, H.
1963 "Das Apollonrakel in Didyma." In *Festschrift für Friedrich Smend*. Berlin: Merseburger.

Hopkins, Donald R.
1983 *Princes and Peasants: Smallpox in History*. Chicago: University of Chicago Press.

Hopkins, M. Keith
    1961   "Social Mobility in the Later Roman Empire: The Evidence of Ausonius." *Classical Quarterly* 55:239–249.

Humphreys, S. C.
    1978   *Anthropology and the Greeks*. London: Routledge & Kegan Paul.

Hunt, E.D.
    1972   St. Silvia of Aquitaine: The Role of a Theodosian Pilgrim in the Society of East and West." *Journal of Theological Studies*, n.s. 23:353–7.

Johnson, Paul
    1976   *A History of Christianity*. New York: Atheneum.

Jones, A. H. M.
    1963   "The Social Background of the Struggle between Paganism and Christianity." Pp. 17–37 in *The Conflict between Paganism and Christianity in the Fourth Century*. Ed. A. Momigliano. Oxford: Clarendon.
    1964   *The Later Roman Empire, 284–602: A Social, Economic, and Administrative Survey*. 2 vols. Norman: University of Oklahoma Press.
    1971   *Prosopography of the Later Roman Empire* [=PLRE]. Ed. A.H.M. Jones, et al. Cambridge: Cambridge University Press.

Jones, C. P.
    1971   *Plutarch and Rome*. New York: Oxford University Press.

Jongman, Willem
    1988   *The Economy and Society of Pompeii*. Amsterdam: Gieben.

Junod, Eric
    1981   "Les vies de philosophé et les actes apocryphes poursuivent-ils un dessein similaire?" Pp. 209–19 in *Les actes apocryphes des Apôtres*. Ed. François Bovon. Publication de la Faculté de théologie de l'Université de Genève 4. Geneva: Labor et Fides.

Kaestli, Jean-Daniel
    1981   "Les principales orientations de la recherche sur les actes apocryphes." Pp. 49–67 in *Les actes apocryphes des Apôtres*. Ed. François Bovon. Publication de la Faculté de théologie de l'Université de Genève 4. Geneva: Labor et Fides.
    1986   "Response." *Semeia* 38:119–31.

Kee, Howard Clark
1980 *Christian Origins in Sociological Perspective*. Philadelphia: Westminster.
1983 *Miracle in the Early Christian World*. New Haven: Yale University Press.

Kelly, J.N.D.
1975 *Jerome: His Life, Writings, and Controversies*. New York: Harper & Row.

Knoch, Otto
1973 *Die Testamente des Petrus und Paulus: Die Sicherung der apostolischen überlieferung in der spät neutestamentlichen Zeit*. Stuttgart: KBW Verlag.

Koester, Helmut
1982 *Introduction to the New Testament*. 2 vols. New York/Berlin: De Gruyter; Philadelphia: Fortress.

Landé, Carl H.
1977 "The Dyadic Basis of Clientelism." Pp. xiii-xx in *Friends, Followers, and Factions*. Ed. S. H. Schmidt. Berkeley: University of California Press.

Laumann, Edward O. and Pappi, Franz U.
1976 *Networks of Collective Action: A Perspective on Community Influence Systems*. New York: Academic.

Lechat, H.
1889 "Bas-reliefs du Musèe du Constaninople." *BCH* 13:518–19.

Lefkowitz, Mary R. and Maureen B. Fant
1982 *Women's Life in Greece and Rome: A Sourcebook in Translation*. Baltimore: The Johns Hopkins University Press.

Levick, Barbara
1967 *Roman Colonies in Southern Asia Minor*. Oxford: Clarendon.

Lipsius, Richard
1883 *Die Apokryphe Apostelakten: Ein Beitrag zur altchristlichen*
/90 *Literaturgeschichte und zu einer zusammenfassenden Darstellung der Neutestamentlichen Apokryphen*. 2 vols. Braunschweig: C.A. Schwetschke.

Littman, R. J., and M. L. Littman
 1973 "Galen and the Antonine Plague." *American Journal of Philology* 94:243–255.

Lofland, John and Rodney Stark
 1965 "Becoming a World-Saver: A Theroy of Conversion to a Deviant Perspective," *American Sociology Review* 30:862–875.

MacDonald, Dennis Ronald
 1983 *The Legend and the Apostle: The Battle for Paul in Story and Canon.* Philadelphia: Fortress.

MacMullen, Ramsay
 1966 *Enemies of the Roman Order.* New Haven and London: Yale University Press.
 1974 *Roman Social Relations.* New Haven and London: Yale University Press.
 1981 *Paganism in the Roman Empire.* New Haven and London: Yale University Press.
 1984 *Christianizing the Roman Empire.* New Haven and London: Yale University Press.
 1985 "Conversion: A Historian's View." *The Second Century* 5: 67–81.
 1986a "Personal Power in the Roman Empire." *AJP* 107:512–524.
 1986b "Women's Power in the Principate." *KLIO* 68:434–443.
 1988 *Corruption and the Decline of Rome.* New Haven and London: Yale University Press.

Macridy, Th.
 1905 "Altertümer von Notion." *JOAI* 8:155–73.
 1912 "Antiquités des Notion II." *JOAI* 15:36–67.

Magie, David
 1950 *Roman Rule in Asia Minor.* 2 vols. Princeton: Princeton University Press.

Malherbe, Abraham J.
 1983 *Social Aspects of Early Christianity.* 2nd ed. Philadelphia: Fortress.

Malina, Bruce J.
 1981 *The New Testament World: Insights from Cultural Anthropology.* Atlanta: John Knox.
 1986 *Christian Origins and Cultural Anthropology: Practical Models for Biblical Interpretation.* Atlanta: John Knox.

Marks, Geoffrey and William K. Beatty
　1976　*Epidemics*. New York: Scribner's

Marrou, H.
　1965　*Histoire de l'education dans l'antiquité*. 6th ed. Paris: Seuil.

Marshall, Peter
　1987　*Enmity at Corinth: Social Conventions in Paul's Relations with the Corinthians*. WUNT 2.23. Tübingen: Mohr/Siebeck.

Martin, Dale
　1990　*Slavery as Salvation: The Metaphor of Slavery in Pauline Christianity*. New Haven: Yale University Press.

Mattingly, Harold
　1976　"The Emperor and His Clients." Pp. 159–186 in *Essays on Roman Culture*. Ed. A.J. Dunston. Toronto: Hakkert.

Mayer, Adrian C.
　1966　"The Significance of Quasi-Groups in the Study of Complex Societies." In M. Banton, ed., *Social Anthropology of Complex Societies*. London: Tavistock; New York: Praeger.

McNeill, William H.
　1976　*Plagues and Peoples*. Garden City: Doubleday.

Meeks, Wayne
　1983　*The First Urban Christians: The Social World of the Apostle Paul*. New Haven and London: Yale University Press.

Millar, Fergus
　1965　"Epictetus and the Imperial Court." *JRS* 55:141–48.

Mitchell, J. Clyde, ed.
　1969　*Social Networks in Urban Situations: Analyses of Personal Relationships in Central African Towns*. Institute for Social Research of Zambia. Manchester: Manchester University Press.
　1969a　"The Concept and Use of Social Networks." Pp. 1–50 in *Social Networks In Urban Situations*. Ed. J. Clyde Mitchell. Manchester: Manchester University Press.
　1973　"Networks and Institutions." Pp. 14–38 in *Network Analysis: Studies in Human Interaction*. Ed. J. Boissevain and J C. Mitchell. The Hague: Mouton.
　1974　"Social Networks." *Annual Review of Anthropology* 3:279–99.

Moine, Nicole
    1980   "Melaniana." *Recherches Augustiniennes* 15:18–34.

Montegu, J. C.
    1965   "Oracles in Asia Minor under the Empire". Unpublished Ph.D. dissertation, Harvard University.

Mooney, James
    1896   *The Ghost Dance Religion and the Sioux Outbreak of 1890*. Fourth Annual Report of the Bureau of Ethnology to the Secretary of the Smithsonian Institution. Washington, D. C.: U. S. Government Printing Office.

Murphy, Francis X.
    1945   *Rufinus of Aquileia (345–411). His Life and Works*. Washington, D.C.: The Catholic University of America Press.
    1947   "Melania the Elder: A Biographical Note." *Traditio* 5:67.

Muyldermanns, Joseph, ed. and trans.
    1952   *Evagriana Syriaca. Textes inédits du British Museum et de la Vaticane*. Louvain: Université de Louvain. P. 30.

Naumann, R.
    1973   *Didyma Führer*. Istanbul.

Neel, James V., et al.
    1970   "Notes on the Effect of Measles and Measles Vaccine in a Virgin Soil Population of South American Indians." *American Journal of Epidemiology* 91:418–429.

Niebuhr, B.G.
    1855   *The History of Rome*. English trans. London: Walton and Maberly.

Niemeijer, Rudo
    1973   "Some Applications of the Notion of Density to Network Analysis." Pp. 46–49 in *Network Analysis*. Boissevain and Mitchell, eds. The Hague: Mouton.

Noble, Mary
    1973   "Social Network: Its Use as a Conceptual Framework in Family Analysis." Pp. 3–13 in *Network Analysis*. Boissevain and Mitchell, eds. The Hague: Mouton.

Nock, Arthur Darby
   1933   *Conversion: The Old and the New in Religion from Alexander the Great to Augustine of Hippo.* Oxford: Clarendon Press.
   1972   "Soter and Euergetes." Pp. 720–35 in *Arthur Darby Nock: Essays on Religion and the Ancient World.* Vol. 2. Ed. Zeph Steward. Cambridge: Harvard University Press.

Oldfather, W. A.
   1925   *Epictetus. The Discourses as Reported by Arrian, The Manual, and Fragments,* Vol. 1. Cambridge: Harvard University Press.
   1928   *Epictetus. The Discourses as Reported by Arrian, The Manual, and Fragments,* Vol. 2. Cambridge: Harvard University Press.

Oliver, James H.
   1970   "Arrian and the Gellii of Corinth." *GRBS* 11:335–38.
   1977   "Roman Emperors and Athenian Ephebes." *Historia* 26:89–94.

Page, D.L.
   1968   *The Greek Anthology. The Garland of Philip and Some Contemporary Epigrams.* Ed. A. S. F. Gow and D. L. Page. 2 vols. Cambridge: Cambridge University Press.

Parke, H. W. and D. E. W. Wormell
   1956   *The Delphic Oracle.* 2 vols. Oxford: Blackwell.

Picard, Ch.
   1922   *Ephèse et Claros.* Paris: Boccard.

Pike, K.
   1954   *Language in Relation to a Unified Theory of Human Behavior.* Glendale, CA: Summer Institute of Linguistics.

Pitt-Rivers, Julian
   1968   "The Stranger, the Guest, and the Hostile Host." Pp. 13–30 in *Contributions to Mediterranean Sociology.* Ed. J. G. Peristiany. The Hague: Morton.
   1973   "The Kith and the Kin." Pp. 89–105 in *The Character of Kinship.* Ed. J. Goody. Cambridge: Cambridge University Press.

Plümacher, Eckhard
   1978   "Apokryphe Apostelakten." Pp. 11–70 in *Supplement* 15 to Pauly-Wissowa, *Real-Encyclopädie der klassischen Altertumswissenschaft.*

Pohlenz, Max
- 1959 *Die Stoa. Geschichte einer geistigen Bewegung.* 2nd ed. 2 vols. Göttingen: Vandenhoeck & Ruprecht.

Price, S. R. F.
- 1984 *Rituals and Power: The Roman Imperial Cult in Asia Minor.* Cambridge: Cambridge University Press.

Radcliffe-Brown, A. R.
- 1952 *Structure and Function in Primitive Society: Essays and Addresses.* London: Cohen and West.

Rawson, Elizabeth
- 1976 "Caesar's Heritage: Hellenistic Kings and their Roman Equals." *Journal of Roman Studies* 66:148–159.
- 1977 "More on the Clientellae of the Patrician Claudii," *Historia* 26: 340–357.

Rayet, O. and A. Thomas
- 1880–85 *Milet et le golfe Latmique.* 2 vols. Paris.

Reitzenstein, Richard
- 1906 *Hellenistische Wundererzählungen.* Leipzig: Teubner.

Rickman, Geoffrey
- 1980 *The Corn Supply of Ancient Rome.* New York: Oxford University Press.

Robert, L.
- 1954a *La Carie II.* Paris: Adrien-Maisonneuve.
- 1954b *Les fouilles de Claros.* Paris: Adrien-Maisonneuve.
- 1955 "Les inscriptions de Claros." *Hellenica* 10:275–75.
- 1959 "Les inscriptions grecques de Bulgarie." *RPh* 33:190.
- 1967 "L'oracle de Claros." Pp. 305–312 in Vol. I of *La civilisation grecque de l'antiquité à nos jours*, ed. C. Delvoye and G. Roux. Brussels: Renaissance du livres.
- 1968 "Trois oracles de la Théosophie et un prophète d'Apollon." *CRAI*, 568–599.
- 1969 "Les inscriptions." Pp. 299–303 in *Laodicèe du Lycos, le nymphée, campagnes 1969–63.* Ed. J. des Gagniers et al. Paris: Boccard.
- 1974a "Les Inscriptions de Thessalonique." *Revue de Philologie* 180–246
- 1974b "Des Carpathes à la Propontide." *Studii Classice* 16:74–80.

Robinson, T. L.
1981 "Theological Oracles and the Sanctuaries of Claros and Didyma." Unpublished Ph.D. Dissertation, Harvard University.

Russell, J. C.
1958 *Late Ancient and Medieval Population*. Vol 48:3 in *Transactions of the American Philosphical Society*. Philadelphia: American Philosophical Society.

Rykwert, Joseph.
1988 *The Idea of a Town: The Anthropology of Urban Form in Rome, Italy and the Ancient World*. Cambridge: MIT Press.

Saller, Richard P.
1982 *Personal Patronage Under the Early Empire*. Cambridge: Cambridge University Press.

Schenkl, Henricus
1916 *Epicteti Dissertationes ab Arriano Digestae*. Leipzig: Teubner.

Schmid, Wilhelm
1909 "Favorinus." *Pauly's Real-encyklopädie der classischen Altertumswissenschaft*. Ed. G. Wissowa. Stuttgart: Metzler. 6:2078–84.

Schmidt, Carl
1903 *Die alten Petrusakten im Zusammenhang mit der apokryphen Apostelliteratur, nebst einem neuentdeckten Fragment Untersucht*. TU 24.1. Leipzig: J. C. Hinrichs.

Schmidt, S. W.
1977 *Friends, Followers, and Factions*. Ed. S. W. Schmidt et al. Berkeley: University of California Press.

Schneemelcher, W.
1965 "The *Acts of Peter*." Trans. G. C. Stead. Pp. 259–75 in vol. 2 of *New Testament Apocrypha*. Hennecke, Scheemelcher, Wilson, eds. Philadelphia: Westminster.

Schuchhardt, C.
1896 "Kolophon, Notion, und Klaros." *MDAI(A)* 11:398–434.

Seeck, Otto.
1883 *Q. Aurelii Symachi quae supersunt*. Monumenta Germania Historica VI.1. Berlin: Akademie Verlag.

Sheid, John
    1975   *Les Frères Arvales: Recrutement et origine sociale sous les empereurs julio-claudiens.* Paris: Bocard.

Sherwin-White, A. N.
    1957   "Pliny's Praetorship Again." *JRS* 47:126–30.
    1966   *The Letters of Pliny. A Historical and Social Commentary.* New York: Oxford University Press.

Silverman, Sydel
    1977   "Patronage as Myth." Pp. 9–11 in *Patrons and Clients in Mediterranean Societies.* Ed. E. Gellner and J. Waterbury. London: Duckworth.

Sjoberg, Gideon.
    1960   *The Preindustrial City, Past and Present.* New York: Free Press.

Skaard, E.
    1931   "Zwei religiös-politische Begriffe Euergetes-Concordia." *Avhanlinger utgitt av Det Norske Videnskap-Akademi i Oslo*, II *Historisk-Filosofish Klasse.*

Söder, Rosa
    1932   *Die apokryphen Apostelgeschichten und die romanhafte Literatur der Antike.* Würzburger Studien zur Altertumswissenschaft 3. Stuttgart: W. Kohlhammer. Rpt. Darmstadt: Wissenschaftliche Buchgesellschaft, 1969.

Smith, J. Z.
    1975   "The Social Description of Early Christianity." *Religious Studies Review* 1:19–25.

Snyder, Graydon F.
    1985   *Ante Pacem: Archeological Evidence of Church Life before Constantine.* Macon: Mercer University Press.

Stadter, Philip A.
    1980   *Arrian of Nicomedia.* Chapel Hill: University of North Carolina Press.

Stark, Rodney
    1986   "Jewish Conversion and the Rise of Christianity: Rethinking the Received Wisdom." Pp. 314–29 in *Society of Biblical Literature 1986 Seminar Papers.* Ed. Kent Harold Richards. Atlanta: Scholars.

Stark, Rodney and William Sims Bainbridge
    1980   "Networks of Faith: Interpersonal Bonds and Recruitment to Cults and Sects." *American Journal of Sociology* 85:1376–1395.
    1985   *The Future of Religion: Secularization, Revival and Cult Formation.* Berkeley: University of California Press.
    1987   *A Theory of Religion.* New York and Bern: Peter Lang.

Stark, Rodney and Lynne Roberts
    1982   "The Arithmetic of Social Movements: Theoretical Implications." *Sociological Analysis* 43:53–68.

de Ste. Croix, G. E. M.
    1954   "Suffragium: from vote to patronage." *British Journal of Sociology* 5:30–40.

Stein, A.
    1931   "Ser. Sulpicius Similis." *Pauly's Real-encyklopädie der classischen Altertumswissenschaft.* Ed. G. Wissowa and H. Kroll. Stuttgart: Metzler. 2nd reihe 7: 871–72.

Stoops, Robert
    1983   "Miracle Visions and Vision Reports in the *Acts of Peter.*" Unpublished Ph.D. dissertation, Harvard University. Ann Arbor: University Microfilms.
    1986   "Patronage in the *Acts of Peter.*" *Semeia* 38:91–100.
    1987   "If I Suffer . . . Epistolary Authority in the Letters of Ignatius of Antioch." *HTR* 80:161–78.

Syme, Ronald
    1939   *The Roman Revolution.* Rpt. and corr.; London: Oxford University Press, 1960.
    1980   *Some Arval Brethren.* London: Oxford University Press.
    1982   "The Career of Arrian." *HSCP* 86:181–211.
    1985   "Correspondents of Pliny." *Historia* 34:324–59.

Tardieu, Michel
    1984   *Ecrits Gnostiques, Codex de Berlin.* Sources Gnostiques et Manichéennes 1. Paris: Cerf.

Taylor, Lily Ross
    1949   *Party Politics in the Age of Caesar.* Berkeley: University of California Press.

Thornton, Russell
- 1981 "Demographic Antecedents of a Revitalization Movement: Population Change, Population Size, and the 1890 Ghost Dance." *American Sociological Review* 40:88–96.

Tran Tam Tinh, V.
- 1964 *Essai sur le culte d'Isis à Pompéi*. Paris: Bocard.

Treggiari, Susan
- 1969 *Roman Freedmen during the Late Republic*. Oxford: Clarendon.

Trouwborst, Al
- 1973 "Two Types of Partial Networks in Burundi." Pp. 111–123 in *Network Analysis*. Ed. J. Boissevain and J. C. Mitchell. The Hague: Mouton

Tuchelt, K.
- 1973 *Vorarbeiten zu einer Topographie von Didyma: eine Untersuchung der inschriftlichen und archäologischen Zeugnisse*. MDAI(I), Beih. 9. Tübingen: Wasmuth.
- 1976 "Tempel—Heiligtun—Siedlung: Probleme zur Topographie von Didyma." *Neue Forschung in griechischen Heiligtümer*. Ed. U. Jantzen. Tübingen: Wasmuth.
- 1977 "Didyma or Branchidai." *Princeton Encyclopedia of Classical Sites*. Princeton: Princeton University Press. Pp. 272–73.

van Velzen, H.U.E. Thoden
- 1973 "Coalition and Network Analysis." Pp. 219–250 in *Network Analysis*. Ed. J. Boissevain and J. C. Mitchell. The Hague: Mouton.

Villain, Maurice
- 1937 "Ruffin d'Aquilée—La Querelle autour d'Origène." *Recherches de Science Religieuse* 27:165–95.

Voigtlaender, W.
- 1975 *Der jüngste Apollontempel von Didyma: Geschichte seines Baudekors*. MDAI(I), Beih. 14. Tübingen: Wasmuth.

Von Dobschütz, E.
- 1902 "Der Roman in der altchristlichen Literatur." *Deutsche Rundschau* 111:87–106.

Walbank, M. B.
    1978   *Athenian Proxenies of the Fifth Century B.C.*. Toronto: Samuel Stevens.

Wallace, Anthony F. C.
    1956   "Revitalization Movements." *American Anthropologist* 58:264–281.
    1966   *Religion: An Anthropological View*. New York: Random House.

Wallace-Hadrill, Andrew, ed.
    1989   *Patronage in Ancient Society*. London: Routledge.

Walsh, Joseph
    1931   "Refutation of the Charges of Cowardice Against Galen." *Annals of Medical History* 3:195–208.

Wardman, Alan
    1982   *Religion and Statecraft among the Romans*. London: Granada.

Weingood, Alex
    1977   "Patronage and Power." Pp. 41–51 in *Patrons and Clients in Mediterranean Societies*. Ed. E. Gellner and J. Waterbury. London: Duckworth.

Wellman, Barry
    1983   "Network Analysis: Some Basic Principles." Pp. 157–172 in *Sociological Theory 1983*. Ed. Randall Collins. San Francisco: Jossey-Bass.

West, M. L.
    1967   "Oracles of Apollo Kareios: A Revised Text," *ZPE* 1: 183–187.

White, L. Michael
    1985   "Adolf Harnack and the 'Expansion' of Early Christianity: A Reappraisal of Social History." *The Second Century* 5:97–127.
    1988   "Shifting Sectarian Boundaries in Early Christianity." *Bulletin of the John Rylands University Library of Manchester* 70:7–24.
    1990   *Building God's House in the Roman World: Architectural Adaptation among Pagans, Jews, and Christians*. Baltimore: The Johns Hopkins University Press.

Whitten, N., Jr. and A. Wolfe
    1974   "Network Analysis." Pp. 717–46 in *Handbook of Social and Cultural Anthropology*. Ed. J. Honigmann. Chicago: Rand McNally.

Wiegand, Theodor
- 1908 "Sechste vorläufige Berichte über die in Milet und Didyma unternommenen Ausgrabungen." *Abh. Berl. Akad.* Pp. 32–46.
- 1911 "Siebte vorläufige Berichte über die in Milet und Didyma unternommenen Ausgrabungen." *Abh. Berl. Akad.* Pp. 37–71.
- 1925 "Achte vorläufige Berichte über die in Milet und Didyma unternommenen Ausgrabungen." *Abh. Berl. Akad.* Pp. 9–25.
- 1941 *Didyma. Erster Teil: Die Baubeschreibung.* Ed. H. Knackfus. 3 vols. Berlin: Gebr. Mann.
- 1958 *Didyma. Zweiter Teil: Die Inschriften*, by Albert Rehm, ed. Richard Harder. Berlin: Gebr. Mann.

Wilmart, D. A.
- 1911 "Les Versions Latines des Sentences d'Evagre pour les vierges," *Revue Bénedictine* 28: 143–151.

Wilson, Brian R.
- 1975 *Magic and the Millenium: A Sociological Study of Religious Movements of Protest among Tribal and Third-World Peoples.* London: Heinemann, 1973; repr. Frogmore, St. Albans: Paladin Press.

Wirth, Theo
- 1967 "Arrians Erinnerungen an Epiktet," *MusHelv* 24:149–89, 197–216.

Wiseman, James
- 1973 "Gods, War and Plague in the Time of the Antonines." *Studies in the Antiquities of Stobi.* Ed. J. Wiseman. Austin: University of Texas Press.

Wistrand, Erik
- 1978 *Caesar and Contemporary Roman Society.* Acta Regiae societatis scientiarum et litterarum Gothoburgensis: Humaniora 15. Göteborg: Vetenskaps- och Vitterhets-Samhället.

Wolf, Eric
- 1966 "Kinship, Friendship, and Patron-Client Relations in Complex Societies." Pp. 1–22 in *The Social Anthopology of Complex Societies*, ed. Michael Banton. London: Tavistock; New York: Praeger.

Wolff, Gustav
- 1856 *Porphyrii de philosophia ex oraculis haurienda librorum reliquae.* Berlin: Springer.

Wood, Neal
　　1988　　*Cicero's Social and Political Thought*. Berkeley: University of California Press.

Zeller, Eduard
　　1922　　*Die Philosophie der Griechen in ihrer geschichtlichen Entwicklung*. 5th ed., vol. 2, pt. 1. Leipzig: Reisland.

Zinsser, Hans
　　1960　　*Rats, Lice and History*. 1934; New York: Bantam.